AS BY A NEW PENTECOST

Golden Jubilee Edition

Patti Gallagher Mansfield

The original book was first published in 1992 by
Franciscan University Press Franciscan
University of Steubenville Steubenville, OH 43952
in the United States of America
This revised and expanded version is published
in 2016 by New Life Publishing, Luton,
Bedfordshire LU4 9HG, United Kingdom

British Library Cataloguing in Publication Data
A catalogue record for this book is available
from the British Library

ISBN 978 1 903623 96 1

Typesetting by New Life Publishing,
Luton, UK www.goodnewsbooks.co.uk

AS BY A NEW PENTECOST

GOLDEN JUBILEE EDITION

THE DRAMATIC BEGINNING OF
THE CATHOLIC CHARISMATIC RENEWAL

PATTI GALLAGHER MANSFIELD

'Share with all in the Church the grace of Baptism in the Holy Spirit'
Pope Francis

NEW LIFE PUBLISHING

DEDICATION

to Mary, Spouse of the Holy Spirit,
Mother of the Church, my Mother

and

to Al Mansfield,
my beloved husband and dearest friend,
who is the reason why this book was written

ACKNOWLEDGEMENTS

I am deeply grateful to those who contributed to this book, both in the first edition and in this Golden Jubilee edition. Your words of testimony bring glory to God and will inspire future generations. What you have written and lived has changed the lives of millions of people.

While working on this book, I have felt the spiritual closeness of Cardinal Suenens, who was so kind to write the foreword in 1992. The last time I saw him, his parting words to me were, 'In heaven,' and from heaven I have experienced his help today.

Heartfelt thanks to Fr. Raniero Cantalamessa, O.F.M., Cap., my dear friend, for the foreword to this new edition. He has helped bring the Baptism in the Spirit into the heart of the Church through his papal preaching and worldwide travels.

I am also greatly indebted to Cardinal Rylko for his beautiful preface. From our first meeting, he has always shown avid interest in the beginnings of the Catholic Charismatic Renewal and has been a tremendous support to the movement.

I am grateful to *Servizio Photografico - L'Osservatore Romano* for permission to re-print the photo of Pope Benedict in the text and to to *Photografia Felici* for the photo of Pope Francis.

I also wish to thank ICCRS to excerpt texts from *Then Peter Stood Up* and to *Libreria Editrice Vaticana* for the translations of most of the texts of Pope Francis.

Thanks to Duquesne University for their permission to re-print photos of the campus. The National Service Committee of the United States has given me permission to re-print from Pentecost Today and Tammie Stevens and Jim Archer have contributed the 2015 photos of the Ark and the Dove.

Finally, from the bottom of my heart, I want to thank my husband, Al Mansfield. It was his idea that this book should be written 25 years ago. Without him I would not have had the courage to undertake the project then or now. His research, counsel, love and support have made *As By A New Pentecost* possible. Thanks also to my four children, their spouses and my nine grandchildren. This book is written to encourage them and others of their generation to open themselves up to the Baptism in the Spirit and to a New Pentecost.

Patti Mansfield

ENDORSEMENTS

After the Ascension of Jesus, when the apostles were choosing someone to join them and bring their number back up to twelve, they looked for someone who was with them from the beginning and who could be a reliable witness to all that Jesus said and did (cf. Acts 1:21-22). As the Holy Spirit is being poured out in our day, we are also blessed to hear from one of the very first witnesses to this action of God. Patti Mansfield tells us of all that the Holy Spirit said and did at the very beginnings of this world-wide outpouring. This account is so important for all of us to hear, to ponder, and to respond to! A very significant - and inspiring - book.
Dr. Ralph Martin
President of Renewal Ministries

As By A New Pentecost documents the birth and early beginnings of Catholic Charismatic Renewal. It is a story of an unfolding history that has been filled with many surprises of the Holy Spirit. This revised Golden Jubilee edition not only takes us back to the extraordinary events of the Duquesne Weekend in 1967. It also leads us forward beyond our Golden Jubilee. The current of grace that we now know as Catholic Charismatic Renewal, is flowing with a greater strength. The move of the Holy Spirit that began among university students in USA has now reached and touched millions of people throughout the world. I highly recommend this book, it is essential reading because it not only details a historic event, it also propels us forward into a new era of the Holy Spirit.
Michelle Moran
President of ICCRS

Lives were changed by the power of the Holy Spirit on that Duquesne Weekend for the fulfillment of God's plan today in his Church. The signs and wonders read about in the pages of Scripture and at different times in the history of the Church were experienced realities in the lives of ordinary, and sometimes the most unlikely people. Good news such as this could not and must not be kept secret. As on that first Pentecost, these new, more fully Spirit-filled Christian Catholics shared what God had done in their lives with others. That message has been heard throughout the world. As a result, the tongues of flame from Pentecost and the fire of the Spirit from Duquesne have literally set ablaze the hearts of millions within the Church.
Most Reverend Sam G. Jacobs, D.D.
Bishop Emeritus, Houma/Thibodaux, Louisiana
Written in 1992

When you love your family very much, you love to read about the history of their origins. This is the same joy that I had when I read Patti's beautiful book. Praise the Lord for all the wonderful signs of love being poured upon his Church in this new Pentecost!
Fr. Emiliano Tardif, M.S.C.
Worldwide ministry of healing and evangelisation
Written in 1992

We are about to celebrate the 50th anniversary of this amazing experience that began in Duquesne University. One of the pioneer students at the beginning was Patti Gallagher Mansfield, whom we call the 'spiritual mother' of this movement. When we look at her, we see faithfulness to the Holy

Spirit and a strong presence of Our Mother Mary. This current of grace has been generating many fruits in the Catholic Church such as new vocations and different ministries. As the President of the Catholic Fraternity in the world now and as Patti's close friend, I would like to thank her for everything she has done for this movement since 1967. I encountered this grace when I was seventeen years old and I consider myself one of her spiritual sons. I am very grateful to her for inspiring me to be a family man and a founder of a charismatic community due to her 'yes' to the Lord at the beginning of this current of grace. I would like to congratulate her for updating the book As By A New Pentecost. We are very happy to receive this gift in our Golden Jubilee. I recommend everyone to read it and announce it so that our history remains generation after generation!

Gilberto Barbosa
President of the Catholic Fraternity

As By A New Pentecost is the amazing story of the beginning of the Catholic Charismatic Renewal as told by an actual participant in the story. This Golden Jubilee edition allows us to relive those historic events and be encouraged by what the Holy Spirit continues to do today. Since the Duquesne Weekend, Patti Mansfield has been spreading the message of the power of the Holy Spirit around the world. Read Patti's account about the lives of those who were there at the beginning and allow your own life to be transformed by the Holy Spirit.

Johnny Bertucci
Chairman of the National Service Committee, USA

ECUMENICAL ENDORSEMENTS

It was an honor and joy to write an endorsement for Patti Gallagher Mansfield's 1992 book, As By A New Pentecost: The Dramatic Beginning of the Catholic Charismatic Renewal. At that time the Renewal was celebrating 25 years since the small beginnings in 1967. Patti was there in the Ark and the Dove Retreat Center near Pittsburgh when the Holy Spirit fell sparking the beginning for the movement. Since that time Patti and her book have become legendary in the Catholic Charismatic Renewal. Her testimony in this book is the most accurate and detailed account of this historic meeting.

Personally speaking, Patti is a shining example of the very best features of the Renewal. Her life of Spirit-filled holiness over many decades has blessed untold multitudes of charismatics in all the churches, but especially in the worldwide Catholic family. Her faithfulness to the Lord and to the Renewal has been an inspiration and a strong guiding light throughout the history of the Renewal.

As By a New Pentecost: Golden Jubilee Edition is a revised and warm account of the beginnings of one of the most incredible religious movements of the entire twentieth century. Now, as the movement approaches the celebration of 50 years, this book will continue to be 'must' reading for anyone inquiring into the roots of the Charismatic Renewal in the Catholic Church, a movement that has touched some 120,000,000 million persons since it began.

Dr. Vinson Synan
Dean Emeritus, Regent School of Divinity

The Holy Spirit is on the move stirring and inspiring so many in so many ways - we are living in fascinating times ..... What you began in 1967 made it possible for the birth of the ecumenical movement of today, and hopefully the ecumenical movement will give birth to a global witness and new evangelisation leading to a the second coming, and beginning of eternity forward..!

So much beauty and mystery.

So much to THANK our Father in heaven for.

Your loving son,

Peace & Good +

+Tony [Bishop Tony Palmer] Written on May 28, 2014

Note from the author:

As I made plans for the Golden Jubilee edition of this book, I intended to ask my friend, Bishop Tony Palmer, to write something. Bishop Tony contacted me in early March, 2014, because he wanted to hear a first-hand account of the Duquesne Weekend. During our meeting by Skype, he knelt down and asked me to pray over him, He said that he wanted the grace that I received in 1967 to pass through me to him. I knelt down as well, we prayed, and from that moment on he called me his mother. Bishop Tony died in a motorcycle accident on July 20, 2014. May he spend his heaven interceding for the unity that he worked so hard to foster among Christians.

CONTENTS

CONTENTS

FOREWORD: FIRST EDITION

Léon-Joseph Cardinal Suenens

During one of the first charismatic conventions in the United States I met a young lady by the name of Patti Mansfield. She told me about the events surrounding the origin of the Catholic Charismatic Renewal at the Duquesne Weekend, which is so noteworthy in contemporary Church history.

I was struck by her testimony — calm, serene, balanced — but even more so by a remark she added in saying that on the day after these events, her first personal reaction was to try to find out what the hierarchical Church thought about this kind of phenomenon, and that she began reading the document *Lumen Gentium* in which Vatican II speaks of the charisms. This reassured her: she felt fully a daughter of the Church open to welcome the Holy Spirit and His surprises.

She also came to realise — and this is equally important — that this grace of spiritual renewal is meant for the entire Church. The Holy Spirit is not the monopoly of any one person and to classify the pentecostal renewal among special 'movements' is to negate its significance.

The initiative to publish the testimonies of those who lived through this famous Duquesne Weekend is an especially happy one. It defines and fixes a point of history.

In her testimony she also links to the Baptism in the Spirit the name and spiritual maternity of Mary, thereby reminding us that Jesus Christ continues to be born mystically 'of the Holy Spirit and of Mary' and that we should never separate what God has joined together.

Father Karl Rahner, S.J., echoing the great tradition, could write that 'the charismatic element belongs to the essence of the Church in a way that is just as necessary and permanent as hierarchical ministry and the sacraments.'

This book helps all of us to re-read the Acts of the Apostles with new eyes. Then we will see more clearly that the story of Pentecost continues and that the pentecostal renewal is indeed, in the words of Paul VI, 'a chance for the Church and for the world.'

+ L.J. Cardinal Suenens

Leon-Joseph Cardinal Suenens, 1972

'I believe in ethe Holy Spirit', Pentecost, 1974

FOREWORD: GOLDEN JUBILEE EDITION

FR. RANIERO CANTALAMESSA, O.F.M. CAP

Like Cardinal Suenens, I too had my small story with the author of this book. I have shared it on many occasions, but can't avoid mentioning it again as I am asked to write a word for the new edition of her book, *As By a New Pentecost*. In July 1977 a lady from Milan offered four tickets to go to America to attend an ecumenical charismatic conference being held in Kansas City, Missouri. One of these tickets was offered to me. On the plane, I was given an issue of the *New Covenant* magazine, published for the tenth anniversary of the beginning of the Catholic Charismatic Renewal. There was an article by someone named Patti Gallagher, one of the students who had participated in the retreat at Duquesne University in Pittsburgh. She summarised her experiences with Jesus' words: 'Blessed are you who see what you see and the ears that hear it.' (Mt. 13: 16). That troubled me. I thought, 'These people must have discovered a secret that is bigger than themselves.' For years afterward, I asked every American I met in the renewal, 'Do you know someone named Patti Gallagher?' No one seemed to know her, until I discovered that she had gotten married in the meantime, so everyone knew her by her married name, Patti Mansfield.

In a recent sermon delivered at the Pontifical Household, in the presence of Pope Francis, I tried to explain in what sense the Charismatic Renewal can be called - as Blessed Pope Paul VI did on May 19, 1975 - 'a chance for the Church and for the world. My answer was this: because it allows us to restore to Christian salvation the rich and inspiring positive content summed up in the gift of the Holy Spirit. The primary goal of Christian life is once again shown to be, as St. Seraphim of Sarov said, 'the acquisition of the Holy Spirit.' It gives a different outward picture of Christian life: it is a joyous, contagious Christianity that has none of the gloomy pessimism that Nietzsche reproved it for.

For this reason I cannot help but rejoice that the event of Duquesne, which started the grace of a New Pentecost in the Catholic Church, is told again by its eyewitness, Patti Mansfield, in a new and enriched edition of her book. Some added testimonies - Kevin and Dorothy Ranaghan, Ralph Martin, Bert Ghezzi, Steve Clark and others - make this new edition really 'new' and even more inspiring. They show how quickly the grace that was manifested at Duquesne University in Pittsburgh spread around 'like a brushfire.' They also show how quick some people were in recognizing in it the fulfillment of St. John XXIII's prayer for 'a new Pentecost,' and of what the Vatican Council had said about the 'charismatic dimension of the Church'. The entire Catholic Charismatic Renewal is indebted to these people and especially to the author of this book.

Fr. Raniero Cantalamessa, O.F.M., Cap.
Preacher to the Papal Household

Fr. Raniero Cantalamessa at the Ark and the Dove in 1992 for the 25th anniversary of the Charismatic Renewal

PREFACE

Stanisław Cardinal Ryłko

We are very grateful to Patti Mansfield for this Jubilee edition of her book entitled *As By A New Pentecost,* in which she presents the long journey of birth and growth undertaken by the Catholic Charismatic Renewal. The book is unique because its author is unique. She was one of the eyewitnesses of the event that in a sense gave rise to this new stream of grace in the Catholic Church: the retreat made by that group of students from the University of Duquesne, Pittsburgh, back in 1967, who were first to experience the gift of the outpouring of the Holy Spirit. So, Patti Mansfield is a special witness of the origins of the Catholic Charismatic Renewal. In these fifty years of history it has experienced extraordinary growth. From a small seed it has become a large and sturdy tree that bears much fruit. So many lives have been changed, of men and women, young people and adults. It has generated so many signs of holiness and has generated so many missionary thrusts by great numbers of the baptised of our time! How can we fail to be amazed at this powerful force of the Holy Spirit in the Church today!

In the life of the ecclesial movements it is very important to remember the origins. It is at the source that the water is clear, and the same applies to the origins of a movement. That is where you best see its deeper nature and identity. To return to the origins of the Catholic Charismatic Renewal is not sentimentality, but an important opportunity to renew our wonder at the beauty of its germinal charism. In this sense, Patti Mansfield is a very valuable guide.

It is significant to note the historical coincidence between the birth of the Catholic Charismatic Renewal and the closing of the Second Vatican Council, the fiftieth anniversary of which we celebrate this year [2015]. Renewal is one of the important fruits of this Council, often called a new breath of the Spirit, a springtime of the Spirit, a new Pentecost in the Church. In fact, the teaching of the Second Vatican Council rediscovers the beauty of our Church rich in many hierarchical and charismatic gifts, the beauty of the vocation and mission of the lay faithful, and it confirms the vocation of all the baptised to holiness. All of this has created very fertile ground for the emergence of numerous ecclesial movements and new communities in the post-Vatican II Church. Saint John Paul II called them 'the gift of the Spirit and hope for humanity', explaining that 'a real movement exists [...] as a nourishing soul within the institution'. Pope Benedict XVI, in turn, called them 'powerful ways of living the faith'. Pope Francis calls them 'a gift and treasure in the Church', indicating in particular the Catholic Charismatic Renewal as 'a great force meant to serve the preaching of the Gospel in the joy of the Holy Spirit. You received the Holy Spirit and he has made you appreciate God's love for all his children; he has also made you love God's word' *(Address to the 37th Convocation of the Renewal in the Holy Spirit, 1 June 2014).*

Mindful of the origins, the Catholic charismatic movement is called to look to the future. Here the biggest challenge that presents itself is to preserve the freshness of the initial charism and to renew the 'first love' of the origins. Pope Francis encourages us by saying, 'As time goes by, there is a greater temptation to become comfortable, to become hardened in set ways of doing things, which, while reassuring, are nonetheless sterile. There is the temptation to cage in the Holy Spirit [...] The newness of your experiences does not consist in methods or forms [...] all of which are important, but rather in your willingness to respond with renewed enthusiasm to the Lord's call. We need always to return to the sources of our charism' *(Address to the third World Congress of the Movements, 22 November 2014).*

Another point on which Pope Francis places strong focus is 'communion'. He explains that 'real communion cannot exist in Movements or in New Communities unless these are integrated within the greater communion of our Holy Mother, the hierarchical Church' (ibid.). It is only when inserted organically into the living fabric of the ecclesial community that a movement can truly fulfil its vocation and mission which is to be 'a nourishing soul within the institution'.

So, thank you to Patti Mansfield for the gift that she is offering us with her book - an eyewitness account of the life of the Catholic Charismatic Renewal. It can help us to relive the wonder of faith in the presence of this immense stream of grace prompted by the Holy Spirit in the Church, a sign of great hope.

Stanisław Cardinal Ryłko
President of the Pontifical Council for the Laity

Duquesne University, 2015
Used with permission Duquesne University

INTRODUCTION

That which was from the beginning, which we have heard, which we have seen with our eyes, which we have looked upon and touched with our hands, concerning the word of life—the life was made manifest, and we saw it, and testify to it, and proclaim to you the eternal life which was with the Father and was made manifest to us—that which we have seen and heard we proclaim to you, so that you may have fellowship with us; and our fellowship is with the Father and with His Son Jesus Christ. And we are writing this that our joy may be complete (1 Jn. 1:1-4).

St. John was able to write these beautiful words in his first epistle because he was a *witness*. He knew Jesus personally. He talked with him and listened to him. He ate with Jesus, witnessed his miracles, stood by his Cross, received his Mother into his home, and touched the Lord's risen body. At Pentecost, John was filled with the Holy Spirit, precisely so that he could fulfill his mission: to be a witness for Jesus Christ and to proclaim his blessed name to the ends of the earth!

I make so bold as to begin this book with these words of St. John, because I too am a witness. Through no merit of my own, I too have had intimate contact with the Risen Lord Jesus by the power of His Holy Spirit. Jesus Christ is 'the same, yesterday, today and forever' (Heb. 13:8). The Jesus whom St. John knew and loved is the same Jesus you and I and all men and women can know and love today.

The testimonies that appear in the following pages are not the stories of saints; they are the stories of ordinary people who have been touched by an extraordinary outpouring of the Spirit of the Living God.

So often during the writing of this book I've asked the Lord to find someone else to do it. 'I'm not a theologian. I'm not an historian. I'm not even a gifted enough writer to do justice to your work,' I've protested. But then the Lord has reminded me of who I am; *I am a witness*. I have seen his glory. And I've gathered here the testimonies of other witnesses, others who were there at the Duquesne Weekend, February 17-19, 1967, when the power of the Holy Spirit fell as by a new Pentecost.

I am encouraged to share these testimonies as I recall the words of Blessed Pope Paul VI in *Evangelii Nuntiandi*, 'Modern man listens more willingly to witnesses than to teachers, and if he does listen to teachers, it is because they are witnesses.'[1] Those whose stories appear here witnessed an event that has left its mark on the Catholic Church in our day.

In 1967, Rev. Don Basham's book, *Face Up with a Miracle*, was published in which he recounted his own experience with the Baptism in the Holy Spirit. In the very last pages of that book, he related the story of his visit to a prayer meeting in the home of Miss Flo Dodge in the North Hills of Pittsburgh on January 20, 1967. Rev. Basham remarked that through such small home prayer meetings, great new moves of the Holy Spirit may come to birth. At that particular prayer meeting, two instructors from

Duquesne University were in attendance, and before the meeting closed, two of these men asked to receive the Baptism in the Holy Spirit. The week before another professor from Duquesne University had already asked to be baptised in the Spirit. These two meetings are the events that led to the Duquesne Weekend the following month which marked the beginning of the Charismatic Renewal in the Catholic Church. Don Basham was right. A great new move of the Holy Spirit *did* come to birth through a small home prayer group.

Rev. Basham closed his book with the comment that the Holy Spirit was moving so rapidly in 1967, written testimony could not keep up with God's miraculous acts. He recommended that more books of testimony be written, more contemporary books of 'Acts' be published, so that the world might come to know that God is alive. As Don Basham finished the last chapter of his book in 1967, the Holy Spirit was beginning the first chapter of a new book of 'Acts' among Catholics.

As By A New Pentecost is just such a book of testimonies. It details the events leading up to the Duquesne Weekend, and then presents the stories of those who were actually there in 1967. Tracking down my friends from Duquesne who are now scattered far and wide has been a bittersweet experience. There's been great joy in renewing old friendships. But there's also been a sense of sadness as we see signs of our own unfaithfulness to the grace of God over the years. Let me make it clear: I'm not holding myself or any one of us from the Duquesne Weekend up as examples of holiness. The lives of the people, named and unnamed in these pages, may not be all that they could be today.

But the sovereign outpouring of God's grace did not depend on our holiness in 1967, and it does not depend on it today. It was God's choice to visit us with a fresh outpouring of the Holy Spirit and his gifts during the Duquesne Weekend. In spite of our own personal shortcomings, the Lord used us to usher forth a move of his Spirit through the Charismatic Renewal in the Catholic Church.

Just recently, I realised how important it is to tell the story of what happened on the Duquesne Weekend when I spoke to a charismatic prayer group for teenagers in New Orleans, Louisiana. I was stunned to realize that all of these young people, born after Vatican II, have grown up in a Church where it is normal to speak about charismatic gifts and Charismatic Renewal. My teenaged friends seemed surprised to learn that prior to 1967, spiritual gifts such as prayer in tongues, interpretation of tongues, healing and prophecy were unheard of in the average Catholic parish. Now, just a relatively short time later, there are few places that have not at least heard of this work of the Holy Spirit.

My husband, Al, was pleased that I finally saw the need to write this book. For years he has encouraged (pestered and cajoled) me to do it. His interest in the Duquesne Weekend dates back to September of 1968 when he was a graduate student at the University of Iowa. At that time a friend, Mike Fitzgerald, gave him an issue of *ACTS* magazine. *ACTS* was a bi-monthly publication of the Full Gospel Business Men's Fellowship International and dedicated to spreading news of the Baptism in the Spirit around the world. This particular issue of September/October, 1967, featured several articles about the work of the Holy Spirit among Roman Catholics. The cover of *ACTS* was a photo of the campus of the University of Notre Dame with several of the early leaders pictured. Inside were a full ten pages written by such people as Kevin Ranaghan, Fr. Ed O'Connor, C.S.C., and Bert Ghezzi. Reading it today, I am impressed by how quickly these Catholics grasped the meaning of the Baptism in the Spirit in terms of Catholic theology.

Years later my husband, Al, told me that when he read ACTS magazine and got to the part describing the experience of a Duquesne co-ed named Patti Gallagher, he said to himself, 'I want to meet this girl and hear her testimony from her own lips.' God certainly answered his prayer, because he not only met me, but he married me! And over the years, Al has heard my testimony hundreds of times from my own lips! He finally convinced me to put the whole story in writing, with the help of my friends from Duquesne and University of Notre Dame.

Although the story of the Duquesne Weekend has been published briefly in other books, there has never been an extensive eyewitness account about the Duquesne Weekend which might serve as a primary source for future reference. The first edition of this book was published for the Silver Jubilee in February, 1992, but as we approach the Golden Jubilee in 2015, a new edition seemed fitting.

This new Golden Jubilee edition includes more of the historical background, including the prophetic intuition of some notable Catholics. It also has been enriched by testimonies of nine additional people who were influential either before or after the Duquesne Weekend event.

I must confess that working on this Golden Jubilee edition, I have often been moved to tears. I am in amazement at the action of God! For instance, as I picked up Fr. Edward O'Connor's book, *The Pentecostal Movement in the Catholic Church,* I read about one of the first prophecies given at University of Notre Dame. It was at the conclusion of the Michigan State Weekend, April 7-9, 1967, which was attended by only about 85 people. The prophetic word was something like this: 'This is only the beginning. You are going to see greater works than this.' Imagine! How marvellously that prophecy has been fulfilled in a movement which now has spread to millions of people around the world!

This book has four parts. *Part One: Renew the Face of the Earth* describes briefly those events which led up to the Duquesne Weekend beginning with the intense prayer to the Holy Spirit at the turn of the century. *Part Two: We Cannot Help but Speak of What We Have Seen and Heard* is a collection of eyewitness accounts from those who were on the Duquesne Weekend. *Part Three: We Too Have Seen Him* contains testimonies of others who were involved in the events immediately preceding and following the Duquesne Weekend. *Part Four: Current of Grace* is my own reflection on the Baptism in the Holy Spirit as a grace for the whole Church. The new appendix includes some of the encouraging words for the Charismatic Renewal by our recent Popes.

As I was working on the first edition of this book I felt moved to make a novena of intercession between Ascension and Pentecost, 1991. My specific intention was that the Holy Spirit would fall afresh on those who contributed to this book, on those who would read it, and on the whole Church. My novena consisted of a Holy Hour, usually before the Blessed Sacrament exposed. As I asked Jesus to send upon all of us the living water of his Holy Spirit to refresh and empower us, I was encouraged by his words: 'If anyone thirst, let him come to me and drink. He who believes in me, as the Scripture has said, 'Out of his heart shall flow rivers of living water.' Now, this he said about the Spirit, which those who believed in him were to receive…' (Jn. 7:37).

I hope you're thirsty! I am! It's a pre-requisite for receiving more of the Holy Spirit. The Lord longs to give his Spirit to us without measure, if only we would open ourselves up to him without measure.

Our Holy Father, Pope Francis, met with 52,000 people from the Catholic Charismatic Renewal at the 37th Convocation of Renewal in the Spirit, June 1, 2014 in Olympic Stadium, Rome. He gave us this tremendous mission:
'I expect you to share with everyone in the Church the grace of baptism in the Holy Spirit (a phrase we find in the Acts of the Apostles).'

I pray this book will introduce many more brothers and sisters in the Church to the grace of Baptism in the Spirit. 'May God grant that I may speak with judgment and have thoughts worthy of what I have received, for he is the guide even of wisdom and the corrector of the wise. For both we and our words are in his hand...' (Wis. 7:15-16).

Patti Gallagher Mansfield, Solemnity of the Assumption of the Blessed Virgin Mary, August 15, 2015

NOTES

1. Pope Paul VI, Apostolic Exhortation Evangelii Nuntiandi, (Dec. 8, 1975), No. 42

2. Edward D. O'Connor, C.S.C., The Pentecostal Movement in the Catholic Church, (Notre Dame, Indiana: Ave Maria Press, 1978), p.70.

SEQUENCE HYMN FOR PENTECOST

Come, thou Holy Spirit, come
And from thy celestial home
Shed a ray of light divine;

Come, thou Father of the poor;
Come, thou source of all our store;
Come, within our bosoms shine;

Thou, of comforters the best;
Thou, the soul's most welcome guest;
Sweet refreshment here below;

In our labor, rest most sweet;
Grateful coolness in the heat;
Solace in the midst of woe.

O most blessed light divine,
Shine within these hearts of thine,
and our inmost being fill;

Where thou art not, man hath naught,
Nothing good in deed or thought,
Nothing free from taint of ill.

Heal our wounds, our strength renew;
On our dryness pour thy dew;
Wash the stains of guilt away;

Bend the stubborn heart and will;
Melt the frozen, warm the chill;
Guide the steps that go astray.

On the faithful, who adore
And confess thee, evermore
In thy sev'nfold gift descend;

Give them virtue's sure reward;
Give them thy salvation, Lord;
Give them joys that never end.

Amen. Alleluia.

The participants in the Duquesne Weekend around the dining room table on Sunday morning, February 19, 1967, at the Ark and the Dove Retreat Center. Seated in front are Patti Gallagher Mansfield and David Mangan. This photo was taken by John Rossmiller and is the only photo of the entire group taken that famous weekend.

PART ONE:

RENEW THE FACE OF THE EARTH

'Renew your wonders in this our day,
as by a new Pentecost. Grant to your Church that,
being of one mind and steadfast in prayer with Mary,
the Mother of Jesus, and following the lead of blessed Peter,
it may advance the reign of our Divine Saviour, the reign
of truth and justice, the reign of love and peace. Amen.'
Pope Saint John XXIII

The Ark and the Dove Retreat Center, Gibsonia, Pennsylvania, 1967

I Never Thought It Would Change My Life

April 29, 1967

Dear Monsieur Iacovantuno,

Ça va?! Please forgive me for not writing sooner, but it's been *unusually* busy for me this semester. I'd really rather sit down with you and tell you the marvellous things that have happened to me of late. However, this short letter will have to suffice.

Perhaps I mentioned to you that I'm a member of a Scripture study group on campus. We had a coed Study Weekend, February 17-19. In preparation, we read the Acts of the Apostles 1-4 and a book entitled *The Cross and the Switchblade* by David Wilkerson. I was impressed by the power of the Holy Spirit and the strength and courage with which the apostles were able to spread the good news after Pentecost. I naturally thought the weekend would be profitable, but I must admit that I never thought it would change my life!

During our discussion groups one of the leaders brought out the fact that we must constantly reaffirm our Baptismal and Confirmation vows and make ourselves more open to God's Spirit. I found it intriguing, but a little hard to believe, when I was told that the charismatic gifts given to the apostles are still given today — that there are still signs and wonders — and that God has promised to pour forth His

Spirit on *all* flesh. We decided to have a renewal of Confirmation and Baptismal vows as part of the closing services Sunday night. However, the Lord had something else in mind for us!

Saturday night we were to have a birthday party for some of the kids, but things just couldn't get going. One by one we were drawn into the chapel and received what is called the Baptism in the Holy Spirit in the New Testament. It happened to different people in different ways. I became struck by a deep awareness that God is real and that he loves us. Prayers poured forth from my lips that I would have never had the courage to say aloud before. I know now what Claudel meant by 'a voice inside more ourselves than we are.' This *wasn't* just a good weekend, but rather a real life-changing experience which has continued and is spreading and growing.

The gifts of the Spirit *are* manifest now — I can testify to this because I have heard people pray in tongues, heal, discern spirits, speak with extraordinary wisdom and faith, prophesy and interpret. I now realize that there is nothing we have to bear ourselves, no prayer that God doesn't answer, no need that the Lord is not rich enough to fill! And I feel such tremendous freedom in depending on him, in truly praising God.

We can try to live as Christians and to die to ourselves and sin, but without the power of the Spirit it can be a rather discouraging struggle. There are still temptations and problems, but now I have the confidence and trust in God — now I have the strength from the Lord to really change and live with him. It's true we receive the Holy Spirit at Confirmation and that we are His temples, but we do not open enough to his gifts and his power in our lives. It's true that the Spirit is a teacher because I've learned so much in such a short time from him! Scripture lives! I'm sure that I could never come by so much knowledge alone, despite good intentions and efforts.

This is why I've cancelled my trip to Europe for the summer. I'm quite sure that I will eventually teach French and visit France. However, at the moment I've lost interest in it. It seems that for the present, the Lord has given me certain gifts which I must use to bring people closer to him. I've found myself talking to people about Christ and really seeing results! I could have never dared to do such things before, but now it's impossible not to. Like the apostles said after Pentecost, *'How can we keep from telling about the things we've seen and heard!'*

The greatest thing is the complete lack of anxiety! Never before have I been so unsure of the future, yet never before have I been so unafraid and happy. If you get a chance, try to read the book I suggested earlier and another one by John Sherrill, They Speak with Other Tongues. I'd love to hear from you, and see what you think. Take care!

Love and prayers, Patti

THE DUQUESNE WEEKEND

I wrote this enthusiastic description of the Duquesne Weekend just two months after the retreat took place. My friend, Mr. Val Iacovantuno, was my high school French teacher. I knew he was Catholic, but we had never before discussed religion. Since he had inspired me to major in French and was helping me with my itinerary for a summer in France, I wrote him to explain my sudden change in plans. God's presence had broken into my life in the Baptism in the Holy Spirit. I knew that my life was no longer my own. To my amazement, when Mr. Iacovantuno answered, he told me to put everything else aside and follow the Lord Jesus unconditionally. In fact, he was one of the few people I witnessed to who truly seemed to understand what had happened.

The retreat of February 17-19, 1967, which I describe in my letter, has come to be known around the world as the Duquesne Weekend. I don't know who began to call it by this name, but I suspect it was some people from the University of Notre Dame who were among the first to hear about it. I am not personally aware of other spontaneous outpourings of the Holy Spirit among a group of Catholics that took place before or at the same time as the Duquesne Weekend. The Duquesne Weekend has been generally accepted as the beginning of the Charismatic Renewal as a post Vatican II movement in the Catholic Church. While there were individual Catholics who were baptised in the Spirit prior to the Duquesne Weekend (see Ralph Martin's testimony later in this book), this was the first event at which a group of Catholics experienced the Baptism in the Spirit together with the manifestation of charismatic gifts. The Duquesne Weekend sparked a widespread experience of the baptism in the Spirit among Catholics in the United States and around the world.

I was not the only Catholic giving exuberant witness to the new outpouring of the Holy Spirit and his gifts in 1967. Through letters, phone calls, and personal visits, word was spreading like wildfire about the pentecostal experience. One of the professors who was a leader on the Duquesne Weekend reported to his friends at the University of Notre Dame, *'I don't have to believe in Pentecost; I've seen it.'*

THE POPE'S PRAYER

Many people who reflect on the outbreak of the Catholic Charismatic Renewal in 1967 call to mind the prayer of Pope John XXIII at the beginning of the Second Vatican Council. They see the Charismatic Renewal as one of the providential answers to the Holy Father's prayer for a new Pentecost:

'Renew your wonders in this our day, as by a new Pentecost. Grant to your Church that, being of one mind and steadfast in prayer with Mary, the Mother of Jesus, and following the lead of blessed Peter, it may advance the reign of our Divine Savior, the reign of truth and justice, the reign of love and peace. Amen.'[1]

Just what did Pope John XXIII have in mind when he prayed for a new Pentecost? What was he longing for? And where did this longing come from? Since that first Pentecost when the Church was born, the Holy Spirit has been continually at work. Throughout the centuries, the Lord has raised up great saints, men and women filled with the Holy Spirit, who have manifested extraordinary charismatic gifts. There have also been communities of Catholic believers in the past who have experienced the presence of the Holy Spirit acting in their midst as he did in the early Church. Pope John XXIII was well aware of this when he implored the Holy Spirit to renew his signs and wonders in this our day. He knew that a lived experience of Pentecost was possible. He had witnessed it for himself.

A Spirit-Filled Village

While he was still Bishop Angelo Roncalli, Pope John XXIII used to visit a tiny Czechoslovakian village of approximately three hundred people where a dear friend of mine, Mrs. AnnaMariea Schmidt, was living.[2] For many centuries all the Catholics in this village had experienced the full spectrum of charismatic gifts as recorded in 1 Corinthians 12-14. It was part of normal Christian life for them. Pentecost was a daily reality.

AnnaMariea related to me the circumstances surrounding the first manifestation of charismatic gifts in the eleventh century. When the villagers were in danger of starvation due to the severe cold which ruined their crops, they prayed for God's help. A beautiful lady, who did not identify herself, appeared on the mountain and taught them how to implore the Holy Spirit.

As they followed her instructions, they were all filled with the Spirit and received charismatic gifts, such as discernment of spirits, prophecy, and the gift of tongues. They also experienced a growth in the sanctifying gifts of the Holy Spirit, especially love. The bread which they baked that winter was blessed, and their supply lasted miraculously until the next harvest

Each successive generation of villagers manifested the charismatic gifts of the Holy Spirit. They did not realize that their charismatic experience was unique, since their village was fairly isolated. AnnaMariea describes how the power of prayer and the presence of God's love were so strong that they needed no jails nor hospitals. When someone was sick, the entire village united in prayer, expecting God's healing. Children were welcomed into families; there was no divorce. Peace and love reigned. Sunday Mass was a glorious celebration of Jesus in their midst and was followed by a sharing of food and fellowship. Scripture was read in the homes and children were instructed to live in the power of the Holy Spirit.

It was into this charismatic environment that Bishop Roncalli came for visits in the 1930's. He was joyfully received as a spiritual father. AnnaMariea, who was a child at the time, remembers him as a priest imbued with God's love. She delighted to sit at his feet and listen to him speak about Jesus. He seemed perfectly at home amidst the manifestations of the charismatic gifts as he prayed with her family and the other villagers.

When I asked AnnaMariea if she thought that Pope John XXIII's prayer for a new Pentecost was inspired by his visits to her village, she said that she thought it would be presumptuous to draw such a conclusion. AnnaMariea believes that this desire for a new Pentecost was born in his heart long before he visited them. It seemed to her as though he knew full well what was possible when people turned to God with repentant, humble hearts and implored the Holy Spirit to act in their midst.

AnnaMariea's description of Bishop Angelo Roncalli is confirmed by many other people. Certainly, Pope Saint John XXIII is widely regarded as one of the most charismatic figures of the twentieth century. He has been called by Cardinal Suenens, 'a man completely docile to the Holy Spirit, a man who, completely free from himself, followed the path of the Holy Spirit.'

Pope Saint John XXIII was canonized on April 27, 2014 by Pope Francis to the joy of the People of God.

It was prophesied in the 1930's that a severe testing would come upon AnnaMariea's village to empty it, but that there would be joy as the villagers stood firm through the trial. This prophecy was fulfilled when Nazi troops came in 1938 and killed almost every villager. The power of the Holy Spirit sustained them, and not one person renounced his faith. I am grateful to God for sparing the life of Mrs. AnnaMariea Schmidt, who survived both Nazi and Russian concentration camps, and who has allowed me to share this portion of her amazing testimony.

The Apostle of the Holy Spirit

The first person to be beatified by the good Pope John was a woman religious named Sr. Elena Guerra. Fr. Val Gaudet[4] who has written about Elena Guerra believes that Pope Saint John XXIII may well have been influenced to pray for a new Pentecost thanks to the efforts of this humble religious sister, called by Pope Saint John XXIII *'the Apostle of the Holy Spirit'*. Blessed Elena Guerra lived from 1835 to 1914, a time of significance in Pentecostal history, as we will see.

Sister Elena Guerra was foundress of a religious order in Lucca, Italy, at first called the Sisters of St. Zita and later renamed the Oblate Sisters of the Holy Spirit. It was in 1886, that Sister Elena began to be aware of her prophetic task, to write to Pope Leo XIII urging him to renew the Church through a return to the Holy Spirit. However, she did not yield to this inspiration until many years later when the Lord revealed to a devout woman from the convent staff named Erminia Giorggetti what he wanted Elena to do. With the encouragement of her spiritual director, Msgr.Volpi, Sister Elena wrote a number of confidential letters to the Holy Father between 1895 and 1903 calling for renewed preaching on the Holy Spirit, 'who is the one who forms the saints.' The Oblate Sisters of the Holy Spirit say that the number of these letters is somewhere between ten and twelve.[5]

Sister Elena told the Pope Leo XIII of her desire to see the whole Church unite in constant prayer, as were Mary and the apostles in the upper room, awaiting the coming of the Spirit. She wrote,

'Pentecost is not over. In fact, it is continually going on in every time and in every place, because the Holy Spirit desired to give himself to all men and all who want him can always receive him, so we do not have to envy the apostles and the first believers; we only have to dispose ourselves like them to receive him well, and He will come to us as he did to them.'[6]

She also wrote, 'Oh, if the invocation *Veni!* (Come)...would only become as popular a prayer as the *Ave* (Hail Mary of the Rosary)!'[7]

Pope Leo XIII heard the Lord's call through Sr. Elena, and he responded to her first letter by publishing *Provida Matris Caritate*, on May 5, 1895 in which he asked the entire Church to celebrate a solemn novena to the Holy Spirit (nine consecutive days of prayer) each year between the feasts of the Ascension and Pentecost. After her third letter, the Pope responded with the publication of the Encyclical *Divinum Illud Munus* on May 9, 1897, which also concerned the doctrine on the Holy Spirit. Sr. Elena was pleased with the Holy Father's efforts but disappointed with the bishop's poor response to the call for an annual novena. Following the ninth letter of Sr. Elena, the Holy Father wrote a letter to the bishops, *Ad Fovendum in Christiano Populo*, April 18, 1902, reminding them of the obligation of the preceding Encyclical.[8]

Sister Elena began to form prayer groups which she called 'Permanent Cenacles'. She also used the term 'Universal Cenacle', 'Cenacle of Universal Prayer' or 'New Cenacle'. Often she was heard to exclaim, 'Let us go to the Cenacle!'[9]

From her early years as an educator, she wrote many pamphlets and books urging people to return to the Holy Spirit. In 1880, she had even approached Don Bosco who was passing by Lucca. He encouraged her to continue her apostolate with the youth but also in her activity as a writer and he said, 'You have a pen of gold….'[10]

That 'pen of gold' was wielded to compose not only letters to the Pope but many beautiful prayers to the Holy Spirit. Elena used the invocation of Pope Leo XIII and wrote a Novena to the Holy Spirit. It is a plea for each of the seven sanctifying gifts of the Holy Spirit with a prayer that is repeated seven times for each gift: 'Father, in the name of Jesus, send forth your Spirit and renew the world.' This prayer is still used today by the Oblate Sisters of the Holy Spirit. In November, 2014, I had the privilege to be present with them at their Motherhouse in Lucca at 5 Piazza S. Agostino while they prayed this powerful prayer together.

And They Were Filled With the Spirit

In her ninth letter to Pope Leo XIII, October 15, 1900, Elena begged the Pope exhort all Catholics to pray for the new century and to place it under the sign of the Holy Spirit. 'Most Holy Father, I humbly present with confidence to your Holiness that the new century may begin with the hymn *Veni Creator Spiritus* to be sung at the beginning of the Mass of the first day of the year.[11]

On January 1, 1901, the first day of the first year in the twentieth century he intoned the hymn *Veni Creator Spiritus ('Come Creator Spirit')* in the name of the whole Church. On the same day, an event took place in Topeka, Kansas, that marked the beginning of a great revival in the power and gifts of the Holy Spirit destined to sweep throughout this country and around the world.

In Topeka, at 17th and Stone Avenue, (now the site of Most Pure Heart of Mary Catholic Church), stood a huge three-story, thirty room mansion. It was nicknamed 'Stone's Folly' after the builder, Erastus Stone, discovered he could not afford to live in it. The mansion then became the home of the Bethel College and Bible School in September, 1900. Rev. Charles Fox Parham and his students dedicated themselves to prayer and the study of God's word concerning the Baptism in the Holy Spirit. In fact, the highest of the three towers in the mansion was designated as a prayer tower, and a marathon prayer vigil was organised. Twenty-four hours a day, seven days a week, these young people were asking God to baptise one or all of them in the Holy Spirit. [12] Now that's a continual cenacle—the kind Elena Guerra was thinking about!

On New Year's Day, 1901, at about 11 o'clock in the evening, Agnes Ozman, one of the students, reported that the 'presence of the Lord' was still there, 'stilling hearts to wait upon him for greater things.' She asked Rev. Parham to lay his hands on her head and pray that she would receive the Baptism in the Spirit. That's precisely what happened. She wrote, 'It was as through rivers of living water were proceeding from my inmost being.'[13] She began to speak in tongues and the following day, a Bohemian recognized her to be speaking his native language. During the next few days many others at the school were baptised in the Holy Spirit, including Rev. Parham. This event is generally accepted as the beginning of Pentecostalism.

God answered the fervent prayer of those who cried out to him day and night. Despite the poor response among Catholics to the call of Pope Leo XIII for continual prayer to the Holy Spirit, there were believers of other denominations who were humbly seeking and gladly receiving the outpouring of the Spirit and his charismatic gifts as the twentieth century began.

In 1906, a continued outpouring of the Holy Spirit occurred in Los Angeles, and is commonly referred to as the Azusa Street Revival. Those who accepted this pentecostal experience were, for the most part, driven out of the established churches. They congregated in new churches and denominations, which are usually categorized as 'Pentecostal'. Pentecostalism is regarded by many historians as a rapidly-growing 'third force' in the Christian world, along with Protestantism and Catholicism.[14]

During the fifties, as charisms began to be received by members of established churches who refused to withdraw from their denominations, a 'neo-pentecostal' movement came into being. The experience of the Baptism in the Holy Spirit began to take place among Episcopalians, Lutherans, Presbyterians, and others who remained in their churches, hoping to work for renewal from within. Therefore, it was not altogether surprising that by the mid-sixties, the Catholic Church would begin to experience a Charismatic Renewal in its midst as well. What did amaze many observers, however, was how rapidly the Baptism in the Spirit spread among Catholics and the openness the Charismatic Renewal met with among the hierarchy of the Catholic Church.

A Network of Friendships

A network of friendships formed among people from Duquesne University in Pittsburgh, Pennsylvania, and University of Notre Dame in South Bend, Indiana in the mid-sixties. Several members of the Duquesne faculty had done their graduate studies at Notre Dame — among them, Patrick Bourgeois of New Orleans, Louisiana. Then there were certain Notre Dame graduate students who had been undergraduates at Duquesne, notably Dorothy Garrity Ranaghan and Bert Ghezzi, both natives of Pittsburgh. Dorothy and Bert had retained personal ties with some faculty members from Duquesne.

In addition to this network of friendships, there was also a preparation for the Charismatic Renewal that had taken place on a spiritual level. Prayer meetings had been going on in the Notre Dame and South Bend communities long before March of 1967. Fr. Edward O'Connor, C.S.C., a leader from the early days of the Catholic Charismatic Renewal, describes the situation this way:

A wave of enthusiasm for Bible vigils and prayer meetings had gone across the country during the early sixties. At Notre Dame, during the year 1963-1964 especially, such activities seem to have flourished. Prayer meetings were held weekly by a group of graduate students, among whom were several who would eventually play a major role in the Pentecostal Movement. These early meetings consisted of Scripture readings, spontaneous prayer, singing and discussion. However, the prayer was less spontaneous, and the discussion more prominent and more humanistic than in the later pentecostal meetings.

A special Mass for the graduate students was also organised each Sunday morning, in which many participated with a lively spirit that was remarkable for those days. It was followed by a breakfast that was real *agape*. A number of students also recited vespers together daily.

That same year, the Cursillo was brought to South Bend, largely through the instrumentality of a graduate student named Steve Clark.Over the next few years, it had a powerful spiritual impact on several hundred people in the city and on the campus. For a while, these *cursillistas* used to meet one evening a week for Mass in Pangborn Chapel at Notre Dame. Out of the Cursillo sprang the Antioch Weekend, designed to confront undergraduate students with what it means to be a Christian. Both the Cursillo and the Antioch Weekend stressed a follow-up programme that was carried out largely through weekly group meetings for discussion, self-examination, mutual encouragement and prayer. Another group which began in that same year was located at Moreau Seminary, where several students began to hold bi-weekly meetings to foster spiritual growth inspired by the example and patronage of Our Lady...

Thus, the pentecostal fire which blazed out in the spring of 1967 had been prepared by a considerable ferment of discussion, prayer, and apostolic activity... Most of the activities undertaken died out after a year or two, only to be succeeded by other endeavors, equally short-lived... Nevertheless, [they] were of real importance in preparing for the Pentecostal Movement, both by exercising people in the life of prayer and apostolate, and by forming friendships which would serve as conductors of the pentecostal spirit when it arrived.'[15]

THE CURSILLO CONNECTION

It's important to note how deeply the Cursillo Movement impacted the people from Notre Dame and Duquesne who were later to become leaders of the Catholic Charismatic Renewal. A *New Covenant* article from February, 1973, describes the men who were involved in the Cursillo at Notre Dame:

> The men who formed around the Cursillo Movement at Notre Dame in the mid-sixties came from varied backgrounds with some significant common threads. They were all highly-educated intellectuals who achieved considerable academic distinction. Most professed a Catholicism of an orthodox type. They were concerned about liturgical and personal spiritual renewal, although several had acquired progressive theological educations and most had worked in social action and civil rights movements...

> There were some exceptions to this pattern. One was Ralph Martin, a brilliant philosophy student and crusading campus editor, who had no concern for the Church at all. By early 1964, he finally felt free from the repressions of his Catholic upbringing, and had gained a reputation as an argumentative atheist around campus. The first time Martin met Steve Clark, they got into an argument about Christianity in a student restaurant near campus.
>
> Martin's conversion occurred suddenly and dramatically during the second Cursillo at Notre Dame. It was a conversion so dramatic that Bert Ghezzi, who was there, at first doubted its authenticity. 'I never saw such a complete U-turn in my life. I didn't believe such things were possible.'[16]

Ralph Martin recalls that after encountering the Risen Lord Jesus on the Cursillo, he felt filled with *'power from on high'*, and he proclaimed, *'I want to be His witness'*.[17] Men like Ralph Martin and Steve Clark from University of Notre Dame realised that what the founders of the Cursillo Movement foresaw was essentially a new Pentecost. Eduardo Bonnin, one of the Cursillo founders, said this explicitly:

> Christianity, afterwards as before, is essentially an outpouring of the Holy Spirit. It is essentially the miracle of Pentecost. And where you cannot see the outpouring of the Spirit, there the 'Counsellor' has not passed. There you might find men who believe in the Father, and, because of

> an ingenious egocentricity, are convinced about a practice of Christianity when they go to beg gifts from the Father. You might also have men who believe in the 'Word' and in the sense of all the things which have been revealed in Him. Inspired by their newly acquired idea of Him, these men try to model their lives on His with a laborious fidelity. They are industrious men of moral probity. But they are not men of the Holy Spirit of overflowing love; they are not men with flashing eyes. For them, Pentecost has not yet come.[18]

But for many of the *cursillistas* at Notre Dame, Pentecost had indeed come! In fact, at one of the prayer meetings held at Phil O'Mara's apartment in 1965, there was an instance of glossalalia (speaking in tongues). It was stopped by the leader of the meeting, who did not understand it. After Ralph had his dramatic conversion on a Cursillo, he too spoke in tongues a month later. However, he did not realize what it was at the time. 'Miraculous events, healing, discernment of spirits, answered prayer accompanied the Cursillos of that era at Notre Dame. Most of the leaders had personal encounters with Jesus at least as intense as their later experiences with the Baptism in the Spirit. George Martin sums up the experience of those days by calling them 'incredibly grace-filled times.'[19]

During the Christmas holidays in 1965 Ralph Martin and Steve Clark met at Martin's home in New Jersey and decided to spend the summer in prayer at Mount Savior Monastery in Elmira, New York. During their stay at the monastery, they felt the Lord leading them to leave graduate school (Clark had remained at Notre Dame and Martin was at Princeton) to make themselves more available for Christian service. Once their decision was made, they were invited to give the opening and closing talks at the National Cursillo Convention in Kansas City, Missouri. They joined the staff of St. John's Student Parish at Michigan State University and the National Secretariat of the Cursillo, also located in East Lansing, Michigan. Between 1965 and 1970, Ralph and Steve presented dozens of Cursillo workshops throughout the United States.[20] Contacts made through the Cursillo were later useful in spreading the news about the Baptism in the Holy Spirit.

LIFE-CHANGING BOOKS

There were two key paperback books destined to lead Ralph, Steve and their network of friends from Notre Dame, Duquesne and the Cursillo into the experience of the Baptism in the Spirit. One is *The Cross and the Switchblade* by David Wilkerson with John and Elizabeth Sherrill, originally published in 1963 by Pyramid Publications for Fleming H. Revell. The other is *They Speak with Other Tongues,* by John Sherrill, originally published by McGraw Hill in 1964. There is a more recent version published in 2004 by Chosen Books, a division of Baker Publishing Group.

Both books make for fascinating reading; they're hard to put down. In *They Speak with Other Tongues,* John Sherrill details his research into the unusual phenomenon of speaking in other tongues 'as the Spirit gives utterance'. During the years of Sherrill's research he was baptised in the Spirit himself and describes the experience first as an observer, then as a participant. This book is considered a neo-pentecostal classic.

The Cross and the Switchblade is the dramatic story of a small town Pentecostal preacher named David Wilkerson who is led by the Spirit to work among the street gangs in the Bedford-Stuyvestant section of New York City. It is a powerful testimony to Wilkerson's dynamic faith and an intriguing introduction to the power released in the Baptism in the Holy Spirit. Wilkerson describes the various ways the Holy Spirit works through divine guidance and the charismatic gifts.

The story of how these books first came to be known in Catholic circles is quite interesting, and shows once again the great debt we Catholics owe to our Protestant and Pentecostal brethren. Peter Collins, a 1966 graduate of Notre Dame, was spending a few weeks during the summer of 1966 in Toronto, Canada, when he came across *They Speak with Other Tongues* while visiting a Pentecostal church with a co-worker. Peter describes in detail how this happened in his testimony later in this book. Suffice it to say here that Peter gave Sherrill's book to Steve Clark in June of 1966, when he met Steve and Ralph at a training session for Extension Volunteers in San Antonio, Texas.

Steve Clark had already obtained a copy of *The Cross and the Switchblade* from a Campus Crusade worker at Michigan State University. He was impressed with the effects that the Baptism in the Spirit had on the lives of drug addicts. He and Ralph had even considered visiting Wilkerson at his Teen Challenge Ministry in New York City, but never did. Steve gave Peter a copy of Wilkerson's book.

Because of this initial exchange of books in June, 1966, a number of other students at Notre Dame began to read the books and wonder about this 'Baptism in the Holy Spirit'. Jim Cavnar and Gerry Rauch, undergraduates at Notre Dame, were spending the summer of 1966 in East Lansing with Ralph and Steve. As Jim shares in his testimony later in this book, he believed that the events he was reading about were probably true, but he was content for someone else to investigate them. And that's precisely what happened.

Spiritual Hunger at Duquesne

A few months before the exchange of books described above, that is, in the Spring of 1966, two faculty members from Duquesne University had entered into a period of intense prayer and discussion about the vitality of their faith. One was a history professor; the other was a theology instructor. They felt the need for a greater inner dynamism, a new power to live as Christians and to give witness to Christ. Both men had been committed to the Lord for a number of years; both were *cursillistas*. In fact, the history professor was instrumental in bringing the Cursillo Movement to Pittsburgh. Eileen Karl's testimony found later in this book gives greater detail on this point. They were also moderators of the *Chi Rho* Society on Duquesne's campus which was founded years earlier to stimulate prayer, participation in the liturgy, Christian witness and social action. Yet they still wanted 'something more'. They weren't sure exactly what it was, but they made a pact to pray for one another.

Each day from the spring of 1966 on, they prayed that the Holy Spirit would renew in them all the graces of their Baptism and Confirmation, that he would fill up in them the vacuum left by human effort with the power and love of the Lord Jesus Christ.[21] Daily, these men prayed the beautiful Sequence Hymn of Pentecost, sometimes called the 'Golden Sequence', which is used by the Church in the Pentecost Liturgy. It may be found in the beginning of this book.

A New Discovery

The National Cursillo Convention in August of 1966 was destined to be an important meeting for the two professors from Duquesne. It was there that they met up with their friends, Ralph Martin and Steve Clark. They were given copies of the two books about the pentecostal experience and urged to read them, which they did. God had already been preparing them for a new dimension of life in the Spirit by awakening in them a deep spiritual hunger and leading them into concerted prayer.

The Holy Spirit was at work. In the course of reading *The Cross and the Switchblade,* one of the men from Duquesne decided to check the scriptural references about the work of the Holy Spirit and how to receive the Baptism in the Holy Spirit. He turned to

St. Luke's Gospel and to the Acts of the Apostles. Later he wrote, 'I then began to flip like mad all through the Bible, particularly through the New Testament, and found, for four solid hours, that the whole Bible was opened to me in a way it had never been before. I don't think I moved from my chair.'[22]

They saw more clearly than before, the role of the Holy Spirit in the life of the believer as the teacher, the one who empowers and guides. 'It seemed so clear, so compelling, so overwhelming. It was almost like discovering Christianity for the first time.'[23]

A Bold Step

Fr. Ed O'Connor recounted to me about a little known fact concerning these two Duquesne professors. In November, 1966, the two men decided to spend some time in prayer at the Ark and the Dove Retreat House. In the middle of the night each of them awakened with an inner urging to go into the chapel. While they were there in prayer in the presence of Jesus in the Blessed Sacrament, they experienced 'the glory of God' coming down and filling that chapel. It was a very strong manifestation of the presence of God for each of them. They shared this experience of God's glory filling the chapel in the middle of the night with Fr. O'Connor. I have not seen any other reference to this experience of 'the glory' coming down in any other book or resource.

The Duquesne professors were then faced with several possibilities. They could continue praying and discussing this deeper life in the Spirit themselves, but that didn't seem too promising. They had already been praying and talking for some time. Perhaps they thought they should lay hands on each other and pray for a release of the Holy Spirit. They weren't convinced that this would be the best alternative either. Another option was to attend a Pentecostal church, but they were reluctant to do so. In the end, the most attractive alternative seemed to be to find some neo-Pentecostals, those who had remained within their own denominations after the Baptism in the Spirit. It was a bold step, but they decided to take it.[24]

There was an Episcopalian priest who had come to Duquesne's campus once to give a lecture. As a 'long shot', they called Fr. William Lewis of Christ Church in the North Hills of Pittsburgh, to inquire whether or not he was familiar with Wilkerson's and Sherrill's books. In fact, he was familiar with them, and although he was not baptised in the Spirit himself, he offered to introduce the men to one of his parishioners who was baptised in the Spirit. Fr. Lewis described her as a fine woman in very good standing in his parish, the mother of an Episcopalian priest, and a member of an interdenominational charismatic prayer group which met in a home just across from his church.[25]

Because a meeting over the Christmas holidays was not opportune, they decided to wait until Friday, January 6, 1967. The date was significant to the men from Duquesne as they recalled that January 6 was the feast of the Epiphany, the manifestation of Jesus Christ as Son of God, as One baptised by the Holy Spirit and the One who baptizes in the Holy Spirit. The two from Duquesne arrived at Fr. Lewis' office and were introduced to his Spirit-filled parishioner. The witness she shared with them was simple, straightforward, and scriptural; they were impressed. As the meeting ended she invited them to a charismatic prayer meeting the following Friday night. It was a meeting that would change their lives.[26]

Where Two or Three Are Gathered in My Name

I am deeply grateful to Flo Dodge, who lived in Lower Burrell, Pennsylvania, in 1992 and who provided me with the following background about her prayer group (later referred to as the Chapel Hill prayer group). It was this prayer group which gave birth to such a powerful move of the Holy Spirit among Catholics.

Flo, a Presbyterian, was sovereignly baptised in the Holy Spirit in 1962.[27] She had been raised in a fine Christian home which was often the gathering place for foreign missionaries and various Christian activities. It was especially significant to Flo's mother, who was living with her in 1967, that once again their home, now in Chapel Hill, would be used for a mighty work of God.

Two and a half to three years prior to the famous visit of the Duquesne faculty members, Flo had felt led to form a prayer group. At the time, she held a responsible position as training director at a large Pittsburgh department store and was active in her church as well. One by one, the Lord brought women from different denominations to the prayer meeting in her home where He dealt with each one in a wonderful way. There was a core group of seven women who were baptised in the Spirit, but at times the meeting numbered as many as thirty people.

Flo said that the Lord trained the core group in intercession and put them under a strict discipline. They experienced a deep unity in the Holy Spirit as He moved in their midst. The women were being prepared through prayer and fasting to be very obedient and docile to the Holy Spirit.

In October of 1966 the Lord led Flo in prayer to read all of Isaiah 48. Her sense was that it held an important message for the prayer group. In this passage the Lord proclaims:

> Things of the past I foretold long ago,
> they went forth from My mouth,
> I let you hear of them;
> then suddenly I took action and they came to be.
> Because I know that you are stubborn
> and that your neck is an iron sinew
> and your forehead bronze,
> I foretold them to you of old:
> before they took place I let you hear of them,
> That you might not say, 'My idol did them
> my statue, my molten image commanded them.'
> Now that you have heard, look at all this
> must you not admit it?

From now on I announce new things to you,
hidden events which you knew not. . .
See, I have refined you like silver,
tested you in the furnace of affliction.
For my sake, for my own sake, I do this
why should I suffer profanation?
My glory I will not give to another.
Is. 48:3-6, 10-11

Flo felt the Lord was stressing four things through this passage and she taught about them at the prayer meeting:

1. He was doing a new thing.
2. They must not say, 'My idol did it.'
3. A refining process was taking place.
4. No one should touch God's glory by moving in the flesh instead of in the Spirit.

In retrospect, she sees how the Lord was preparing this Chapel Hill prayer group for the role they were to play in bringing the Baptism in the Holy Spirit to Catholics. God clearly had a plan in mind for them although they didn't realise it at the time. The passage from Ephesians 2:10 was especially meaningful to Flo. 'For we are His workmanship, created in Christ Jesus for good works, which God prepared beforehand, that we should walk in them.'

Shortly before the meeting of January 13, 1967, Flo received a phone call from the Episcopalian woman who had met with the people from Duquesne. This sister in Christ was very excited and anxious to do something special the night the Catholics would be visiting. Flo felt that the prayer group needed to be 'prayed up' and proceed as usual. But when she hung up the phone, she asked the Lord what was happening and if she should contact the core group. She recalls that the Lord seemed to say, 'Ask them to fast and pray and be obedient to the Holy Spirit and history will be made.'

The night of January 13, 1967, around 7:30-8:00 p.m., four visitors from Duquesne arrived at Flo's townhouse, 25 Chapel Drive in the North Hills. There were the two faculty members already mentioned, one of their wives, plus another theology instructor, Patrick Bourgeois. Flo recalls that when her mother opened the door that night and saw the men, she felt a deep love for them and received them as sons. They welcomed each other with a warm embrace. The Lord gave Flo's mother some sense of the unity in the Spirit He desired to bring about. The love of the Lord came over the whole group and lasted all evening.

Flo was deeply touched by the spiritual hunger she saw in the two men who had been fasting and praying for a renewal in the Holy Spirit. The theology instructor commented to Flo's friend that he was amazed at the insight with which lay people at the meeting could discuss Scripture. The evening proceeded as usual with hymns, spontaneous prayer, brief testimonies, sharing from Scripture and prayer in tongues.

It was customary toward the end of the prayer meeting to get a chair and place it in the middle of the room for anyone who wanted to request prayer for a special need. But that night, Flo felt the Lord ask her to forego this custom. She remembered that passage from Isaiah, *'My glory I give to no other'*. Flo wanted to obey the Lord's prompting that there be no laying on of hands that night. It was important that no one member of the prayer group 'take the credit', so to speak, for being the person to lay hands on the Catholic visitors for the Baptism in the Spirit.

But as she tried to bring the meeting to a close, the history professor from Duquesne leapt up. Flo Dodge vividly remembers that he reached out with the sweep of his hand as if to stop her and said, 'Oh, no you don't. I've waited a long time for this. I came to receive the Baptism in the Holy Spirit, and I'm not leaving until I have it.'

Flo then asked Jim Prophater, a commercial artist who happened to be present that night with his wife, to meet with this professor and to ascertain if, indeed, he was ready for the Baptism in the Spirit. According to Flo, Jim asked him to state what he believed about Jesus Christ. The professor replied that he loved the Lord with all his heart and that he was eager to receive more of His Holy Spirit.

All those present joined hands in a circle and Jim Prophater offered a simple prayer, asking the Holy Spirit to come. Flo recalls that Jim said, 'Lord, You know his heart and need. Fill him now to overflowing with Your Spirit.' She said that she could sense the Holy Spirit falling upon the professor, however he did not pray in tongues and no one laid hands on him. But there was such a power in the room that night that everyone present received more of God. In a spirit of rejoicing, everyone stood up and gave thanks for what the Lord was doing. One of the theology instructors sang a hymn and the meeting closed.

For the four Catholics who attended that first meeting, it was significant that this prayer for one of them to be baptised in the Spirit should take place on January 13, the octave day of the Epiphany, set aside in the Catholic liturgy to celebrate the baptism of Jesus in the Jordan River.[28]

Another Description

It's often interesting to see how different people describe the same event. We are fortunate to have the following account of one of the original four Catholics who attended the Chapel Hill prayer meeting at Flo Dodge's home. This was written by the theology instructor who had made the original commitment to pray for a renewal in the Holy Spirit:

> My wife, two colleagues and I walked cautiously into a 'pure suburbia' home and were immediately struck by the warmth of the people there. It was like a family gathering, and we belonged. I remember that they sang four or five traditional mainline Protestant Sunday school type hymns to open the meeting. A lengthy spontaneous prayer session followed. There was one person leading out at a time, and while it was certainly not babble there was an undertone of voices, and a little praying in tongues. This, too, was done quite softly and unobtrusively.

They then began to share biblical passages in a most remarkable way. They shared what they had read in the last week and related it to a variety of experiences both past and present. What startled us about this is that the theology of Christian life which emerged was excellent.

It was a resurrection-oriented grace theology of the kind usually found in Cursillos and in good textbooks in theology; yet, it was neither contrived nor from a textbook. The operative theology of the group as it met and prayed together was positive, natural, and joyful, since it was grounded in the Pauline epistles. I winced once or twice when someone mentioned intelligence and how 'dangerous it is, etc.' In fact, I was about to start grinding my teeth till someone said, 'You know, I think the Lord means to use that too…' and this began a very positive discussion.

My only other objection seemed to centre on the way they were using Scripture. Fundamentalist is not the right word. It was much more that they were tending to read the Scriptures like the Fathers of the Church did, in a highly allegorical manner. It put me off for a while. But even through this I could see a real testimony of the sense of the presence of God. Maybe that's why it bothered me. I fear a 'super-direct pipeline to God' mentality. Yet as one of my friends said after the meeting, maybe we over-emphasise secondary causality too much so that we never have a sense of God working in anything. In all it was not

> an extraordinary evening. Yet, it led us to think and to pray. We were left with an abiding sense that here was a movement of God.[29]

I have been told by several people who were present that this professor left Flo's home to walk outside by himself for a while during the time of fellowship after the prayer meeting. He had had an overall positive experience of the meeting as is recorded here. But certain elements caused him enough emotional upset that he felt the need to be alone and think them through.

Coming Back for More

The following Friday, January 20, 1967, two of the four Catholics returned to Flo's house in Chapel Hill. The theology instructor shared his impressions of that second meeting with his friends in a letter:

> Of the four of us who attended this first meeting, for a number of reasons only Patrick Bourgeois, a fellow instructor in the theology department, and I were able to make it to the next meeting. We returned to find the prayer and discussion centered this time upon the Epistle to the Romans.
>
> The only way I can express the way we felt about this discussion was that it was not all clouded up by Reformation issues. They weren't saying anything that I felt to be a problem. It was a strikingly non-denom-

inational meeting. It ended when Pat and I asked to be prayed with for the Baptism in the Holy Spirit.
They broke up into several groups because they were praying over several people. They simply asked me to make an act of faith for the power of the Spirit to work in me. I prayed in tongues rather quickly. It was not a particularly soaring or spectacular thing at all. I felt a certain peace — and at least a little prayerful — and truthfully, rather curious as to where all this would lead.

They broke out food afterwards and had a little party. I remember that my comment to them that night was, 'See what you do when you have Catholics here, you have rites and ceremonies.' They had never done that before. They had always sort of just broken up and gone home. That night, however, was a sort of celebration.

To me, praying in tongues was a rather minimal aspect, a purely concomitant phenomenon which seemed naturally to go along with this. I was interested in it mainly because I felt my faith needed 'livening.' That was the prime concern — speaking in tongues didn't really present an intellectual problem because I knew historically that it had been a phenomenon which was widely accepted in the Church in its beginning. And from what I knew of Church history the New Testament phenomenon was not limited to the New Testament by any means.

My personal difficulty had been the reverse. I couldn't

> understand why this charismatic phenomenon didn't occur more frequently, as one would expect. This seemed to be more in line with what I had come to expect of New Testament Christianity.[30]

Ask and You Shall Receive

In the following week, the professor whose narration you have just read, prayed with his wife and the history professor with the laying on of hands. They too received a new outpouring of the Spirit. The history professor described it this way:

> Talk about a baptism, it was just like I was being plunged down into a great sea of water, only the water was God, the water was the Holy Spirit...
>
> All in all it is not a new experience. It is not a revolutionary experience because it reaffirmed all the things which I'd been trying to hold on to for years and to affirm for so many years: my appreciation of Scripture, my appreciation of the Eucharist, my appreciation of praying and working with other people.
>
> The difference is that it seems to me that everything is easier and more spontaneous and comes from within. It is not so much that I am trying to work with people or that I am trying to advert to God or to pay attention to him, to make him the center of my life. This seems to be now a much more spontaneous welling up of these aspirations

> and this power from within. This is not saying that I've overcome all my difficulties, not by a long shot, it's just that there's more inwardness and spontaneity, more power in a word than there ever was before.
>
> And this has lasted and endured. It can be lessened or weakened by lack of faith because I am sure that God doesn't work despite us. We have to cooperate with him and let him act, let him have his own way because there is nothing automatic, nothing mechanical, nothing magical, nothing superstitious about it. It is still the old-fashioned, Christian life which was first taught to me when I was a child, and yet it has a certain new dimension, a new strength and a new power and interiority which it did not have before, for which I thank him with my whole heart.[31]

ANOTHER EYEWITNESS

I am grateful to have yet another description from one of the original four Catholics who attended that famous Chapel Hill prayer meeting at the home of Flo Dodge. It is the testimony of Dr. Patrick L. Bourgeois, a native of New Orleans, Louisiana, who was for many years a professor of philosophy at Loyola University of the South. Pat had done summer graduate studies at University of Notre Dame and he was a graduate student in philosophy and a full-time theology instructor at Duquesne in 1966. Therefore, he had many of the same friends and acquaintances alluded to earlier. Pat was invited by his colleagues to come along to the prayer meeting on the night of

January 13, 1967, and he felt impelled to go. In fact, he was one of the two who returned and were prayed over the following week. Pat's story is found later in this book and provides not only an eyewitness account of the meeting at Flo Dodge's home, but also Pat's reflections as a professor of theology and philosophy.

As you may remember from Flo's description, one of the original four from Duquesne asked for the Baptism in the Spirit at the first prayer meeting they attended. Pat's own intense inner response to the Spirit took place when he and his colleague returned to the prayer group the next week and actually asked for the Baptism in the Spirit with the laying on of hands. An interesting note is that Rev. Don Basham and his wife, Alice, were living in Sharon, Pennsylvania, at this time. Basham was a Spirit-filled minister and author. Flo recalls that when there were no special activities being held at Pastor Basham's church, he occasionally joined the Chapel Hill prayer group for their meeting. He and Alice 'just happened' to be there on January 20, the second time the Catholic visitors attended. Rev. Basham later commented on this meeting in his book, *Face Up with a Miracle*. He wrote, 'I found myself praising God who had taken what began as a simple prayer of faith over two sincere young men who were seeking more of Him, and seemed to be turning it into a spiritual renaissance of major proportions among future leaders of the Roman Catholic Church.'[32] Mrs. Basham told me in a personal conversation in 1991 that she and Don realised history was in the making that night in January of 1967, and they felt privileged to be a part of it.[33]

We Cannot Help But Speak of What We Have Seen and Heard

In the weeks following these meetings a number of things happened. The theology instructor who was a Chi Rho advisor returned to South Bend on business in mid-February. While he was there, he shared his experience of the Baptism in the Spirit with some of his friends from Notre Dame. Kevin and Dorothy Ranaghan describe their encounter with him in the following words:

> The quiet fire burning in him was obvious to both of us. In a real way he was a new person, a man more centered on Christ. For two days we talked of Pentecostalism and what it all could mean. Long into the nights, over many cups of coffee, we raised every intellectual, aesthetic and psychological objection we could muster to fend off this intrusion into our religious complacency. We were curious, but quite happy to stay at a distance from the whole thing. Yet, we now had seen for ourselves a man changed by the power of the Holy Spirit. [34]

Fr. Edward O'Connor, C.S.C., met this professor from Duquesne during his visit to South Bend quite by accident. Fr. O'Connor had remembered him from his days as a student at Notre Dame. Fr. O'Connor commented on the encounter. 'He didn't say a word to me about the pentecostal happenings. However, there was a strange, joyous light in his eyes I had never seen before. I didn't really advert to it at the moment, but somehow it haunted me for a while thereafter. Later when I got into the Charismatic Renewal, I realised what lay behind it.' [35]

A Week before the Duquesne Weekend

In addition to his visit to South Bend, this same theology instructor wrote a letter to a friend describing his experience with the Baptism in the Spirit and the charismatic prayer group. It is dated February 11, 1967 — exactly one week before the Duquesne Weekend took place. The theological and pastoral reflections are interesting, since they come from a man who describes himself as a 'fledgling theologian' who has just received the Baptism in the Spirit.

> [I understand] that you are interested in our impressions of contacts with a Spirit-filled prayer group.
>
> Essentially, I think, it has been simply a discovery of all that we already knew of Christ and Christian life. I hope all this doesn't sound too enigmatic, but the whole experience has been rather like having all our suspicions about the truth of Christianity confirmed; gaining a new depth of awareness of who Christ is and what it means to be a Christian.
>
> A deep sense of need for prayer and sacraments, a joy and confidence in witnessing, a serious confrontation with my own sinfulness, have been what I have noticed most about myself. I have been given a couple of the charisms— prayer in a tongue, discernment of spirits, and power to

cast them out. I mention these because I trust your discretion, and because I believe you deserve the full story on what is happening here.

My impression of prayer in a tongue is that when I pray in this way He is doing something deep inside where I can't reach, that somehow it makes intercessory prayer more effective, and that prayer in the usual sense and prayer in a tongue are complementary and foster and feed one another. The other gifts have been helpful. I gratefully accept them, pray that I may use them to God's glory, and have no idea whether they are permanent or only transient signs. My conviction is that these are all gifts to be used and not to be talked about.

My wife began to speak in a tongue when I laid hands on her and prayed over her, just two days after the same thing had happened to me at a prayer meeting. It happened to both of us in the same way; a couple of phrases came to mind, and when we used them, more came. It develops with frequent use, rather like a baby learning to talk.

What I have noticed most about her is a quite remarkable attraction to the Scriptures, to spiritual reading, and to prayer, as well as a spiritual wisdom which I find (by way of understatement) quite helpful to me.

The whole experience has brought much joy and confidence; but I would say that there has been nothing that has been exhilarating (in any frothy emotional sense).

It has been, on the whole, calm, quiet, and sometimes painful...

How I relate all this to my Catholicism should be fairly obvious from what I have said above. Anything else can best be summarised by saying that I find Thomas Aquinas, the Roman Liturgy, and the lives of the saints helpful and relevant.

Perhaps some of my observations as a fledgling theologian might be helpful.

First of all, the prayer group is super-orthodox. Their understanding of the Trinity, of Christ, of the life of grace, of the relation between nature and grace, of election, of human freedom before God, is a Catholic understanding of those realities.

Secondly, I would relate the Baptism of the Spirit to Confirmation as follows. Our Sacrament of Confirmation is identical to the New Testament Baptism of the Spirit. That we notice no effects, or minimal ones, in many cases, is due, not to a failure of the sacrament, but to a failure to seek or respond to the gifts to which the sacrament gives us a claim (the whole scholastic bit about co-operating with the grace of the sacraments.) If a confirmed Catholic is later transformed in a context such as we have experienced, this is simply a revival of the grace of the sacrament (again a traditional scholastic notion). The laying on of hands is no repudiation of Confirmation, any more than the Asperges is a repudiation of Baptism. If we are not mere ritualists, it is obvious that sacramentals can be used by God as means of activating what He has already done through the sacraments.

Thirdly, in an ecumenical perspective, this could be the Spirit's way of leading us into unity with one another. All of the people we have met in the group are active in their own churches; we have found no sectarian spirit, no repudiation of the larger institutional church. We are 'learning from one another' in the deepest sense, and in the deepest sense we 'need one another'. At the same time I find three hours a week when all the divisions between the churches are gone, and I find myself becoming more and more committed to the Catholic Church.

Finally, a pastoral concern. People will go where the action is. Those Catholics whose ties with the Church are loose or shaky, and who have come in contact with the genuine Christians in these prayer groups, may well sever their ties with Catholicism — to their loss and ours — if there is nobody to show the way. It is well to remember that to many Pentecostals and Evangelicals, we represent at best a dead institutionalism, and at worst the Anti-Christ. Unless they know and respect real Catholics, they will not direct fringe Catholics back to their own Church. Formed Catholics, I think, will find their Catholicism enhanced by contacts with these groups; but they will also serve their

> Church by creating a climate of understanding and love, and by retrieving the strays.
>
> By way of closing, I find it difficult to say how much joy it gives me to share this with you, since you are responsible for starting me on the path to all this. Our prayers go with you.'[36]

THE CHI RHO SOCIETY

Another significant development concerned plans for a retreat of Duquesne students scheduled for February 17-19. As has already been mentioned, the two professors who have figured so prominently in the events just recounted, were advisors to the *Chi Rho* Society. *Chi Rho* took its name from the first two letters in the Greek word for Christ. Bert Ghezzi had been the first president of the organization while still an undergraduate at Duquesne. Dorothy Garrity Ranaghan had also been a founding member of *Chi Rho*.

On a campus where Greek organisations were strong, *Chi Rho* provided an alternative to sorority and fraternity life. Students joined *Chi Rho* to experience Christian fellowship and many members met in the morning or afternoon in the History Department to pray a shortened form of the Divine Office and to study Scripture. One of the students who was a member of *Chi Rho* in 1967 recalls that there was a strong emphasis on social action. David Mangan's brother, Tom, who was a member of *Chi Rho* as an undergrad went to Turkey to serve in the Peace

Corps. Others were active in the Civil Rights Movement and travelled to Selma, Alabama, for the historic march in 1965. Gina Steinmetz Scanlon, whose testimony appears later in this book describes how she and others from *Chi Rho* were active in another Duquesne organisation as well, the Council of Interracial Friendship (COIF). By January, 1967, members of the *Chi Rho* Society were being pulled in different directions and the organisation was struggling to define its identity.

A New Theme

The two professors had had such a profound experience of the Holy Spirit, they suggested a change in the theme of the student retreat — from *'The Sermon on the Mount'* to *'The Acts of the Apostles.'* Several students were part of the committee to plan the weekend — Bill Deigan, the president; Karin Sefcik, the secretary; Marybeth Mutmansky; Pat Bourgeois; Annamarie Nacko; Paul Gray and Mary Ann Springel. Marybeth remembers that during these planning sessions the two professors made no specific reference to the Baptism in the Spirit. Yet they communicated a deep sense of anticipation and joy. She and others began to wonder what was going to happen on this retreat? Pat Bourgeois recalls that the other two professors were hoping and praying that the Holy Spirit might do something special on the retreat weekend, but they had no clear plan in mind.

The Ark and the Dove Retreat Centre

On Friday, February 17, 1967, approximately 25 students left for retreat along with the campus chaplain, a Holy Ghost priest, Fr. Joseph Healy, C.S.Sp., the two professors who were faculty moderators, and one of their wives.

We headed for the Ark and the Dove, a lovely retreat centre nestled in a sixteen-acre wooded area of the North Hills, just fifteen miles north of downtown Pittsburgh. A twenty-eight room, three-story country inn served as the main house and a smaller adjacent cottage housed additional retreatants. The facility was originally built by Bell Telephone Company in 1924 as a get-away for their female employees. In 1944 it was sold to Cyrilla Marismann and M. Jean Seibert who opened a private school called the Maxada School for boys and girls age 4 to 14. I was told by a groundskeeper that the owners were Christian and that they dedicated the large upstairs room as a prayer room. This later became the chapel when the property was acquired by the Diocese of Pittsburgh in 1964. It served as a retreat center and was staffed by an order of religious sisters from Holland, the Ladies of Bethany. These sisters had a special apostolate to care for the poor and to foster ecumenical encounters. Cardinal Wright was eager to foster such ecumenical gatherings in the post-Vatican II church and the Ark and the Dove served such a purpose. I remember being told that they had a cross with a corpus on one side for Catholic services and a side with no corpus for ecumenical services. In 1979, the Diocese of Pittsburgh began to administrate the facility directly and changed its name to 'The John Cardinal Wright Vocation and Prayer Centre.' It was purchased by the Sisters of Divine

Providence in 2000 and renamed 'Providence Villa'. In 2015 the property was put up for sale. The National Service Committee of the Catholic Charismatic Renewal has taken the lead in purchasing the property which will be owned by the Renewal worldwide. It will once again be called The Ark and the Dove and will serve as a home for the Renewal, a meeting place and pilgrimage site. It will house the history of the Charismatic Renewal. [37]

VENI CREATOR SPIRITUS

The retreat opened in the upper room chapel and the students were told that intercessory prayer was being offered on their behalf by the two men who had given the men's retreat the year before—Ralph Martin and Steve Clark. After the Duquesne Weekend, the retreatants learned that the members of the Chapel Hill prayer group had been interceding as well. Flo remembers how excited all the women in the core group were. In Flo's words, 'They knew God was going to move in a burst of power.'[38]

The professors directed the group to sing an ancient hymn to the Holy Spirit entitled, *'Veni Creator Spiritus'*. One of the professors explained that it was more than a song; it was a prayer. The retreatants were asked to sing it at each session, imploring the Holy Spirit to come. Some of the participants remember being told that they should be careful what they were asking for, because God always answers prayer!

The students were taught the traditional Gregorian chant melody but the hymn was sung in our own language as follows:

Come O Creator Spirit blest
And in our souls take up thy rest;
Come with thy grace and heav'nly aid,
To fill the hearts which thou hast made.
Great Paraclete! to thee we cry;
O highest gift of God most high!
O fount of life! O fire of love!
And sweet anointing from above!

Thou dost appear in sev'nfold dow'r
The sign of God's almighty pow'r!
The Father's promise, making rich
With saving truth our earthly speech.

Kindle our senses from above,
And make our hearts o'erflow with love;
With patience firm and virtue high,
The weakness of our flesh supply.

Far from us drive the foe we dread,
And grant us thy true peace instead;
So shall we not, with thee for guide.
Turn from the path of life aside.
Oh, may thy grace on us bestow
The Father and the Son to know,
And thee, through endless times confessed,
Of both th'eternal Spirit blest.

All glory, while the ages run,
Be to the Father and the Son
Who rose from death: the same to thee,
O Holy Ghost, eternally. Amen.

A Sovereign Outpouring of the Holy Spirit

The remaining details of the Duquesne Weekend and the sovereign outpouring of the Holy Spirit are told many times over in the eyewitness accounts found later in this book. A brief sketch of the schedule of daily activities is as follows. The presentations centered on the first four chapters of the Acts of the Apostles. These talks were presented in the sun parlor of the Ark and the Dove Retreat Centre on the first floor. Friday night, after an opening talk, there was a Penance Service in the chapel. On Saturday morning, Paul Gray spoke on Acts 1 in the sun parlor, Mass was celebrated and afterwards Marybeth Mutmansky (Greene) and Karin Sefcik (Treiber) presented meditations on women of the Bible. The talk on Acts 2 was followed by small discussion groups.

Many of the testimonies mention this presentation on Acts 2 because it was a pivotal moment in the Duquesne Weekend. The faculty advisors had invited the Spirit-filled Episcopalian woman they had met at the Chapel Hill prayer group, to come and speak. Her presentation was on the Lordship of Jesus Christ and the Baptism in the Holy Spirit. She may not have used this terminology, but that was her theme.

During the discussion following her talk, David Mangan made a proposal that the participants renew their sacrament of Confirmation as part of the closing ceremony. A plumbing problem threatened to end the retreat early, but it was resolved. Later that night, during what was scheduled as a birthday party for several people, the Holy Spirit began a sovereign work. One by one, about half (but not all) of the young people were drawn into the chapel and experienced the Baptism in the Spirit in a manifest way.

News Too Good To Keep

Shortly after the Duquesne Weekend, one of the two faculty advisors to *Chi Rho* wrote a letter to his friends giving them an update on 'some wonderful things'. He apologised for his use of carbon paper, but he wanted to communicate with many people very quickly. He explained, *'I have news too good to keep'*. Here is an excerpt from that letter:

> ... We have found ourselves on a plane of Christian life all the textbooks call normal and all practice and expectation seems to deny. Our faith has come alive, our believing has become a kind of knowing. Suddenly, the world of the supernatural has become more real than the natural. In brief, Jesus Christ is a real person to us, a real living person who is our Lord and who is active in our lives. (Cf. the New Testament and read it as though it were literally true *now* every word, every line). Prayer and the sacraments have become truly our daily bread instead of practices which we recognise as 'good for us'. A love of the

Scriptures, a love of the Church I never thought possible, a transformation of our relationships with others, a need and a power of witness beyond all expectation, have all become part of our lives.
The initial experience of the 'Baptism of the Spirit' was not at all emotional, but life has become suffused with calm, confidence, joy, and peace...

One of the most startling results has been a Weekend we held for about twenty-five students. Just an ordinary conference and discussion type retreat. But we did one thing different—we centered on Acts 1-4 and *expected* the coming of the Holy Spirit. We sang the *Veni Creator Spiritus* before each conference and meant it. We were not disappointed. What happened in Acts 2 happened there. These, incidentally, were students who three months ago had their doubts about the existence of God, wouldn't hear of prayer, etc., etc. They have already had their effect upon the campus...

We have also been showered with charismata (again, cf. 1 Cor. 12-14). (Cf. also Rahner's theological dictionary on Charism).

This also puts us in an ecumenical atmosphere at its best. Most of our Friday evenings we go to a prayer meeting with Anglicans, Presbyterians, Methodists, Lutherans, and Pentecostals. And for three hours all denominational differences are annihilated, without compromising an inch on our Roman Catholicism... Never have I heard the Church of Rome prayed for with such fervor as I have at prayer meeting. And with such love.

The most helpful people in assisting us with the spiritual direction of the students have been two Pentecostals, a layman and his pastor. They are truly remarkable people. And all the stuff we have heard about emotionalism etc. is a lot of nonsense, as far as the Assembly of God church is concerned.

I could go on and on; but that would take a whole book. To summarise; a little group of Protestants have shown us what it really means to be Catholics. And more than that, the Spirit of God is mightily at work here.

If you should get the books I mentioned, which you should be able to find in a good Protestant bookstore, you will note that the Baptism of the Spirit is often given by the laying on of hands. Where Catholics are concerned, I do not view this as a substitute for Confirmation. I think it is just a sacramental which activates Confirmation... just as any sacramental should be a genuine activation of what is already present.

Nor do I view this as a new gimmick; I view the whole experience as something which should be always and everywhere present, and which we have muffled by our lack of faith. Do we really believe that the Spirit of the Lord has filled the whole world?[39]

WORD TRAVELLED QUICKLY

Dr. Vinson Synan, a Pentecostal Holiness church historian, has commented, 'One never knows the effect of any one meeting when the Spirit of God moves. I believe the Duquesne Weekend will have to go down in history as one of the most important prayer meetings that ever occurred, especially in modern time.[40]

Word travelled quickly among neo-Pentecostals about the new move of the Holy Spirit in the Catholic Church. In early March, Rev. Don Basham received a letter overflowing with good news from Jim Prophater, the commercial artist who had been present the first night the Catholics came to Flo Dodge's meeting. Here is an excerpt of that letter:

> There has been such a tremendous move of the Holy Spirit here in Pittsburgh that it is making our heads swim — because we are right in the middle of it. Remember the two young instructors of theology from Duquesne who received the Holy Spirit at Flo's when you were here last? Well, the tallest of the two, went home that night so full of the Spirit that he was bursting. He told his wife about it — I guess until the wee hours of the morning — prayed for her and she received.
>
> ...Then they took thirty Duquesne students on a weekend retreat, for the purpose of studying the first four chapters of Acts. They had an upper room experience and *twenty or more received the Holy Spirit.*

> Back on campus they have been praying fellow classmates through to receive… They even called Bishop Wright and informed him of what is happening…
>
> They recognise the need for instruction, and we have been helping them. Friday night we went to hear testimonies of some of the students. …Nothing is impossible with God! But, He sure shakes us up sometimes when He moves so quickly and in such power...[41]

As Jim Prophater's letter indicates, after the retreat Weekend, at least for several weeks, some of the faculty members and students attended the prayer meeting at Flo's house and got a real taste of Christian unity in the power of the Holy Spirit. There were also Spirit-filled ministers who passed through Pittsburgh and visited with the students. The most notable of these ministers was Rev. Harald Bredesen, a pioneer in the neo-Pentecostal movement. A group from Duquesne even spent the following summer with Rev. Bredesen in Mt. Vernon, New York, as an ecumenical venture in fellowship and ministry.

FROM CAMPUS TO CAMPUS

As has been mentioned earlier, both faculty moderators from *Chi Rho* had close ties with University of Notre Dame in South Bend, Indiana. On March 4, 1967, the history professor went to South Bend on business and met with a group of about thirty students and friends at the home of Kevin and Dorothy Ranaghan. He witnessed strongly and joyfully about the wonder of Pentecost in our own day. The next night nine people met with him again, including the Ranaghans, Bert and Mary Lou Ghezzi, Gerry Rauch and Jim Cavnar. All present asked to be prayed with to receive the Baptism in the Holy Spirit, and although no charisms were manifested that night, there was a definite breakthrough of the love of Christ in their lives. As one of them put it, *'We have seen the Lord'*.[42] Several of those testimonies may be found later in this book.

On Monday, March 13, 1967, another group made up primarily of those who had received the Baptism in the Spirit the week before and a few newcomers went to a prayer meeting in the home of Ray Bullard in Mishawaka. Ray was president of the local Full Gospel Business Men's Fellowship International. It has been noted that this meeting of men and women from such radically different backgrounds could only have taken place with the grace of God. Ray had invited some Pentecostal ministers to come to his home that night to meet with the Catholics. Before the evening ended most of the Catholics had prayed in tongues. When asked, they also made it clear that they intended to remain in the Catholic Church. Afterwards, Catholic charismatic prayer meetings began taking place at Notre Dame, and word spread about this new pentecostal fire that was burning on campus.[43]

The very next day, March 14, four visitors arrived in Pittsburgh. Jim Cavnar and Gerry Rauch had hitchhiked from Notre Dame to meet Ralph Martin and Steve Clark who had arrived from East Lansing. Jim and Gerry had just received the Baptism in the

Spirit the week before. The Duquesne professors ministered to Ralph and Steve privately, praying for them with the laying on of hands. Ralph recalls that it was obvious that the Holy Spirit had done something with the group from Duquesne. He could see evidence of what Scripture describes as *'power from on high'*. People were aglow with the Spirit; there was an atmosphere of Pentecost. All four visitors also met with the students in an informal prayer gathering on campus. Everyone was quite new at manifesting spiritual gifts. Jim Cavnar relates how he heard that one of the faculty advisors had a charismatic 'word of knowledge'. Jim, not realising how this gift worked, kept careful guard over his thoughts when in this man's presence, for fear that this Duquesne professor might read his mind. Of course, no such thing happened.

Ralph recalls that at Duquesne he witnessed in a community setting what he had experienced before, personally. The visit gave him hope that an environment could evolve to foster a real life together in the Holy Spirit. The four young men returned to Notre Dame and Michigan State University, respectively, and the Pentecostal Movement in the Catholic Church, as it was then called, began to spread.

The Wind Blows Where It Wills

It is interesting to note that the Chapel Hill prayer meeting at Flo Dodge's home disbanded about six weeks after the Duquesne Weekend. Flo said that she sensed it had fulfilled its purpose and the Lord moved her on. At the same time on Duquesne's campus, the *Chi Rho* meetings were taking on more of a charismatic quality. This upset some of the members who had not experienced the Baptism in the Spirit, and before long the chaplain's office asked that the prayer meetings be held off-campus. The group moved to the home of one of the faculty advisors, then to Pat Bourgeois' apartment.

To the dismay of the fledgling prayer group in Pittsburgh, both professors who had been so instrumental in fostering the work of the Holy Spirit on the Duquesne Weekend moved to new locations by that summer. Catholics from around the world who have been baptised in the Holy Spirit since 1967 owe a debt of gratitude to these two professors and to the many other people whose stories appear in the pages of this book. ***They dared to pray for, to believe in, to receive and to proclaim a new Pentecost!***

NOTES

1. Prayer of Pope John XXIII to the Holy Spirit for the success of the Ecumenical Council. The last paragraph of this prayer is also found in Humanae Salutis, the apostolic constitution by Pope John XXIII convoking the Second Vatican Council, dated December 25, 1961. Cf. Walter M. Abbott, S.S., General Editor, The Documents of Vatican II, (New York: The American Press, 1966), pp. 709 and 793.
2. Personal conversations of the author with Mrs. AnnaMariea Schmidt of Milo, Maine. AnnaMariea's testimony has appeared in New Covenant, (November, 1985), pp. 20-22.
3. Léon-Joseph Cardinal Suenens as reported in The Catholic Messenger (Davenport, Iowa) May 7, 1964.
4. Fr. Val Gaudet, 'A Woman and the Pope', New Covenant, (October 1973), pp 4-6.
5. Oblates of the Holy Spirit, 'Come Holy Spirit', a pamphlet about Bl. Elena Guerra, no other data available about publication.
6. Bl. Elena Guerra, Rebirth in the Spirit (The Cenacle Community, Sisters Oblates of the Holy Spirit, Lucca, Italy, 1985), p.27.
7. Domenico M. Abbrescia, O.P., Elena Guerra (1835 – 1914): Prophecy and Renewal, (Makati, M.M., Philippines, 1982), p.131.
8. Oblates of the Holy Spirit, op. cit.
9. Domenico M. Abbrescia, O.P., p. 131.
10. Oblates of the Holy Spirit, op. cit.
11. Ibid.
12. John W. Ripley, 'Erastus Stone's Dream Castle - Birthplace of Pentecostalism', found in Topeka at the Turn of the Century, Shawnee County Historical Society, Bulletin No. 52, (Topeka, Kansas, n.d.), pp. 42-53.
13. Edward D. O'Connor, C.S.C., The Pentecostal Movement in the Catholic Church, (Notre Dame, Indiana: Ave Maria Press, 1971), p. 22.
14. Ibid., p. 23.
15. Ibid., pp. 44-47. When Fr. O'Connor wrote this book, the term 'Pentecostal Movement in the Catholic Church' was still in use. When he describes 'pentecostal meetings', he is referring to Catholic Charismatic Renewal prayer meetings. The Antioch Weekend was originally called a Study Weekend and is mentioned elsewhere in this book.
16. Jim Manney, 'Before Duquesne: Sources of the Renewal', New Covenant, (February 1973), p. 13.
17. Personal conversation of the author with Ralph Martin.
18. Jim Manney, op. cit., p. 15.

19. Ibid., p. 17
20. Ibid., p. 17
21. Kevin and Dorothy Ranaghan, Catholic Pentecostals, (Paramus, NJ: Paulist Press, 1969), p. 8.
22. Ibid., p. 9.
23. Ibid., p. 10.
24. Ibid., pp. 11-12.
25. Ibid., p. 12.
26. Ibid., p. 13.
27. Personal conversation of the author with Flo Dodge, June 10, 1991. Additional Scripture passages which formed the Chapel Hill prayer group are: 1 Cor. 11-14, Eph. 4:11-16, Heb. 4:12, and Jn. 14-17. This prayer group is no longer in existence. Flo Dodge is founder of The Lydia Fellowship, a teaching ministry, and has been active in Women's Aglow Fellowship as well.
28. Kevin and Dorothy Ranaghan, op. cit., p. 13.
29. Ibid., pp. 14-15.
30. Ibid., pp. 15-16.
31. Ibid., pp. 16-17.
32. Don Basham, Face Up With A Miracle, (Monroeville, Pennsylvania: Whitaker Books, 1967), p. 184.
33. Alice Basham, Personal letter to author, June 25, 1991.
34. Kevin and Dorothy Ranaghan, op. cit., p. 39.
35. Fr. Edward O'Connor C.S.C., Personal letter to author, June 3, 1991.
36. Personal letter, February 11, 1967.
37. The Ark and the Dove Retreat House is located in Pine Township, Allegheny County, between Exits 3 and 4 of the Pennsylvania Turnpike, approximately six miles from the Wexford, Route 910 exit of Interstate 79. The address is: Babcock Blvd., Gibsonia, PA 15044.
38. Personal conversation of the author with Flo Dodge, June 10, 1991.
39. New Covenant, (February 1973), p. 1.
40. Dr. Vinson Synan, Personal letter to author, February 27, 1991.
41. Don Basham, op. cit., p. 183.
42. Kevin and Dorothy Ranaghan, op. cit., p. 40.
43. Ibid., pp. 41-42.

PART TWO

WE CANNOT HELP BUT SPEAK OF WHAT WE HAVE SEEN AND HEARD (ACTS 4:20)

'Whenever the Spirit intervenes,
he leaves people astonished.
He brings about events of amazing newness;
he radically changes persons and history.'

Pope Saint John Paul II, meeting with
Ecclesial Movements and New Communities
St. Peter's Square, Rome. May 30, 1998

EVENTS OF AMAZING NEWNESS

In early January, 1991, I began to contact all the participants in the Duquesne Weekend who are now scattered far and wide. I asked them to share in as much detail as possible their recollections about that famous retreat. The following pages contain twelve eyewitness accounts of the Duquesne Weekend. As you will see, there was a wide range of reactions to what happened among us that weekend. People remember different details or were able to understand only certain parts of the retreat accurately. Most of these testimonies were written 25 years after the event. Some of the testimonies will use the term 'Study Weekend' instead of 'retreat'. In 1966 there had been a 'Study Weekend' for the men. Two of the participants I contacted were gracious enough to respond, but did not wish to offer a testimony since they said that the Duquesne Weekend was not 'a decisive religious event' in their lives. There were still others that I was never able to reach.

My own testimony, which is the first in the collection, is by far the longest and most detailed. By God's providence, I still have the notebook we were given during the Duquesne Weekend in which I recorded all that transpired during those days. I continued to use this notebook as a spiritual journal. Therefore I have a record of many of the key events, graces and struggles of those early weeks and months. I cover the events of the first year after receiving the Baptism in the Holy Spirit.

After reading through my own notebook and swapping stories

with my friends from Duquesne, one thing has become clear. God certainly had a sense of humor in choosing to send the power of His Spirit on such a motley group of people! Most of us at Duquesne were young and immature emotionally and spiritually. Looking back, it seems to me that the miracle was not that God sovereignly moved to renew the work of the Spirit in the Church. *The real miracle was that this grace ever got beyond the Duquesne Weekend!* What I mean is, considering our lack of maturity and wisdom, it's a wonder that God was able to use us to 'proclaim His marvellous deeds.' But then, that's the message, isn't it?

> For consider your call, brethren; not many of you were wise according to worldly standards, not many were powerful, not many were of noble birth; but God chose what is foolish in the world to shame the wise, God chose what is weak in the world to shame the strong, God chose what is low and despised in the world, even things that are not, to bring to nothing things that are, so that no human being might boast in the presence of God. He is your source of life in Christ Jesus, whom God made our wisdom, our righteousness and sanctification and redemption; therefore, as it is written, 'Let him who boasts, boast in the Lord' (1 Cor. 1:26-31).

Permit us to boast in the Lord. We weren't 'wise, powerful or well-born'. Most of us were just college kids who made a retreat in 1967. God caught us by surprise. He sovereignly intervened. We use words to describe His coming as fire, flame, heat, blinding radiance, dynamite, a waterfall of light. What follows are personal stories of how the Holy Spirit visited us on the Duquesne Weekend as by a new Pentecost!

MY SOUL MAGNIFIES THE LORD

A TESTIMONY BY PATTI GALLAGHER MANSFIELD

Patti Gallagher Mansfield graduated from Duquesne in 1968 with a B.S. in education as a French major. She has been engaged in fulltime evangelistic work with the Catholic Charismatic Renewal since then. She and her husband, Al, are based in New Orleans, Louisiana and have four children and nine grandchildren. She is an international conference speaker and author. Testimony, 1992. Photo, 1967

'God who is mighty has done great things for me, and holy is His name' *(cf. Lk. 1:49)*. I begin this testimony by echoing Mary's own words in the *Magnificat*. My l ife the Lord has been characterised by many gifts from God. I've known the love of family and friends, the blessings of good health and a wonderful home, academic success and the gift of my Catholic faith.

Because I attended a large public high school in Irvington, New Jersey, I was exposed to people from other faiths. In fact, most of my closest friends were Jewish. There was a young Jewish man that I cared for very much but his parents objected to our relationship because I was a 'gentile'. This was my first experience of being discriminated against because of my faith. I began to wonder what made Christianity distinctive. I knew that being a Christian meant believing in Jesus Christ, and I did. But as I finished high school, I felt a growing desire to deepen my understanding of Catholicism. To that end, I decided to search out a Catholic university where I could learn more Catholic theology and form relationships with other young Catholics.

At that tender age of 18 I had my whole life planned out. I wanted to go to a Catholic university in a big city, study to be a French teacher, spend at least a semester or summer in France to perfect my French accent, meet and marry a rich Frenchman and live 'happily ever after' in his chateau! I even prayed about the future. But my prayer would go something like this: 'Dear Lord, please bless my plans and do my will according to my timetable. Amen!'

My first choice for university studies was Boston College, but a full-tuition scholarship to Duquesne University in Pittsburgh, Pennsylvania, lured me there instead. The University's full title is Duquesne University of the Holy Spirit and the motto on the Duquesne emblem is: *'Spiritus Est Qui Vivificat',* or 'It is the Spirit Who gives life'. The school is administrated by the Holy Ghost Fathers, now known as the Spiritans, a missionary order. I later realised how appropriate this connection between Duquesne and the Holy Spirit would prove to be!

While I found it helpful to study theology at Duquesne, I quickly realised that theology alone could not satisfy my hunger for God. What I really desired was not simply to know more ABOUT God, but to KNOW God... to know Him in a deeper, personal way.

During my sophomore year, my friend, Mary Ellen Belfiore, began inviting me to meetings of the *Chi Rho* Society, a Scripture study group on campus. I devised numerous creative reasons why I couldn't attend. Basically, I was stalling. I felt drawn to know God better, but I was also afraid... afraid of what he might ask. What if his plans for my life conflicted with my own plans? What if he wanted me to be a nun? What if I got identified as being overly religious? What might that do to my social life? Finally, on Ascension Thursday, 1966, I agreed to attend a *Chi Rho* picnic. I was impressed by the friendliness and kindness of the kids in *Chi Rho* and I decided that I would join them when I returned to campus as a junior.

I'll never forget my first *Chi Rho* meeting in September, 1966. The group discussed some passages from the Bible while I sat quietly by, hoping that no one would call on me to share an insight. I was totally ignorant of Scripture and preferred keeping my ignorance hidden. Before leaving, we chanted a shortened form of the Divine Office using the book *Morning Praise and Evensong*. Intoning that Gregorian chant resonated deeply within me. 'There's something so right about this', I thought. 'This is what I was created for'. I considered myself very much a novice in *Chi Rho*, but I was warmly welcomed and quickly made wonderful friendships.

Getting Ready

I became nervous when plans were announced for the *Chi Rho* retreat to be held February 17-19, 1967. Believe it or not, as a public school girl, I had never been on a retreat before in my life! I struggled with conflicting emotions. On the one hand, I felt drawn to go and experience God's presence. But on the other hand, I was afraid that something might happen to change my life.

As I read Acts 1-4 and *The Cross and the Switchblade* in preparation, I was deeply impressed. In David Wilkerson's book, I missed all the references to the Baptism in the Holy Spirit and to spiritual gifts such as speaking in tongues. What captivated my attention was the fact that a man living in our own time could really know God's will. It amazed me to think that God would actually speak to David Wilkerson in prayer and guide him by means of various signs. As I read, I found rising in my heart the desire to be led by the Lord myself. I thought, 'Wouldn't it be wonderful if an ordinary person like me could actually know the guidance of God in my life?' But I concluded that this kind of guidance must be reserved for special people, people with a mission, like priests, religious sisters and ministers.

But after finishing the book, I had a little mustard seed of faith to reach out to God in prayer. Alone in my dormitory room, I knelt next to my bed and said, *'Lord, as a Catholic, I believe that I've already received your Holy Spirit in Baptism and Confirmation, but if your Spirit can be more at work in my life than he's been up until now, then I want it!'* After I prayed that prayer, I opened my eyes and looked around the room expectantly. There was no vision, no angel, no voice; I was disappointed. After reading *The Cross and the Switchblade*, my expectations were high. I thought, 'I'll never tell a soul I prayed this prayer. I guess it didn't work'. I mistakenly concluded that because I didn't experience anything dramatic in that moment, God hadn't heard my prayer. But he had heard. And he *did* answer... in a way more glorious than I could have ever imagined. What I was actually praying for was the grace to be baptised in the Spirit even though I didn't know that terminology yet.

VENI CREATOR SPIRITUS

A few days later, about twenty-five students from *Chi Rho* left for the Ark and the Dove Retreat Center, a lovely three story structure in Gibsonia, Pennsylvania. My room was in the little house, 'The Dove'. When I unpacked my bags, I was dismayed to discover that I had forgotten my makeup; and this was a co-ed retreat! Then I reminded myself that I was there to seek God, not to seek a new boyfriend.

Before each presentation we sang the beautiful hymn *'Veni Creator Spiritus' (Come Creator Spirit)* in English, using the Gregorian chant melody. One of our professors told us Friday night that this was more than a song; it was a prayer. He wanted us to sing it repeatedly as an invocation to the Holy Spirit. It was as if he were saying, 'We're going to keep on praying this until the Holy Spirit comes.'

I later learned that this hymn, written in the ninth century and attributed to Rabanus Maurus, is the Catholic hymn to the Holy Spirit. One of my friends said it is like a 'mysterious thread' woven into the lives of the saints. St. Teresa of Avila writes in her *Autobiography* how she prayed the *Veni Creator Spiritus* when she was at an impasse in her prayer and for the first time she experienced a rapture. St. Louis-Marie Grignion de Montfort recommends praying this prayer to the Holy Spirit when one is preparing to consecrate one's life to Jesus through Mary.

The *Veni Creator Spiritus* is sung at all important gatherings in the Church, such as the openings of synods and the ordination of prists and bishops. It is the most powerful prayer to the Holy Spirit in the Church.

MARY, SPOUSE OF THE HOLY SPIRIT

Friday night in the chapel, our other faculty advisor held up a statue of Our Lady which depicted her with her hands lifted up in a very charismatic gesture of prayer. He described Mary as a woman of faith and prayer. As he spoke, I was amazed by the change I saw in him. When I was a student in his class, this theology instructor always seemed to be so nervous and high-strung. That night as he spoke about the Blessed Virgin Mary, he had a new peace and joy radiating from his face. I thought, *'He looks and sounds like he's filled with the Holy Spirit.'* I'd never used that expression *'filled with the Holy Spirit'* before, but it seemed to capture what I saw in him. Of course, none of us realised that both these professors had, in fact, been *'filled with the Holy Spirit'* just a few weeks earlier.

I believe it was significant to have our attention drawn to Mary at the beginning of our retreat. She was there at the Annunciation when the Word became flesh. She was there at the Nativity to bring forth Jesus to the world. She was there at the Cross when our redemption was won. She was there in the upper room at Pentecost when the Church was born. In God's plan, it was necessary for Mary to be 'with us' in an explicit way in our own upper room as we experienced a sovereign move of the Holy Spirit that weekend. The Fathers of the Church call Mary *'the Spouse of the Holy Spirit'*. How can she fail to be present when the Holy Spirit is at work?

He Will Convict the World of Sin

After the meditation on Mary I experienced my first communal Penance Service, and I was quite moved. Such communal Penance services were new for us in 1967. Even though *Chi Rho* members were wonderful young people, the group still had much need of repentance. We had our share of factions, judgements and grumbling. It was clear that the Holy Spirit was at work in the Penance Service, because he was convicting us all of sin. As I listened to my friends pray and admit their sinfulness, I realised how much alike we all were in our need for God's mercy. For the first time in my life I offered a spontaneous prayer aloud and immediately shed tears of embarrassment. I scolded myself for this display of emotion. I wanted something deep and lasting to take place in me during the retreat, not a mere emotional experience.

Jesus, Be Real For Me!

Saturday when I heard that the talk on Acts 2 was being given by an Episcopalian woman, I must admit that I was sceptical. My scepticism increased when she began by saying, 'I don't know what to say, but I've prayed for the Holy Spirit to lead me'. Indignantly, I thought, 'Why didn't she have the courtesy to prepare a talk?' I sat there thinking, 'Impress me with your Holy Spirit.' Yet, as this beautiful woman spoke, God was moving. Really moving. At first I thought she couldn't be for real as she spoke about knowing Jesus Christ personally. She said that the power of the Holy Spirit could be experienced in our daily lives.

'It can't be that easy,' I reasoned. 'She looks old enough to know that life isn't that simple'. But before she finished speaking I was longing to have what she had and I wrote in my notes, 'JESUS, BE REAL FOR ME.'

I still have the notebook I kept during the weekend. Here are my notes from her talk on Acts 2 exactly as I wrote them.

1. The apostles met *in unity*. Christ is with us. *We need the power.* To get the power *we have to ask for it*. Christ wants each and every one of us to receive this power.
2. You have to *co-operate,* be willing to surrender your life and every aspect of it to the Lord. The joy of receiving the Lord is your life given back... increased a hundredfold.
3. JESUS, BE REAL FOR ME.
4. What happens when you receive the Spirit? From Scripture we see heat, fire, gift of tongues. The gifts aren't used *for ourselves,* but for the Lord.
5. If you don't *use* it, you *lose* it. If you *dare* to believe, *dare* to receive.
6. I rejoice in my infirmities.
7. You're not holy afterwards, but you have the power.

After her talk we broke into small discussion groups. The people with me asked why there was so much mention about *receiving* Jesus and receiving the Holy Spirit. Hadn't we already *received*

Jesus in Baptism, and the Holy Spirit in Confirmation? One of the faculty moderators happened to be in my group and he answered our questions this way. He said that although we had received Jesus and the Spirit in the sacraments, these were moments of decision which we probably didn't fully enter into because of our youth. As young adults we needed to ratify, and activate what had already been given to us.

Who Do You Say that I Am?

The professor shared something else too that hit me full force. He said that he asked a young man once to describe who Jesus Christ was in his life. The young man replied, 'Jesus is like a big band around me, holding me together. If it weren't for Jesus Christ, I'd fall apart'. I was stopped dead in my tracks by these words. I was face to face with the BIG QUESTION, the ULTIMATE QUESTION. 'Who is Jesus Christ in *your* life?' I was thunderstruck. It was as if Jesus himself were asking me the same question he asked his disciples long ago. *'And you, Patti, who do you say that I am?'*

I had to admit that although I knew and loved Jesus, he wasn't actually at the center of my life. I didn't experience him as the one holding me together, the one around whom all other people, interests and plans revolved. Quite frankly, I was still the one in control, or so I thought. My relationship with Jesus was one of convenience... *my own!* It could be characterised by the kind of prayer I used to pray: 'Lord, bless my plans. Do my will.

According to my timetable, which means right now. Amen.' In short, I realised in the midst of that discussion that I needed a conversion. I needed to surrender the control of my life to Jesus Christ... to let him be the Lord and Master over everything.

Renewal of the Sacrament of Confirmation

I'm including here the notes I took during our discussion. They indicate some of our reflections at this crucial point in the weekend.

1. To turn over our free will is the greatest gift we can give to God.
2. Take me as I am. He sent them out 'two by two'.
3. Acts 4: A miniature Pentecost. 'The house rocked'.
4. We've administered the 'decision sacraments', Baptism and Confirmation, to babies, to children. We're trying to activate our baptismal spirituality now.
5. 2 Cor. 3:17 'This Lord is the Spirit and where the Spirit of the Lord is, there is freedom'.
6. David Mangan's proposal: A renewal of our sacrament of Confirmation as part of Sunday prayers.
7. Our advisor's question: Are you ready for what the Spirit may do to you? My response: I'M SCARED.
8. Are we ready to be fools?

We ended our discussion having been asked the question, *'Are you ready to be fools'?* No wonder we were scared! As you can see from the notes, David Mangan made a proposal that as young adults we invite the Holy Spirit, who had already come to us in the sacrament of Confirmation, to be released. He suggested that we ask our chaplain if we could conclude our retreat with a ceremony in which we would renew our Confirmation, much the same way we renew our Baptismal promises at the Paschal Vigil. I had the task of reporting our discussion to the whole group. When I mentioned David's proposal, there wasn't an enthusiastic response. One of our professors asked, *'Are you ready for what the Holy Spirit can do for you'?* I didn't know exactly what it would mean, but I knew I wanted more of God. I was scared, but I was ready.

After the reports from each discussion group were completed, David and I took a walk on the grounds, still pondering all that had transpired. He and I agreed that even if none of the others present wanted to renew their Confirmation, we did. And we would! When we got back to the house we saw the history professor who had been in our discussion group and we told him of our decision. 'That's good', he said. 'God sent His people out two by two'.

I Want A Miracle!

With expectations high, I wrote on a sheet of paper: *'I WANT A MIRACLE!'* and tacked it up for everyone to see. I didn't know exactly what the miracle would be; I just wanted God to act with power. I noticed later that another retreatant wrote on the bottom of my paper, 'Me too'.

It's interesting to note that as the Holy Spirit moved later in the evening on Saturday, He chose to fall upon David Mangan and then upon me in very rapid succession and in a similar way. We were the two who agreed to renew our Confirmation and to seek a release of the Spirit even if no one else did. The Lord himself took note of our desire and he didn't wait for a closing ceremony Sunday to answer our prayer.

Saturday night a birthday party was scheduled in honour of some of the students. But the party just never materialised. There was a kind of listlessness in the group; people were milling around. In fact, we had some trouble with the water at the retreat house just prior to the party. The plumbing had broken and we were told that the whole group might have to go home early. But some students went to the chapel and prayed that the water would be restored. After praying, they turned on the tap and out came the water, full force! Some thought it was a miraculous intervention but we later learned it was the intervention of a plumber. I wasn't part of the group that went to the chapel to pray for water. But I do know the effect it had on the entire group. We felt that God wanted us to stay and that he had made it possible for us to do so.

I've often reflected on the fact that water is a scriptural image for the Holy Spirit. Jesus said, 'If anyone thirst let him come to me and drink. He who believes in me, as Scripture has said, 'Out of his heart shall flow rivers of living water.' Now this he said about the Spirit, which those who believed in him were to receive...' (Jn. 7:37-39). Some people might say of the Church today, 'The water is gone. It's all dried up. There is no life'. But in the name of Jesus, there is still a fresh flow of the Spirit's living water among us! The Duquesne Weekend was a dramatic illustration of this fresh outpouring of the Holy Spirit in today's Church.

In the Upper Room

Because the birthday party never really got started, I decided to go to various parts of the retreat house and call all the students to gather downstairs for the celebration. Even though I was a newcomer to *Chi Rho,* I had been president of my class each year in high school and had experience in leading groups and organising activities. I thought that if we all assembled in the same place, the party might happen. It was at this point that I wandered upstairs to the chapel. I wasn't going in to pray... just to tell any students there to come down to the party. When I entered the chapel I saw a few people sitting on the floor praying. It was a small carpeted room with no pews, just a few cushions. The Blessed Sacrament was in the tabernacle on the altar in the center of the room near the front. I knelt down in the presence of Jesus in the Blessed Sacrament. Then something happened I wasn't expecting.

I'd always believed by the gift of faith that Jesus is really present in the Blessed Sacrament, but I had never experienced his glory before. As I knelt there that night, my body literally trembled before his majesty and holiness. I was filled with awe in his presence. He was there... the King of Kings, the Lord of Lords, the one through whom all things came into being! I remember thinking, 'God is holy and I'm not holy. If I stay in his holy presence, something is going to happen to me.' I felt really frightened and I said to myself, 'Get out of here quick'. But overriding this fear, was the desire to remain before the Lord.

Then Bill Deigan, the president of *Chi Rho,* came into the chapel and knelt next to me. I described to him what I was experiencing. He said, 'I was just talking to a few other people. Something's going on here; something we didn't plan. Just stay and pray until you feel you should leave'. Bill left the chapel.

As I knelt there before the Lord Jesus Christ in the Blessed Sacrament, for the first time in my life, I prayed what I would call 'a prayer of unconditional surrender'. I prayed in the quiet of my heart, *'Father, I give my life to you, and whatever you want of me, that's what I choose. If it means suffering, then I accept that. Just teach me to follow your Son, Jesus, and to learn to love the way he loves'.*

When I prayed that prayer, I was kneeling before the altar. The next moment I found myself prostrate, flat on my face, stretched out before the tabernacle. No one had laid hands on me. I had never seen such a thing happen before. I don't know exactly how it took place, but in the process, my shoes came off my feet. Later

I realised that, like Moses before the burning bush, I was indeed upon holy ground. As I lay there, I was flooded from my fingertips to my toes with a deep sense of God's personal love for me... His merciful love. I was especially struck by the foolishness of God's love. It is so completely undeserved, so lavishly given. There is nothing that you and I can ever, ever do to earn or merit God's love. It is freely given, generously given, out of the abundance of his mercy. Our God is a God of love. He's created us out of love and destined us for love. We are his people. We belong to him. His love is *for us* no matter what we've done, no matter who we are.

As I think back over my experience in the chapel that night, the words of St. Augustine so beautifully capture what I felt in those moments: '*You have made us for yourself, O Lord, and our hearts are restless until they rest in you*'. Within me echoed the fervent plea, '*Stay! Stay! Stay!*' I felt as if I wanted to die right then and go to be with God in heaven. Yet I knew that if I, who am no-one special, could experience the love and mercy, the tenderness and compassion of God in such a way, it was possible for *anyone,* yes *anyone,* to experience God as well. Although I just wanted to remain and bask in the presence of the Lord, I knew that I needed to share this experience with others. Like the apostles after Pentecost, I wanted to 'proclaim his marvellous deeds', to give witness to the living God.

I rose to my feet and said to the other students in the chapel, 'I pray this will happen to you'. That one brief encounter with the Spirit of the Lord taught me more than a lifetime of study could ever have done. I felt myself captivated by the beauty and goodness of the living God. The mercy and love of Jesus had overwhelmed me.

Whom Should I Tell?

I immediately recounted my experience to the chaplain and he told me that David Mangan had been in the chapel before me. David had an almost identical experience. He too was overwhelmed when the Holy Spirit came upon him and he fell to the ground. Some people in the Charismatic Renewal now use the expression 'being slain in the Spirit' or 'resting in the Spirit' for the phenomenon of falling down under the anointing of the Holy Spirit. I prefer to say that I was 'swept off my feet by the love of God'. Neither David nor I had anyone lay hands on us. It just happened. That was the only time in my life I have had such an experience.

Father'. I asked our chaplain, 'with whom should I share this?' His answer has echoed in my mind over these decades since that retreat: 'The Lord will show you'. Then I asked him how the Lord could use someone as insignificant as me in his work. Father reminded me that when Jesus came into Jerusalem he was seated on a *donkey*. He can use whomever and whatever he chooses!

Immediately thereafter, two girls from La Roche College who were newcomers to the *Chi Rho* retreat approached me and said, 'What's happened to you? Your face looks different'. In the Bible we read about how Moses' face glowed after he had been in the presence of God. St. Paul writes, *'We all, with unveiled face, beholding the glory of the Lord, are being changed into his likeness from one degree of glory to another; for this comes from the Lord who is the Spirit'. (2 Cor. 3:18).* I didn't realise that I looked different, but apparently these girls saw a reflection in my face of what God had done in my heart.

Since our chaplain had just told me that the Lord would lead me in witnessing, I launched out. 'I've just experienced all that we've been talking about during this weekend'. For a girl who had been afraid of speaking about Jesus, I suddenly became very bold. Taking each of them by the hand I beckoned, 'Come into the chapel with me'.

The three of us knelt before the Lord in the Blessed Sacrament, and I began to pray out loud. I didn't have the correct terminology; I just prayed from my heart. *'Lord, whatever you just did for me, do it for them!'* I was asking the Lord to baptise them in the Holy Spirit without even realising it. That was probably the shortest Life in the Spirit Seminar on record!

A Sovereign Move of the Holy Spirit

Although no one ever called the birthday party downstairs to a halt, within about an hour, approximately half of the students were up in the chapel praying. The Holy Spirit had drawn them to the real birthday party which was in the 'upper room'. Just as the Church was born at Pentecost in an upper room, the Catholic Charismatic Renewal was born in an upper room too. God was moving sovereignly.

As we knelt there, a number of things were happening. Some people were weeping. Later they said that they felt God's love for them so intensely, they couldn't do anything but weep. Others began to giggle and laugh for sheer joy. Some people, like myself, felt a tremendous burning going through their hands or arms like fire. Others felt a clicking in their throats or a tingling in their tongues. I didn't know anything about charismatic gifts. Apparently some did pray in tongues in the chapel that night but I did not hear them. I suppose all of us could have spoken in tongues right away if we had understood how to yield to this gift. Others testify that the professors went around the room laying hands on the students there. I do not remember anyone laid hands on me that night. As I knelt in the presence of Jesus in the tabernacle, his awe inspiring presence was all that I remember.

One of the professors entered the chapel and commented, 'What's the bishop going to say when he finds out that all these kids have been baptised in the Holy Spirit?' The Bishop of Pittsburgh at the time was Bishop (later Cardinal) John Wright. I heard the professor use that term, 'baptised in the Holy Spirit', and I wondered what it meant. We still didn't fully realise what was happening to us, and never did we dream that what was transpiring would have an impact on the entire Church.

Even in the midst of this sovereign move of the Holy Spirit, the enemy was at work. One young woman later told us that while the rest of us were praying, she felt filled with hatred and was compelled to leave the retreat house. She wandered down a road alone, until someone went after her to bring her back. The next day she was still not at peace. As we were getting ready to leave the retreat, I spotted her huddled on the ground. The theology instructor came and got me. 'Come on, Patti, we have to go and cast out the evil spirit'. I was stunned by his words. I didn't even know if I believed in evil spirits, much less casting them out! But he seemed to know what he was doing, so I trusted him. As we approached her he said to me, 'Command, in the name of Jesus, that this evil spirit depart'. I did as he said and immediately the girl relaxed. She was relieved, but bewildered. Then she told us that the night before while everyone in the chapel was happy and joyful, she felt a terrible hatred for what was happening. 'Although I hated everyone in the room', she said, 'I hated Patti most of all'. We barely knew each other. I was grateful that the Lord had allowed me to be part of the prayer that restored her to peace.

Magnificat

Sometime in the wee hours of the morning, those of us who were in the chapel were sent to bed. If we had not been ordered to leave, I think we would have remained there all night. Back in my room, I couldn't sleep, so I picked up my copy of *Morning Praise and Evensong* and opened it at random. My eyes fell upon the *Magnificat,* Mary's song of praise. From that moment on, her song has become my song. I've never shared my testimony over all these years without using a portion of this beautiful passage. Mary said:

> *My soul magnifies the Lord, and my spirit rejoices in God my Savior,*
> *for he has regarded the low estate of His handmaiden.*
> *For behold, henceforth all generations will call me blessed;*
> *for he who is mighty has done great things for me, and holy is his name.*
> *And his mercy is on those who fear him from generation to generation.*
> *He has shown strength with his arm,*
> *He has scattered the proud in the imagination of their hearts,*
> *He has put down the mighty from their thrones, and exalted those of low degree;*
> *He has filled the hungry with good things, and the rich he has sent empty away.*
> *He has helped his servant Israel, in remembrance of his mercy,*
> *as he spoke to our fathers, to Abraham and to his posterity forever.* (Lk. 1:46-55)

I was overflowing with wonder and awe at what God had done in me and in my friends. We were 'the hungry who had been filled with good things'. I picked up my pen and underlined these words, 'His mercy is from age to age on those who fear him'. His mercy had extended to our own generation through this dramatic outpouring of the Holy Spirit!

Sober Intoxication of the Spirit

Still unable to sleep, I recorded in my notebook everything that was in my heart. Here is a very personal description of the Baptism in the Holy Spirit just hours after my experience in the chapel. This is exactly the way I recorded it.

> I guess it must be after two or three a.m. maybe, I've lost count of time.
>
> THANK YOU LORD!
>
> I asked for a miracle and you gave it to me — You came and now I know *God is real!*
> You have seized me Lord. You've rocked and knocked me over.
> You've made me mad with great joy — the light of YOU!
>
> Why me? I *really* didn't believe, I didn't really think a miracle could happen!
> NOW, HERE — least of all TO ME.
>
> Maybe that's why you came — so that others might believe.
>
> For if you came to me, selfish and sinful as I am, you can come to all. Help us to ask, to beg you to fill the longings of our hearts. Fill us. Make us overflow with profound

utterances of foolishness. Use us as signs. Make us sacred dwellings for Your Holy Spirit. Help us to use our gifts for you alone. To realise our nothingness before you, O God!

It's so *peaceful* to be with you.
STAY, STAY, STAY, STAY.
I don't deserve this but I thank you. Now I taste your goodness.

I fall prostrate before your presence, my hands burn, my heart beats.
I rant and rave. I think I'm mad. I am, Lord, I'm mad with the giddiness of your love.

Help ALL OTHERS EVERYWHERE to know you,
O God of Gods, flame, fire. ALLELUIA!

There's new power in me. I speak with a voice from within that's a new me - your Spirit. May others hear me speak of you, think I'm a fool - I AM! I'm a fool for you, for your love is foolish.
Who else could take us with all our faults, our weaknesses, our neglect?

It's so easy to pray. It overflows. It pours out.
It's your Spirit of Love uniting you, Jesus Christ, with the Father.
Glory be to the Father and to the Son and to the Holy Spirit *now* and *forever*. Amen!

I know I'm still weak, that I'll face many difficulties in the future - many dry spots in my search for you. But never let me stop seeking you - Great Comfort. PEACE, CALM.

HOW GOOD IS THE LORD!

All you needed was my commitment - without asking for return. You were there all the time, just waiting until I came around.
Perhaps I can help others to know you, Lord, but keep me humble! Let me realise that it is no longer me, but you in me.
This means suffering. Funny, that's the first time I thought of that.

BUT YOU ARE REAL. You exist - You live now. You listen. You give us miracles.

Let us pray for the fulfillment of your will in all men.
Let Your Spirit come to each and every one -
but when you will, how you will. I KNOW YOU WILL.

Thank you, Thank you, Thank you for the gift of yourself!

Constantly increase the spark within my heart.
Help me not to be afraid, cowardly, sinful -
for your revelation has shown me how good you are, Lord
- I want to rest with you in eternity.
AMEN.

SENDING US FORTH

After a few hours of sleep, I awakened Sunday morning and my hands were tingling and burning. At first I thought I might have slept on them, but the sensation remained for many hours. When I asked our theology instructor what this meant, he replied, 'You, too? Come on, you need to lay your hands on people and pray'. Just as I followed his lead the day before, I did whatever he told me. I remember he pointed to one of the Chi Rho members, Gina Scanlon, who was pregnant at the time. 'Let's pray for her', he suggested. 'We can get two for one'. And we did. *(Note that in Gina Scanlon's testimony later in this book she recounts that this child has always had a special closeness to God. By his providence about 30 years after the Duquesne Weekend, I met this child, now a young woman at a Catholic Charismatic Conference in Los Angeles!)*

At some point Sunday, the Episcopalian woman who had spoken on Acts 2 returned to the Ark and the Dove. No longer was she a 'Protestant stranger' to be held in suspicion. Instead, she was 'a sister in Christ' and we embraced her, overflowing with gratitude for her witness. I held my hands out to her which were still burning and asked her what I should do with them. 'Don't look at your hands', she warned me. 'Look at the Lord'. Good advice. We discovered that her prayer group had been interceding all weekend for us. No doubt their prayers helped usher forth our personal Pentecost. That afternoon our faculty moderators gave us some parting advice. When one of them recommended John Sherrill's book, *They Speak with Other Tongues,* I was stunned. 'You mean you knew all along that this

'The Dove', where some of the women students stayed during the Duquesne Weekend, 1967

The foyer at the Ark and the Dove, 1967

was going to happen to us?' I asked. Apparently, they were praying for God to act, but they did not anticipate the sovereign move of the Holy Spirit in the way it had transpired. Here are notes from that parting advice Sunday:

1. A miracle requires faith, but sometimes a miracle is used to arouse faith.
2. *Living* in the Spirit is as important as receiving the Spirit. The Spirit is given that Christ may be proclaimed.
3. The devil's going to try to tempt us because he thinks he's losing us ... the Precious Blood. Psalm 91.
4. The Lord will give you Scriptures if you ask for them.
5. PRAISE CHRIST FOR SOMETHING THAT DOESN'T *SEEM* TO HAVE HAPPENED YET.
6. Other gifts may appear later. Pray for all the gifts, especially the higher gifts.
7. Don't rely on your own efforts. To witness with wisdom doesn't mean to do what's safe.
8. Pray to Mary, for the Spirit overshadowed her. Her *fiat* was needed. So is ours.

Too Much New Wine

When I think about our return to Duquesne's campus, the words of Psalm 126:1-3 come to mind:

The dining room at the Ark and the Dove, 1967

The living room at the Ark and the Dove, 1967

> When the Lord brought back the captives of Zion, we were like men dreaming.
> Then our mouth was filled with laughter, and our tongue with rejoicing.
> Then they said among the nations.
> 'The Lord has done great things for them.'
> The Lord has done great things for us; we are glad indeed.

The day after we returned, a friend asked me what had come over me. He was walking me home after an early morning French class. 'If I didn't know you better, Patti, I'd say you were drunk!' he exclaimed. Of course, I was quick to point out to him that this was *the very thing* said of the apostles after Pentecost. 'They have had too much new wine!' *(Acts. 2:13)*

Yes, I was drunk, but not on wine! 'Taste and see that the Lord is good' *(Ps.34:9),* wrote the psalmist. I had tasted the intoxicating love of God when the Holy Spirit came upon me. I knew for myself, *yes from personal experience,* the goodness of the Living God.

My friend seemed frightened. 'You're not going to be a nun, are you?' he asked. 'I don't think so,' was my reply. Then I opened my Bible (an action which in itself startled my friend), and I read to him Joel's prophecy quoted in Acts 2:17-19:

> It shall come to pass in the last days, says God,
> that I will pour out a portion of my spirit on all mankind:
> Your sons and daughters shall prophesy,

your young men shall see visions
and your old men shall dream dreams.
Yes, even on my servants and handmaids
I will pour out a portion of my spirit in those days,
and they shall prophesy.
I will work wonders in the heavens above
and signs on the earth below.

I know this friend wasn't the only person I frightened with my enthusiastic witness in those early days. I lacked prudence and sensitivity in the way I shared about the extraordinary events that had taken place. When Fran, my room-mate of three years, asked me how the retreat went, I looked at her intently. 'Do you really want to know?' I inquired. When she nodded, I locked our door, grasped her hand, and recounted to her with eyes aglow the dramatic events. As a result, she decided not to room with me our senior year. I later discovered that she had even spoken to my parents and questioned my mental stability.

Catholic and Charismatic

Immediately after the weekend, Fran told me she didn't like 'the whole operation', and was afraid we were leaving the Church. Quite the contrary, I felt that I was discovering the Church in a wonderful new way. One of the first things I did after the weekend was to take *The Documents of Vatican II* and look up every reference to 'Holy Spirit', 'charisms', and 'spiritual gifts'.I said to myself, 'As intense as my experience of the Holy Spirit on the Weekend was, if the Church tells me this is not authentic,

I would rather renounce my own experience than ever leave the Catholic Church.' To my delight, I found nothing but encouragement in the Council documents. I rejoiced as I read the following from *Lumen Gentium,* Article 12 (the italics are mine):

> The holy People of God shares also in Christ's prophetic office. It spreads abroad a living witness to Him, especially by means of a life of faith and charity and by offering to God *a sacrifice of praise,* the tribute of lips which give honor to His name *(cf. Heb. 13:15)...*

Yes! A sacrifice of praise!... The Holy Spirit had placed just such words of praise on our lips! Praise God!

> It is not only through the sacraments and Church ministries that the same Holy Spirit sanctifies and leads the People of God and enriches it with virtues. Allotting His gifts 'to everyone according as He will' *(1 Cor. 12:11),* He distributes special graces among the faithful of every rank. *By these gifts He makes them fit and ready to undertake the various tasks or offices advantageous for the renewal and upbuilding of the Church, according to the words of the Apostle: 'The manifestation of the Spirit is given to everyone for profit' (1 Cor. 12:7).* These charismatic gifts, whether they're the most outstanding or the most simple and widely diffused, are to be received with thanksgiving and consolation for they are exceedingly suitable and useful for the needs of the Church...

Yes! Charismatic gifts are to be received with thanksgiving and consolation! It's all right!

> Still, extraordinary gifts are not to be rashly sought after nor are the fruits of apostolic labour to be presumptuously expected from them.
> In any case, judgement as to their genuineness and proper use belongs to those who preside over the Church, and to whose special competence it belongs, *not indeed to extinguish the Spirit, but to test all things and hold fast to that which is good (cf. Th. 5:12, 19-21).*

Yes! The Church is to discern the gifts, but not to quench the Holy Spirit! Alleluia!

The Church was clearly telling me through *The Documents of Vatican II* that my experience of the Holy Spirit was valid, even if certain individuals were looking at me askance. *What a relief to know that I could be both Catholic and Charismatic.* No choice had to be made. I later discovered that it was Cardinal Suenens whose intervention at the Vatican Council made these statements on the charisms so explicit. We are all deeply indebted to him.

God's Word Is Spirit and Life

For years I'd been longing to read the Bible, but I always felt too ignorant and intimidated to try. Now, words from Scripture were jumping off the page; Jesus was speaking to my heart.

I literally stayed up until the wee hours of the morning, night after night, pouring over Scripture. In the margins of my Bible next to certain texts I wrote, *'This is true!' 'This is for me!' 'This is real!'* It was my own personal *'Amen'* to the Word of God. One passage I underlined in my Bible during those days is from Acts 4:20, 'We cannot possibly give up speaking about he things we have seen and heard.' And we couldn't! The Word of God was a banquet and I was hungry.

YOUR SONS AND DAUGHTERS SHALL PROPHESY

We began to literally 'stumble' into the charismatic gifts. For example, Marybeth Mutmansky showed me a piece of paper on which she had jotted down some words that kept coming to her mind during the day. As we began to share these 'messages' with one another, we realised that this was the charismatic gift of prophecy. I still have a few of those early prophecies recorded. They were very simple messages from the Lord, yet they had a profound effect on us. Here you can see the kind of things the Lord was teaching us.

> My love exceeds all you can imagine, my love for you. How much I give to all who ask. Do not be too proud to come for help. I am with you always - just waiting for your surrender, your 'yes'. Come, come to me. Live a new life of trust. Hope *will* keep you joyful. You will see the fruits of my Spirit blossom and grow in your hearts. You will know me. And in me, my Father. And in me, my Spirit.

And in me, all your brothers. How I long for you to know - to live in me.

Listen, my children, to the sound of my voice. You know me - I live in the depths of your being. It is I who have been with you since the beginning of time. I made you - I created you - you are my own.

Nothing can compare with my love for you. Nothing you have ever known. Never fear, for you are continually in my presence. I cannot be known to my children unless they open their hearts to me, unless they listen to my voice and answer my call. Love me - Love each other in Me. Know the meaning of life - the very essence of your existence. Apart from me you can do nothing. For all your being is rooted in mine. I am all in all... The beginning and the end... the bread of life... food and drink for the hungry... refuge from the storm... comfort for the afflicted... solace for the troubled... peace for the oppressed... joy for all who seek me. I never fail, and love like mine cannot be found but in me, through my Cross, the wood on which I was crucified, where I offered myself to the Father in love for you. If only you would trust me, you would see how simple life is moment by moment.

They Will Speak in New Tongues

Apparently some people prayed in tongues on the Duquesne

Weekend; I did not. At first, I thought that 'speaking in tongues' meant praying in your own language with special fervor. The Monday after the retreat, I experienced a terribly depressed feeling and an inability to pray at all, even to remember the words of the Lord's Prayer. Deep down inside I sensed the Lord saying, 'Just keep talking to me'. On my way to class I met a friend from Chi Rho, John Rossmiller. As he grasped my hand in passing, the depression lifted immediately and I could pray with ease. Because such fervent prayer was pouring out of me in those weeks following our retreat, I saw no need for the gift of tongues. As a French major, it bothered me to think that some people could acquire another language supernaturally when I was working so hard to master a foreign tongue. The Lord had to teach me how to view this properly, and He did.

One night at a prayer meeting I sat next to David Mangan who had already received the gift of tongues. I was flabbergasted as I heard David pray in beautiful, flowing French. It sounded like the words of a psalm, praising the kindness of the Divine Child, extolling the streams of living water. The cadence of his French was different, but his pronunciation was perfect. After the meeting I asked David if he knew he had been praying in French; he didn't. I was impressed by the authenticity of this charismatic gift. It was a sign to me that God was at work.

Soon I began to long to praise God more, to go beyond my own limited abilities to extol His goodness. St. Paul advises, 'Earnestly desire the spiritual gifts' *(cf. 1 Cor. 14:1)*. I asked God for the gift of tongues, but I failed to realise that I needed to move my lips and use my voice in order to yield to tongues. I thought that a prayer language would force its way out of me if I waited in silence long enough.

Mary's Song

When I woke up on March 13, 1967, I was excited by the sound of clicking in my throat. I hoped it might be the gift of tongues, but I was afraid to be in the middle of a class when it 'overtook me'. I cut class and went above the University Chapel to pray in the oratory, one of our favorite places for prayer in those early days. I was determined I would stay there as long as it took until I prayed in tongues... I was alone kneeling before a crucifix and I prayed, 'Lord I am not getting off my knees until I am praying in tongues', I remained there with my mouth open... waiting.

The clicking became louder; my mouth started to move and then I began to grunt. 'Oh no', I thought, 'don't tell me the Lord is going to give me an ugly, guttural tongue after I majored in French because of the beauty of the language!' But I kept grunting away until finally I was singing in tongues, a lovely song which flowed from the depths of my being. It was a beautiful language, different from the tongue I pray in now. Although I didn't recognise the words, in my heart I *knew* I was singing the *Magnificat* - the very passage the Lord had given me the night I was baptised in the Spirit. 'My soul magnifies the Lord and my spirit rejoices in God my Saviour, for He has regarded the low estate of His handmaiden. For behold all generations will call me blessed. For he who is mighty has done great things for me, and holy is his name.' *(Lk. 1:46- 49)*. It was confirmed. Mary's Magnificat had become my Magnificat. Her song had become my song. In some mysterious, yet very real way, I was incorporated into Mary's magnificent surrender to God. *'Fiat!* Yes! Be it done unto me according to Your word!'

I hurried downstairs praying softly in tongues, afraid that if I stopped I might not be able to start up again. In the chaplain's office I whispered my gift of tongues into the secretary's ear. Who knows what she must have thought! She avoided me in the future. Later I understood that the gift of tongues was under my control to start and to stop at will.

They Will Lay Their Hands On The Sick

We began to 'stumble' into the charismatic gift of healing as well. In our prayer meetings we would pray for healing and expect results. My own introduction to the gift of healing took me by surprise. Shortly after the Duquesne Weekend, I saw a note on the bulletin board of St. Ann's dormitory that Mrs. Jones, our housemother, was in Mercy Hospital with phlebitis. The hospital happened to be right next to our dormitory. As I read the note, a thought went through my mind: 'Go, lay your hands on her, and she will be healed'. I immediately dismissed such a foolish notion, but it kept returning. I was panic stricken. What if this was actually the Lord speaking to me? I had never felt comfortable with the faith healers on television who would lay hands on an ailing person's head and shout, 'Heal! Heal!' I knew there must be another way to pray for healing, but I didn't know what it was. Nor did I want to find out. How could I find the courage to pray over Mrs. Jones, I wondered? What should I do?

Then I remembered that in *The Cross and The Switchblade,* David Wilkerson would 'lay a fleece before the Lord' like Gideon did and ask for a sign to know God's will. I obviously needed guidance so I prayed, 'Lord, if it's Your will for me to pray over Mrs. Jones for healing, let me wake up early for class tomorrow morning'. I figured this was an easy way out, since I was notorious for sleeping late.

Sure enough, bright and early the next morning I awakened with the words blazing in my mind, 'Lay your hands on her and she will be healed'. Reluctantly, I walked over to Mercy Hospital and entered Mrs. Jones' room. 'What's been happening, Patti?' she asked. 'Miracles have been happening, Mrs. Jones', I replied. 'I believe in miracles', she responded. But before we could pursue our conversation, another visitor arrived. As they spoke, I sat in the corner, feeling foolish and awkward. Yet my hands were on fire, burning and tingling, and in my heart was the growing conviction that Mrs. Jones would be healed.

As I rose to leave I approached her bed and said, 'I know you're going to be all right, Mrs. Jones'. Then I took my right hand and traced a tiny cross on her forehead like my mother used to do in blessing us as children. It wasn't exactly laying my hands on her, but it was the best I could muster. She seemed appreciative.

Shortly thereafter I saw her in the cafeteria back on campus. I almost dropped my tray of food! 'What are you doing out of the hospital already?' I asked. She told me that the swelling had gone down more quickly than expected, and the doctors had discharged her. I believe my prayer helped speed the healing process already begun through her treatment. Of course, in the gift of healing as in deliverance, much wisdom and discernment is needed. As young people, we didn't always approach these topics with the greatest prudence. But we were learning by experience, with very little guidance.

I Will Instruct You and Teach You

One of the most amazing things that happened right after the Duquesne Weekend is that the Spirit began to teach me directly, often speaking to me through Scripture. As Jesus says in John 16:13, 'When the Spirit of Truth comes, he will guide you into all the truth...' And in Psalm 119:130 we read, 'The unfolding of your words gives light; it imparts understanding to the simple.' I approached the Lord as a child needing instruction, and he revealed himself to me.

For instance, one day I was thinking about my Jewish friends from high school and wondering about God's plan for the Jewish people. I began to pray for understanding and opened the Bible at random to Romans 9-11 where St. Paul speaks about his beloved Jews and what God intends for them.

Another time, Marybeth and I were puzzling over what we should do during the summer of 1967. 'Lord, where should we go?' we asked. Into my mind came a mental image of a Scripture passage. It was as clear as if it were in neon lights. 'Psalm 32:8' Having no idea what it was, I looked it up and read, 'I will instruct you and teach you the way you should go; I will counsel you with my eye upon you.' Amazing grace! It's as if Jesus came into the room to speak to us personally, assuring us of his guidance.

Several days in a row the Lord would call my attention to certain Scripture passages in the morning. Later at Mass, I would discover that these 'just happened' to be the readings for the liturgy of the day. I knew I was being taught by the same Holy Spirit who breathed in the universal Church. It was very reassuring. I can't help but recall St. Luke's words at the beginning of the book of Acts. He writes that after the Resurrection Jesus showed his disciples *'in many convincing ways that he was alive... '* Well, Jesus used *'many convincing ways'* to show us that he was alive too! Of course, we didn't limit our reading of the Bible to this method of praying for passages, but the Lord was very gracious in revealing himself to us through his word.

He's Alive!

I found it difficult to engage in theological speculation or theoretical questions with other students in theology class. When I heard questions such as, 'What would Jesus say if he were alive today?,' I wanted to shout, 'But he is alive today! If we want to know what's on his mind for us, *let's ask him.* He'll reveal his will if we have expectant faith!' After the weekend, I continued to use my notebook as a journal. I wrote the following: *'I know now what others have longed to know. I see what others have longed to see. Thank You, Lord.'*

How reminiscent this is of the time that Jesus rejoiced in the Holy Spirit and thanked the Father for *hiding things from the wise and understanding and revealing them to mere children.* To His disciples Jesus then said privately, *'Blessed are the eyes that see what you see! For I tell you that many prophets and kings have longed to see what you see, and did not see it, and to hear what you hear, and did not hear it' (Lk. 10:23-24).* One week after our retreat I wrote: *'I can't possibly recall all the miracles of the past week.'* Every day was filled with amazing new discoveries about the Lord.

On Friday, 5th March, 1967, I attended my first inter-denominational prayer meeting at the home of Flo Dodge, accompanied by Patrick Bourgeois, a theology instructor, and David Mangan. Here's my description:

> Thank You, Lord. Before-hand I prepared myself to guard against prejudice or fear of any kind. The people were so warm and friendly. In prayer they said, 'Give us another chance, Lord.' I'm really starting to think of Christian unity as a reality to be attained with the help of the Holy Spirit.

> The meeting started with spontaneous prayer, then they asked us to witness. They really seemed delighted for us. Almost everyone spoke in tongues. It was very natural and flowing. I was startled when everyone prayed in tongues at the same time.
>
> Then they asked for prayer. A woman got in the middle and people laid hands on her. For some reason I started doubting all this. After all I've witnessed, I dared doubt. I asked Pat to pray for me that I might believe, and almost immediately the Spirit came to David in a visible way. I knew that sign was for me. My hands and mouth felt anointed.

Perhaps more than the presence of the charisms, the overflowing love I experienced there was a sure sign that the Holy Spirit was in their midst.

In mid-March, some friends of our moderators came to campus. I didn't even know their last names, but God gave me a prophetic sense of how He planned to use them to spread the work of the Holy Spirit. In my notebook the day before they came, I wrote:

National leaders of the Cursillo are coming tomorrow, Ralph and Steve. Should be big happenings this week. Praise You, Lord! Praise your name! When you come to them, you'll come to the States and to the world.

In fact, God *did* use Ralph Martin and Steve Clark to promote the news of the Baptism in the Holy Spirit through their contacts in the Cursillo, and their work on campus ministry. Two other young men from University of Notre Dame visited with us at the same time, Jim Cavnar and Gerry Rauch. Jim spoke to Marybeth Mutmansky and me about the possibility of joining the four of them to work on campus ministry after we graduated from Duquesne. It was a new and exciting prospect to consider.

I still smile when I think of my conversation with Ralph Martin during that visit. Here was Ralph, a dedicated Christian leader, sitting down to talk with a newly converted young student... namely me. For some reason Ralph began to share with me his concerns about one of his sisters. I pulled out my Bible and read to him from Romans 8:28, a passage I had just discovered. *'We know that in everything God works for good with those who love him, who are called according to his purpose.'* Then I proceeded to 'counsel' him to trust the Lord for his sister. I was too new in the Spirit to realise the humour of the situation. He wasn't asking me for advice, but he got it anyway!

About two weeks later I met Ralph Martin again while we were both visiting our families in New Jersey. Ralph brought me to a prayer gathering of students from Fordham University in New York City. As we mounted the steps to the meeting he said to me, 'I want you to share your testimony'. I drew a complete blank. 'What's my testimony?' I asked. 'Just tell them what happened to you in the chapel during the retreat,' he replied.

So, that night I learned from Ralph what it meant to give a personal testimony and I've been doing it ever since.

Actually, that Easter vacation precipitated something of a crisis within my family. I felt much more inclined to stay at Duquesne and celebrate the Paschal Triduum with my friends from *Chi Rho*. But when I broached the subject, my family was quite upset. I later learned that my sister, Gail, cried because she thought I was entering the convent. My Mom wondered who all these newfound friends were. Daddy teased that I'd have to become a Cardinal before I could be Pope. Despite my deep desire to be a good witness to my family, I'm afraid that many of my early attempts to share the grace of the Baptism in the Holy Spirit were quite clumsy.

The Man Who Held Nothing Back

Right after the Easter holidays we had another visitor to Duquesne's campus, Rev. Harald Bredesen, a pioneer in the neo-Pentecostal movement from the time he had been baptised in the Holy Spirit in 1946. Although we didn't realise it then, our group at Duquesne was already deeply indebted to Pastor Bredesen because of his boldness in witnessing to the release of the Holy Spirit.

In 1959, the Lord spoke to Harald Bredesen, who was a Lutheran at the time, and told him in prophecy to 'hold nothing back' concerning the Baptism in the Spirit. Bredesen shared his experience of the Spirit with Dr. and Mrs. Norman Vincent Peale. Then John Sherrill, the senior editor of *Guidepost's* magazine, heard Harald's testimony and was led to seek the Baptism in the Holy Spirit for himself.

Sherrill in turn 'held nothing back' in his testimony. He was writing a neo-pentecostal classic, *They Speak With Other Tongues,* when Harald Bredesen introduced him to a street preacher named David Wilkerson. *Voila!* Sherrill helped Wilkerson tell his amazing story in *The Cross and the Switchblade.* These two books were instrumental in leading the professors from Duquesne and many others into the Baptism in the Holy Spirit in early 1967. So it was only right that Pastor Bredesen should come and see some of the fruit of his apostolic toil... a room full of 'Catholic kids' on fire with the Holy Spirit. He was a delight.

Bredesen's visit was very significant in my life. He explained how to discern personal prophecy and how to tell if what you're hearing is really God's voice or simply your own imagination at work. Harald told us that once he had had a personal prophecy indicating which woman he should marry. The only problem was, she was in love with someone else! Pastor Bredesen went on to explain that decisions aren't made on the basis of one personal prophecy. Rather, a personal prophecy usually prepares for or confirms something which is unfolding along with many other indications that it is of God.

This was an important lesson for us to hear from a man who had been moving in the gifts of the Holy Spirit for many years. In our little group of young men and women at Duquesne, there were already a number of romances. After the Duquesne Weekend many of us were receiving 'words from the Lord,' or so we thought, that 'X should marry Y,' or 'Y should marry Z,' or 'X should be a priest,' or 'Y should be a nun'. It was confusing to know how to make our way through all these conflicting 'revelations'. Harald Bredesen helped us appropriate some rules for discernment.

The other significant thing about his visit was the proposal that a group of Catholics from Duquesne live in his church in Mt. Vernon, New York, for the summer. He spoke to us about the wonderful ecumenical witness we could give and also of the desperate need for young people to do street evangelisation. It was quite a vision, so reminiscent of what we had read about in *The Cross and the Switchblade*.

Come Follow Me

As Pastor Bredesen spoke, my friend, Karin Sefcik, poked me. 'That's for you, Patti', she said. At first, I felt annoyed with her suggestion that I should go to Mt. Vernon. I'd been saving money to travel to France during the summer of 1967 to study at the Sorbonne in Paris. As a French major, I wanted to perfect my accent. But I had to admit that, in light of the Duquesne Weekend, nothing interested me as much as serving the Lord in the direct work of evangelisation. I asked the Lord to show me what he wanted. And he did so quickly and dramatically.

The Monday after Pastor Bredesen's visit, I had three French classes in a row. In each class I was called upon to read aloud, and as I did, I was amazed! My French accent sounded better than ever! It was almost as if someone else were speaking French through me! As I walked home that afternoon I sensed the Lord's voice in the depths of my heart. 'Patti, French accents are easy for me to perfect. You, come follow me.' I cancelled my trip to France. The decision was made. My life belonged to Jesus. If I never had a chance to go to France, it didn't matter.

You might be wondering what happened to my studies at this point. I found that my awareness of God's presence was so intense sometimes that I could think of nothing else. I felt absorbed in God. I'm afraid this was probably a source of scandal to some people, even in *Chi Rho*. I'd lecture myself about getting back into my French, but my heart was no longer in it. Perhaps if I were more mature spiritually, I could have handled this integration of study and spiritual growth better.

One day during French class, my professor even upbraided me publicly. *'Nous attendons le réveil de Mademoiselle Gallagher'*, he announced to everyone. (We're awaiting the awakening of Miss Gallagher.) I assume I looked like my mind was elsewhere, and it was! How could I tell him that it was my *réveil'* my 'awakening' to God that was causing the trouble? It was as if my experience of God in the Baptism in the Holy Spirit had replaced other kinds of knowledge. After I was baptised in the Spirit, I found my attention more and more drawn to the things of God and less toward secular pursuits, however valid and good they may have been. I expressed this reality in my notebook:

> YOU, Lord are MOST important to me.
> You've given us 'knowledge of your secrets' —
> a knowledge which surpasses all else.
> Praise and thank you.
> Order my life, Lord.
> Help me to apply myself better to my studies
> and not to waste time.
> *But,* if you call me away to do your work
> I willingly leave everything and everyone,
> even though it's hard.
> *You alone* are my Creator, my Lord and God.
> There is none other but you.

A few of us even considered quitting school after the Duquesne Weekend but, thank God, we continued through to graduation. That might seem drastic, but in light of the unfolding work of the Holy Spirit, personal career plans seemed insignificant for some of us.

The Lord Is Near

I have an entry in my notebook from those early weeks after the Duquesne Weekend that indicates the intensity of the experiences some of us were having:

> Last night I felt drained... so full of your love I could die.

It's almost TOO much.
How good Heaven must be Lord... so close to you
Your brilliance... your perfect, all-consuming love.

Sometime in mid-April, 1967, one of my friends and I went for a walk along the Bluff on campus in the evening and this is what happened:

Praise you, Lord! It's hard to be brief about your wonders, but I'll try… a friend and I decided to walk outside. Our attention was drawn to the sky where we saw puffs of clouds. At first we thought it was nothing special, but then, in front of the Philosophy Department, the puffs gathered and formed a dove. Praise God!

Father, I'm more aware all the time of how little we deserve and how much you give… how generous you are… how greatly you love!

By late April a friend and I had another unusual experience. We both felt sick and uncomfortable on the same day. Then we discovered that someone from *Chi Rho* had just quit smoking. We were apparently bearing some of his withdrawal symptoms. This same thing happened to me again years later when my mother, living in another state, quit smoking and I experienced a variety of withdrawal symptoms without knowing of her decision to quit.

The Lord's presence would 'overtake' me almost anywhere. In

my notebook I describe the following experiences. Sometimes at Mass I would feel 'like my heart would burst' at the moment of encounter with the Lord Jesus. Even at recreation, the Holy Spirit would visit me. One night I went with some friends to see a play. As I sat there I became keenly aware of the Lord's presence and felt as if I were 'on fire with a desire for God'. Or sometimes, while walking on campus or in the midst of a conversation, I'd hear a high-pitched sound that would attract my attention. It was as if the Lord were saying, 'Pay attention!' Only in recent years have I read in St. Teresa of Avila's *Autobiography*, a description of a voice that made a whistle-like sound, but spoke no words. She experienced God communicating an answer to her prayer through this whistle-like voice. It reminded me of the high-pitched whistle I've heard at times since the Duquesne Weekend.

PENTECOST PRAYER AND PROPHECY, 1967

A few days before the great feast of Pentecost, 1967, I wrote this prayer, rejoicing in the experience of possessing God, or rather, of being possessed by God.

> Your goodness overwhelms me!
> Your mercy is beyond comprehension!
> How my soul longs to be yours!
> How my heart nearly bursts with joy!
> For you have richly poured forth your blessings.
> You have manifested your presence.
> O wonderful light of love!

O blinding radiance of truth!
your comfort,
your understanding,
your peace are mine.
I praise you, Lord, for your gifts of love!
I acknowledge my nothingness before you.
I rejoice in your strength and power.
I cling to you as my Father, my brother, my friend,
my God.

I wanted to believe that the Baptism in the Holy Spirit, this immersion in God's love, was meant for all God's people. But because there wasn't an enthusiastic reaction to us on campus, even among the priests, I used to wonder if God really intended this experience for the whole Church. On Pentecost Sunday, May 14, 1967, the Lord spoke to me in a prophecy which I recorded.

My Spirit is for *all* men. I have promised, I will give. But you must ask, you must seek. Open your eyes, open your hearts, open your hands, lift them up to me. Know that I have delivered you from your sins, that I am now reigning in power and glory with my Father. Call on me... Jesus. I am always with you. I hear your prayers. My children, what more must I do to prove my love?

It was finally clear to me. *God desired to pour out His Spirit on all men and women.* Since we at Duquesne were recipients of a new release of the Holy Spirit, we had to proclaim it to everyone who would listen. I remember one of our faculty advisors in *Chi Rho* told us, 'The saints are still out there'. He explained that God still had people 'out there', in the world, that He intended to transform and use by the power of His Spirit. It would be our witness that would draw them to God. They'd become saints and accomplish great things for the Kingdom, while we might remain hidden and in the background. Yet, it would be our testimony that would call them forth into God's service.

That certainly has been true. The leadership of the Charismatic Renewal which began at Duquesne passed quickly to fine men and women in various other locations, such as Ralph Martin, Steve Clark, Kevin and Dorothy Ranaghan, Bert Ghezzi, George Martin, Fr. Edward O'Connor, C.S.C., Jim Cavnar, Gerry Rauch, Paul DeCelles, Bobby Cavnar and many others.

I Will Not Plan This

Marybeth Mutmansky and I felt a growing desire to be part of the campus ministry effort of Ralph Martin and the others who had visited us at Duquesne in March. We were open to spending part of the summer of 1967 with them at Michigan State University. News of the Baptism in the Spirit was spreading on that campus and they were experiencing some persecution. I was determined to wait upon the Lord, to follow the Spirit's lead, to resist the temptation to take control and make my own plans. I had always been so quick to map things out for myself in the past. I wrote in my notebook in capital letters, 'I WILL NOT PLAN THIS'. But it was difficult to wait on the Lord's guidance.

One day in late April, 1967, an envelope arrived from Ralph Martin. I opened it eagerly and found half a piece of paper napkin with a note typed on it in just this way, lower case letters and all:

Dear Patti,
thank you for your letter,
come,
in Jesus, our glorious saviour
Ralph

Based on that simple note from Ralph, I decided to join him to work on campus ministry. A young man from Duquesne noticed how I was reordering my life after the Duquesne Weekend. He asked if I minded having God 'interfere' with my life. Mind!! How could I mind? His question amused me because just a few days before I had written a prayer asking the Lord to 'interrupt' and 'interfere' with my life.

And You Shall Be My Witnesses

On Duquesne's campus the Lord was using me as a witness. For instance, right after our retreat, a girl I didn't know asked me where I had been for the weekend. 'Did you meet a boy?' she inquired. When I told her I had met many guys and girls she said, 'You must have met someone special, it shows.' Then there was the ex-seminarian who plied me with theological questions and objections to faith. Realising my own inadequacies, all I could say was, 'I know that God lives because I experience his love in a personal way every day.' He finally stopped arguing.

Another time, as I passed an acquaintance, I felt led to shake her hand in a gesture of friendship. She later told me how that very morning she had said, 'Lord, if you're real, you'll have to show me.' When I grasped her hand without saying a word, she told me it was as if I had wished her the peace of Christ. Apparently she experienced the reality of his presence through my handshake. This same young woman kept after me until I shared with her everything I knew about the Baptism in the Holy Spirit. The Lord was teaching me that I had a duty to evangelise. I wrote:

Jesus, you're showing me that even when I'd
rather not say anything,
I have a responsibility to tell others about you
and your love.
They ask such leading questions,
and all I can see is that *you* are the answer.

Not Peace but the Sword

As the school year drew to a close in May, 1967, those of us baptised in the Spirit were experiencing a certain amount of suffering and rejection. The Holy Ghost Fathers never did seem to welcome the outpouring of the Holy Spirit on campus. The one exception was Fr. Vince Donovan, C.S.Sp., who was a missionary in Africa home for a visit. In fairness to the Holy Ghost Fathers, I must say that we were probably a rather 'wild and woolly' flock for them to try to shepherd.

Our chaplain seemed concerned about the divisions the Duquesne Weekend brought to members of *Chi Rho* and he chose not to identify with us. In the prayer group, we were concerned about our lack of experienced leadership because our two faculty moderators were moving out of town.

Personally, I was struggling with the reaction of my family, especially my mother, to my call to evangelise. She simply couldn't understand why I should give up my trip to France to do 'social work'. The more I tried to explain that it wasn't 'social work', the worse things got. I remember going to my bedroom in tears after one of our discussions during a visit home. I pleaded with the Lord to show me why his will should cause such pain to those I loved. Into my mind came the passage, 'Mark 10:28.' When I looked it up I read:

> 'Lo, we have left everything and followed you.' Jesus said, 'Truly I say to you, there is no one who has left house or brothers or sisters or mother or father or children or lands, for my sake and the sake of the gospel, who will not receive a hundredfold now in this time and in the age to come eternal life.'

The next day, after another upsetting conversation with the family, I was back up in my bedroom crying out to the Lord. This time I opened my Bible right to Luke 9:57-62:

> As they were making their way along, someone said to Him, 'I will be your follower wherever you go.' Jesus said to them, 'The foxes have lairs, the birds of the sky have

> nests, but the Son of Man has nowhere to lay His head.' To another he said, 'Come after me.' The man replied, 'Let me bury my father first.' Jesus said to him, 'Let the dead bury their dead; come away and proclaim the Kingdom of God.' Yet another said to him, 'I will be your follower, Lord, but first let me take leave of my people at home.' Jesus answered him, 'Whoever puts his hand to the plow but keeps looking back is unfit for the reign of God.'

In a way, this is where I see the greatest evidence of the work of the Holy Spirit in my own life in those early days. The Lord enabled me to place him above father, mother, friend, roommate, home, and career, in spite of the pain and embarrassment. This was pure grace because I loved them all very much. I wrote in my notebook:

'If it costs me every relationship in my life, I will not leave you, Lord, even though it hurts. You are worthy. I welcome your discipline.'

We sang a song in those early days entitled, *'I Have Decided to Follow Jesus.'* One of the verses seemed more appropriate as time went by. *'Though none go with me, still I will follow. No turning back, No turning back.'*

Through these difficulties Jesus was inviting us to become true disciples, not merely fair-weather friends who rejoice at his miracles but flee from his Cross. *The Cross.* How could we love Jesus without embracing it? Again from my notebook:

Your Cross . . .
Sign us with it, Jesus,
Imprint it on our hearts . . .
That we may joyfully embrace it
Because it makes our union with you complete.

A Holy Spirit School

In the summer of 1967 a group of us from Duquesne arrived at the parsonage of Harald and Gwen Bredesen in Mt. Vernon, New York. Bredesen's First Reformed Church in Mt. Vernon had been described as the charismatic nerve centre in New York in that era. Christian love was action, not mere words, in the Bredesen household as they graciously moved their entire family into one bedroom to accommodate us. We learned about Christian unity as we shared a time of morning prayer. These dear people even adjusted their style of prayer if it made us uncomfortable.

It was like enrolling in a *'Holy Spirit School'* just to be around Harald Bredesen! Our first grocery bill of $60.00 came from his own pocket. That night someone handed him three $20 bills 'to help with the Catholic kids.' I'm sure the Bredesens suffered from our lack of personal and spiritual maturity during that summer, but they didn't complain. Most of us were really novices in Christian discipleship.

As we watched Pastor Bredesen minister to young people on the streets of Mt. Vernon, we learned how to follow the Spirit's lead in proclaiming the Good News. One day after witnessing to some teenaged boys, my friend and I tried to speak to their girlfriends. The boys whisked the girls off in a car, and we were left standing on the sidewalk. 'What would Pastor Bredesen do?' we asked ourselves. Immediately we knew the answer. Heads bowed in prayer, we said, 'Jesus, if You want these girls to be evangelised, send them back.' Within moments the car returned and the boys called out, 'Okay. We've heard your story, but they haven't. Tell them.' Alleluia! The girls were Jewish.

The weeks I spent with Rev. Harald Bredesen left a lasting impression on my life. His lesson was clear: *The Holy Spirit is in charge! It's worth sacrificing everything to be faithful to His lead!*

The latter part of the summer, Marybeth Mutmansky and I joined Ralph Martin, Steve Clark, Jim Cavnar and Gerry Rauch to work on campus evangelism and to seek God in prayer. Right before Marybeth and I arrived at Michigan State University in East Lansing, Michigan, we received some disturbing news. The men had lost their jobs because of their involvement with the Charismatic Renewal, which was then called the Pentecostal Movement in the Catholic Church. We spent much time in prayer with them during the summer months, asking for the Lord's guidance. The Lord confirmed His call on my life for the work of evangelisation in the Church during that time.

Only This Love Can Transform

When we all returned to Duquesne in September, 1967, the

divisions between the chaplain's office and those of us who were baptised in the Spirit grew more pronounced. In spite of this, we joined together in such ventures as the Antioch Weekend, a student oriented retreat program based on the Cursillo which was developed by our friends from Michigan.

As I look back over my notes from the fall of 1967, it is evident that the Holy Spirit was continuing to work among us to purify our thoughts and actions. There is a prophecy the Lord gave me on October 11, 1967, which I include here because it speaks about this purification:

> Can you not see what is right before you? Do you still not understand what I am doing to you, what I am asking, what I require? Your life - lay it down for me and I will pick it up. Open up your heart and let it be pierced by my love which darts like flaming arrows - the action of my grace. It penetrates, it permeates, it purifies, it purges. It's painful and intense for those I wish to perfect. Give yourself wholly to my love — only this love can transform.

A Call to Intimacy in Prayer

My prayer during those months back on campus in the fall of 1967 reflected a growing awareness of my own sinfulness and a desperate need for the transforming power of God. Here is what the Lord instructed me to do as I have it written in my notebook:

> Be constant in prayer. Be constant in prayer. Persist and

> you will live in my grace. The promises I made you will be fulfilled if you continue to trust. Do not listen to the spirits of this world, to the evil one who will try to rob you of your peace. My word is eternal. I do not give to take away. What you have received shall be increased, but come to me, my child. You are my child. Gaze into my eyes and my love will transform you. Know me. Know me. Know me.

I asked, 'But how Lord?'

> By turning to me in prayer. By trusting in my word. By listening to my voice. By believing the things I tell you. By acting in obedience to my commands. I am the Lord, your God.

Have Your Own Way, Lord

As I began to experience the cost of discipleship I entrusted myself to the Blessed Virgin Mary and turned to the example of the saints. I knew I would need grace to persevere:

> I'm receiving all these warnings from you Lord, like 'Don't be afraid if I take everything away from you, if men hate you, because of the new things I will do to you.'
>
> Lord, I can't run away from you. Where can I go to hide from you? Where can I escape from your glance? As I rise, as I rest, you are with me, and I praise you for this

continual presence, for this relentless love, for this constant pursuit.

It pains me to see my own hesitation to trust you, to say 'yes.'O Lord, even after seeing your wonders and miracles of love I doubt and worry instead of trusting in complete self-abandon.

Mary, help me! With your prayers as by your example - for the courage, the strength to say joyfully, 'Your will be done - Yes - though I don't understand - Yes.'

How many priceless lessons you have taught me, Jesus. Even and especially the most painful have been the most fruitful.

I've thought of St. Thérèse, 'who never denied you anything;' of John the Baptist, who was content to be 'a voice' - a soul you could have your way with, Jesus.

Let me too say, 'Have your way, Lord. Melt the obstacles with the fire of your love! Come Holy Spirit! Come Spirit of wisdom, understanding, counsel! Spirit of faith, hope and love. Come quickly!'

Immersed in the Love of God

Exactly one year after the Duquesne Weekend, I have a prayer recorded in my notebook which reflects my tendency to control my own life. I prayed, *'Forgive my little plans. You, O Lord, are plan enough!'* Yet, in spite of my struggles, I was still experiencing the reality of being immersed in the love of God. St. Paul writes that *'the love of God has been poured into our hearts by the Holy Spirit who has been given to us' (Rm. 5:5).* For me, this passage, Romans 5:5, is the best description of the Baptism in the Spirit. I believe that being baptised in the Spirit is being baptised in the love of God. On February 21, 1968, I describe this experience of being immersed in the love of God:

> Your peace, your life-giving presence settles over me
> like a cloak - a cloak of goodness and love.
> It increases... this longing for you...
> To be with you where you are...
> To be totally surrendered to you, to you alone, O Christ.
> For I am Yours, O Lord my God.
> You have made me and claimed me.
> You are my Shepherd, my Master.
> You have filled me with your Spirit.
> And now I know I shall never be the same.

I've allowed you, through these excerpts from my notebook, to peer into what God was doing in my soul during that first year after the Duquesne Weekend. These are deeply personal experiences, not easily shared. But I want you to see the extent to which the grace of God was being poured out in my life. In spite of my sinfulness, my ignorance, my lack of wisdom and maturity, the Lord Jesus was working in me by His Spirit. *His action was pure gift, totally undeserved and unmerited.* There was an unmistakable call to discipleship, to pick up my cross every day and follow Jesus. Sometimes with joy and praise, at other times in sorrow and tears, I was learning to walk in his footsteps, guided by his Spirit. He was speaking his word to me personally, calling me to purification, to transformation, to holiness, to service.

A Graduation Gift

I graduated from Duquesne on Pentecost Sunday, June 2, 1968. It was another experience of the power of the Holy Spirit at work in my life. My parents drove in from New Jersey with my two sisters and brother for the graduation ceremony at the Civic Arena in Pittsburgh. They were driving back to New Jersey without me, since I was riding home the next day with a friend. As I said goodbye to my family, I felt moved by the Holy Spirit to pray a special prayer of protection for their journey, rebuking Satan in the name of Jesus. I did this silently inside their car. They headed back to New Jersey and I spent the night in Pittsburgh.

But during the night I awakened suddenly with a sense of urgency that I should pray about something serious. A heavy burden of prayer settled over me, so I knelt down and began to pray. Not knowing what I was praying for, I used the wonderful gift of tongues and prayed for a long time. *'Likewise, the Spirit helps us in our weakness, for we do not know how to pray as we ought but the Spirit himself intercedes for us… ' (Rm. 8:26).*

The next day, as my friend and I drove through Pennsylvania, I had a frightening thought cross my mind: 'Your family has been in a car accident and they've all been killed. What will you do now?' A knot formed in the pit of my stomach. But just as quickly as this gloomy thought came, I received a grace of surrender. I turned to Jesus and prayed, 'Lord, I don't believe that this has happened. But even if they were all taken, I would trust you still.' Immediately, peace filled my heart and I dismissed the thought as nothing more than temptation.

Later in the day when I arrived home, all the members of my family were seated in the living room, still in their travelling clothes. They told me that during the night they had had a tyre blow out on the highway. My mother lost control of the car and they swerved all over the road. Miraculously, there were no other cars in sight and their lives had been spared. In the words of the policeman on the scene, 'God must have been with you. This could have been a fatal accident.'

Then I remembered my inspiration to pray for a safe journey, and how I had been awakened during the night. *It was my own family I had been interceding for in tongues!* Immediately I headed to my home parish of Immaculate Heart of Mary, to give thanks to the Lord for his special graduation gift… my family's safety!

Lift Up Your Eyes and See

I never did teach French! After graduation I worked on campus ministry at the University of Michigan in Ann Arbor with Ralph

Martin and Steve Clark. Then I taught religion at Mercy High School in Farmington, Michigan. In 1971, through the prodding of my dear friend from New Jersey, Fr. Jim Ferry, I began to consider full-time work with the Charismatic Renewal. Fr. Harold Cohen, S.J. invited me to New Orleans, Louisiana, where I worked with him in campus ministry at Loyola University of the South. It was a time of explosive growth in the Charismatic Renewal, and I served in prayer group and conference leadership.

I also travelled to witness the tremendous outpouring of the Holy Spirit among God's people around the country and in different parts of the world. At a conference in Aix-en-Provence, France, in 1973, the Lord spoke to me in these words from Scripture, *'Lift up your eyes and see how the fields are already white for harvest' (cf. Jn. 4:35)*. And at our National Catholic Charismatic Conference that same year, a prophecy was given to the whole assembly, *'What you see before your eyes is just the beginning.'*

To God Alone Be the Glory

The first conference of Catholic Charismatics I attended at the University of Notre Dame in South Bend, Indiana, was in September, 1967. There were fifty of us gathered informally in one small panelled room! In 1973, at another Notre Dame Conference, I stood in the football stadium with 35,000 Catholics who had been baptised in the Holy Spirit! Now there are millions of us from all over the world. Only God knows exactly how many people have been blessed with this priceless gift of the Baptism in the Holy Spirit.

It is absolutely clear to me that it is not human strategy or organisation that can be credited for this work. It is not any one of us who was there at the beginning of the Charismatic Renewal, or who has been called forth into leadership since, who can claim any credit. IT IS ALL GOD'S WORK! He is the One we have to praise and thank for the fresh outpouring of the Holy Spirit in this our day as by a new Pentecost.

Take Delight in the Lord

One of the greatest blessings in my personal life has been my marriage to Al Mansfield. For years I had asked the Lord for 'a Spirit-filled saint' and He answered my prayer. Al and I experienced our coming together as an explicit call to be one for the glory of God. The Lord gave me a promise from Psalm 37:4 long ago. *'Take delight in the Lord and He will give you the desires of your heart.'* The Lord was true to His word by sending Al to me and in gifting us with four beautiful children. Together, we are committed to serve the Catholic Church, which we love, and to foster the outpouring of the Holy Spirit in the Charismatic Renewal. We have been privileged to make this our full-time work since 1971.

In his love, the Lord eventually blessed every member of my family and many of my closest friends with the Baptism in the Holy Spirit. He has indeed given my family back to me, along with *'the hundredfold'*, that is brothers and sisters in Christ all over the world.

Saying Yes with Mary

Sometimes I've been asked how it feels to have been at Duquesne when a tiny handful of Catholics were baptised in the Spirit in 1967, and to witness today the spread of the Charismatic Renewal around the world. My answer may surprise you. I feel very humbled, and I feel very united to Mary, the Mother of Jesus. In some mysterious but very real way, I have been caught up in Mary's response to God. It's amazing to see what the *'yes'* of this one simple woman could do! Mary said *'yes'* when the Holy Spirit overshadowed her and as a result Jesus, the Saviour of the whole world, was born. Mankind's salvation hinged on the activity of the Holy Spirit and the response of a creature. Mary's *'yes'* was essential for the unfolding of God's plan, and so is yours and mine.

Each one of us who says *'yes'* to God when the Holy Spirit overshadows us becomes like Mary, another Mary, a dwelling place for Jesus. Our mission now is to bring forth Jesus to the world. My call, your call, is like Mary's call... to embrace and welcome the action of the Holy Spirit, to offer Him no resistance, so that Jesus Christ may be born in us and manifested to the world! To know that my *'yes'* to God has impacted other lives in some way is humbling, because I know how insignificant I am. Yes, *'God who is mighty has done great things for me and holy is His name' (Lk. 1:49).* I close with these beautiful words of St. Paul: 'What no eye has seen, nor ear heard, nor the heart of man conceived, what God has prepared for those who love Him, *God has revealed to us through the Spirit' (1 Cor. 2:9-10).*

David Mangan and Patti Gallagher Mansfield Close up
Dusquesne Weekend 1967

DYNAMITE!

A Testimony by David Mangan

David Mangan graduated from Duquesne University with a B.S. in mathematics and a minor in physics in 1966. David and his wife Barbara live in Ann Arbor, Michigan. They have five children and sixteen grandchildren. David has authored several books and has devoted his professional life to high school education and evangelisation. Testimony and photo, 1992.

The first thing I would like to do is make a slight disclaimer concerning my involvement in the beginning of the Charismatic Renewal at Duquesne; I always feel like I am claiming something that I don't have a right to. There's a rule in baseball that if a runner between bases gets hit by a batted ball, he is automatically out. The fielder who is standing nearest to him gets credit for putting him out, even though he never touched the ball. That's what I feel like. I was in a place when God moved. I happened to be standing close and I get some credit, even though I don't deserve it.

It's also important to point out that this wasn't the first time the Holy Spirit acted among Catholics. There were individual Catholics baptised in the Spirit long before the Duquesne Weekend. Yet, the real significant thing is that God decided to use this event for a specific work.

I had already graduated from Duquesne University at the time of the Weekend, but I was invited to come back as a graduate student. I was twenty-two at the time. I was invited to give one of the talks about the Holy Spirit. Even though I was very active in my parish, teaching catechism at the time, I backed away from the invitation to teach on this retreat. I realised that I didn't know much about the Holy Spirit. In fact, I could say everything I knew about the Holy Spirit in about three sentences and they were all from the Baltimore Catechism. I had a lot of questions about the work of the Holy Spirit myself. I even put off my catechism lesson on the Holy Spirit until after that retreat, hoping that I might learn more during the weekend.

I did the required reading from the Acts of the Apostles, and *The Cross and the Switchblade* by David Wilkerson. I have to be very honest. Even though *The Cross and the Switchblade* has many references to the Baptism in the Holy Spirit and spiritual gifts, it all went over my head. After reading it I still had no idea what speaking in tongues was all about.

It's also important to note that some people attending the Duquesne Weekend were in a time of crisis. As I recall it, some were thinking of leaving the Church and turning away from God. I didn't realise this at the time. For myself, I felt there were a few things I was missing, and I was open to receiving them from God. I had a very simple faith.

As a little kid, I had had experiences of God. After Mass I would often know the presence of the Lord in a very real way. I thought everybody grew up with experiences such as these. I never talked about it, because you didn't really talk about such things. It surprised me on the Duquesne Weekend that some people could consider turning away from Christ. It made no sense to me. Christ is more real than anything else. As a child, I had given my life to the Lord. I had taken various stands as a Christian along the way. I figured that if I didn't understand the Holy Spirit or if the power of God was absent in my life, it was my problem. It wasn't God's problem. I was the one who needed to correct something. That's the attitude I brought to the retreat. I needed to figure out what the problem was and let God do something about it.

We began each session during the weekend by singing the same hymn to the Holy Spirit. We sang it in the old Gregorian chant, which I like and still sing sometimes in my prayer time.

We had four talks during the retreat, one on each of the first four chapters of the Acts of the Apostles. The first talk really struck me. This was the talk I had been asked to give. I received a lot of insight from the person who gave it, but the thing I remember really distinctly, was his comment on Acts 1:8, *'But you shall receive power when the Holy Spirit has come upon you'*. He referred to the Greek word for power which is the same as we would use in English for *'dynamite'*. In other words, the *'dynamite'* of the Holy Spirit would come upon you. This is what he was saying. *Dynamite!* Now, I loved God and tried to love others, but I could hardly characterise my life as *'dynamite'*. Again, I quickly drew the conclusion that the problem must be with me. I am sure God was doing His part.

The second talk on Acts 2 was the Pentecost account. You would think that this would be a particularly exciting talk, but I thought the speaker was rather dull. She was a lady who knew some of our faculty advisors. To us, she was an outsider. All I remember is that she read Acts 2 and said, *'This is still happening today'*. She spoke about fifteen to twenty minutes. When you're a college student, you're used to long lectures. This was just a little chat to me. I was thinking, 'There has got to be more to this than what she's saying'.

We were taking notes during the talks. This is what I wrote in my notebook, almost in defiance of what she was saying, *'I want to hear someone speak in tongues... ME!'* Then the next line reads, *'Be a fool for the Lord'*. Both were about to happen very quickly! I have no more notes from the Duquesne Weekend. There were two more talks, but I wasn't writing anymore. After the talk on Acts 2, we had discussion groups and I went into my discussion group trying to figure out why I didn't have *'dynamite'*. I was still on this *'dynamite'* idea when I came to this conclusion. I reasoned that as a Catholic I received the Holy Spirit in the Sacrament of Confirmation. Being trained as a mathematician and physicist, I tend to be very analytical. I knew that for a sacrament to work, there are three factors: 1. It needs to be a valid sacrament. 2. It needs to be ministered by a lawful minister. 3. It needs to be received in faith. That last point seemed to be the problem... me, my lack of expectant faith. I thought, that must be why I didn't have *'dynamite'*.

Therefore, I made a proposal to our discussion group. I said, 'You know, every year at Easter we renew our baptismal vows because we were baptised as infants and we need to make these vows our own as we mature.' When I was in sixth grade being confirmed, I don't even know if I realised what was happening. I went through the preparation, and answered all of the questions, but I somehow remember I was more concerned about what Confirmation gift I was going to get from my sponsor, than what gifts I might receive from God. I told the others, *'I think we ought to renew our Confirmation'*. In fact, I was determined to do it. Remember, I'd never heard of the Baptism in the Holy Spirit or the gift of tongues. I would not have known to ask for any of that. I just said, *'I want to renew my Confirmation'*. I thought it was a brilliant idea. When we went back to the large group to share the fruit of our discussion, my idea was proposed. Some people thought I might be taking things a little too seriously. I remember feeling disappointed that my idea wasn't really accepted by others.

After lunch I took a walk with Patti Gallagher who had been in my discussion group. We were talking over my proposal and how few people seemed to like the idea. The conclusion I came to right then was that even if nobody else wanted to renew his Confirmation, I was going to do it. I thought I'd approach the chaplain and ask him how to go about it. I made that decision in my heart, but I never had time to act on it. You know, God is so fast, he is always acting before you get a chance.

Back at the retreat house I was greeted with some news. One of the leaders was gathering several people together when I entered. The water pump serving this retreat facility had broken; there was no water. He asked us to go to the chapel and pray. This was dangerous stuff to me. Although I prayed a lot, I don't think I ever prayed for anything specifically, where I really needed an answer right away. I could pray for the conversion of Russia. That was easy. You don't have to face the fact that it might not happen tomorrow. You can be patient with those kind of prayers. This one was a now or never kind of prayer. A few of us gathered in the chapel and we were praying away when I had an interesting experience.

I started to thank God for the answer! No one ever told me about that theologically. That teaching came later in the Charismatic Renewal. I just had this inner conviction that our prayer was answered. As I started thinking this, it was almost as if I caught myself, and reflected on how odd it was to feel so convinced. After we finished praying, I was so sure that the water was there, I ran down to the kitchen and turned on the faucet. It came gushing out with stronger force than it ever had! After the Duquesne Weekend, I was told that while we were praying, a mechanic showed up and fixed it. However, we were informed going into prayer in no uncertain terms that a mechanic could not come until Monday. The fact that the water was there after we prayed obviously made a big impression on me. When I saw the water gushing out I did something I had never done before. I decided that I needed to give thanks. My thanksgiving should be as loud as my groaning. I went back to the chapel and gave thanks to the Lord for what he had done.

When I walked into the chapel, it was like walking into a brick wall. I had just been there a short time before, and I hadn't felt the presence of God in any unusual way. But when I opened the door *this* time, there was something significantly different. To this day, I am not quite sure how I ended up on the floor, but I did. I don't know how much it was me prostrating myself before the Lord, or the Lord prostrating me in his presence. The only thing I could say is that the presence of God was so powerful and manifest, the only sensible place to be was on your face, and I got there. For a calm, quiet, reserved mathematician, I was having a very wild experience. You could cut the presence of

God with a knife. I didn't have any words, I had no theology, all I could say was, *'This is it! DYNAMITE! This is it!'*

I got up and left the chapel, wobbling with a stupid grin on my face and went downstairs. It was February 18, 1967, my brother Tom's birthday. There was supposed to be a party that night for several people who had birthdays. Tom wasn't there; he was in Turkey in the Peace Corps. But everybody on the retreat knew him and he was on the birthday slate to celebrate. Everybody was trying to get into a birthday mood but I certainly couldn't after my experience in chapel. As people stood around chatting, I was leaning against the wall, trying not to fall over, because I still felt really wobbly. I was thinking to myself, 'Mangan, you've flipped out. Mathematicians don't act like this. You've really done it now. You've lost it all.'

Everybody continued talking but I didn't know what they were saying. I was having this inner experience, and all the while I was smiling. Then I began to doubt the whole thing. I said, 'This wasn't real. I just went off the deep end.' Being a mathematician, the natural thing for me to do was to go back to the laboratory and try it again. 'Let's see if this experiment is valid.'

I moved close to the wall, still wobbly, and started making my way back up the stairs toward the chapel. I walked back into the chapel, and 'Wham!' I hit the floor again. I said, 'This is it. This is *definitely* the answer to my prayer.' There I was in the presence of the Lord.

After a while I left the chapel, walked downstairs, leaning against the wall, smiling at all of the people and doubt again crept in. I stood there thinking, 'Oh, this can't be right. Something is not adding up here.' I went back upstairs, and entered the chapel, 'Wham!' It all happened again.

Then something interesting happened. I didn't know anything about the gift of tongues but I needed to express something. I was sitting there on the floor, trying to figure out how to respond. I wasn't sure how to do it, so I yelled a rebel yell at the top of my lungs. I gave out one of the biggest 'hoot and hollers' you would ever want to hear. I found out later it was heard the complete length of the retreat house and everybody else was sure I had flipped out. Somebody came running into the chapel, wanting to know what was wrong with me. I just had a peaceful grin on my face. All I could say was, *'It is so good. It's so good and this is it. This is what I came for and this is the truth.'*

My theology may have been weak, but the experience was valid. I no longer doubted that it was real. But, I began to wonder, 'Was I alone? Was I weird? Could I stand for God alone?' It seemed that everybody else was having a crisis. As I was walking around the retreat house, I saw Patti Gallagher coming down the stairs. I was going to try and tell her what had happened, but as we looked at each other, I saw this same look on her face. I asked, 'You, too?' She replied, 'Yeah, me too.' That was all that passed between us, but we understood completely what had occurred. And at least I was relieved to know I wasn't alone.

I went to the leaders of the retreat and shared my experience. One of them asked, 'Did you try to speak in tongues?' 'What's that?' I answered. I mentioned that I did start to say something prior to the rebel yell that wasn't in English. Not knowing what it was, I stopped. He told me that praying in tongues was scriptural, and if it happened again to let her rip. Those weren't his words, but that's what I took from them. So the next time it happened, I let her rip.

I want to share a few facts about the Duquesne Weekend now, because sometimes when an event is in the past it can be described in a more romantic way than it really happened. What I've recounted here is purely accurate in terms of my own experience. Of the thirty people on the Weekend, only about half were baptised in the Spirit. There were some people on the Duquesne Weekend that thought we were nuts, and others left the Charismatic Renewal early on. It was actually a difficult experience. Yet, the Lord did a mighty work among us.

After you're baptised in the Spirit, you're usually high for a while. My high lasted at least nine months to a year. I didn't think I was ever going to come down. But when I came down, I came down like everybody else. Perhaps the Lord allowed me this time because it was the beginning of the Renewal and He was being gentle with me, leading me along. When I came down, I was very convinced that I had had a genuine encounter with God. I couldn't doubt that anymore. It was really set deep within me. I was able to dedicate myself to a life of prayer and a life of service. When the hard hat end of Christianity started to hit me, I was able to dig in and embrace it and move on. I think I needed that nine months to a year just to be ready.

Immediately after the Duquesne Weekend, I had three basic fears still to deal with. The first one I already mentioned, but it was still there. 'Was I alone?' The second one, a very big question for me, was, 'Could I remain a Catholic?' The third question was, 'What would people think of me?' I was not so strong that I wasn't influenced by the opinion of others. Here's how I handled those things.

The first one was rather easy to handle with God's help. I found out that there were other people just like me. They may have been few in number back then, but I was satisfied. Now I have more people that are just like me than I could count. They are like the sands on the seashore. God took care of the loneliness problem for me very quickly.

The second question was a very crucial one. 'Could I remain a Catholic?' At that time, it was unpopular to be a charismatic and it was very unpopular to be a Catholic in certain circles. I grew up in a good Catholic family. I found out as I moved in Pentecostal circles, as they were called then, that I was challenged. It was very common for people to say, 'You've received the Baptism in the Spirit? That's great. When are you leaving the Catholic Church?' As much as I put those comments aside, they challenged me. The question I was often asked was, 'What would you do if God told you to leave the Catholic Church?' It was a very scary question, especially when I had just said, 'God, I will do anything you want me to do.' Leaving the Church would be like ripping my heart out. It was a very difficult question for me to handle.

Through the crisis though, some very good things happened. I realised that God wasn't asking that at all and this gave me a great sense of peace. The Catholic Church was where I had experienced the Lord as a child, and it was where I had experienced the Lord acting in power. When I came to that realisation, I think I finally became an adult Catholic. It was an important day for me. I became a Catholic by choice and not only by birth. It's fine to be a Catholic by birth, but what should happen at Confirmation is that we become Catholics by choice. I took my adult stand as a soldier for Christ after going through this period of being questioned about my commitment as a Catholic. Something important was completed. It was the completion of my prayer to renew my Confirmation. This scary experience was part of it. I stood up as an adult and said, 'This is who I am in the Lord, and I'm proud to be so.'

As far as what people thought of me, by God's grace I came to the conclusion that I didn't much care, as long as I was obeying God. I didn't come to that conclusion on my own. It took a good deal of grace; it's something I'm still peeling off layers and growing in. I'm learning not to be intimidated by what people think of me, learning to stand strong for the Lord, striking out where he says, finding out what God is doing and following it. That's the way I want to live my life.

Within the first year, we had a situation where all our leaders moved out of town. We needed a new leader and I was anxious for one to be selected. I really wanted to sit at some wise person's feet and learn. As we were praying and fasting for someone to lead the prayer meeting, I was hearing the Lord say to me, 'It's you.' My response was, 'No way! Not this kid. You don't realise what I don't know, Lord. You don't realise how foolish I am and how immature.' But I kept sensing the Lord say, 'It's you.' I did something then I wouldn't dare do now. I said, 'Lord, don't expect me to say anything about being a leader. If you want it to happen, the ball is in your court. I just can't.'

When the prayer group came together to share our discernment, everybody pointed to me and said, 'God wants David to be our new leader.' I accepted it as God's will.

I spent the summer of 1967 in Mt. Vernon, New York, in a household with others from Duquesne. It was a very formative experience for my life, both in household living and in being a fool for Christ. I remember how we went out into the streets to evangelise without knowing what we were supposed to say. We decided we had to go back, pray, and figure out what the Gospel was, at least in a simple form, to talk to people about it. After a few meetings we went back out and were able to put the Gospel in a form that was simple and clear.

There were several learning phases we went through in the early period of the Charismatic Renewal. The first phase could probably be described as fascination with spiritual gifts. They almost seemed like new toys. For instance, it was fascinating to speak in tongues. I remember praying over somebody who was a linguist from Paris, France. He told me, 'You are praying in an archaic form of French that is no longer used.' I thought, 'Wow, that's fun! I want to do that again.' The fact that it was supposed to glorify the Lord somehow escaped me for the moment. Somebody prayed aloud in tongues at a prayer meeting once. Then another person stood up and interpreted it. Finally, a third party who didn't know either person said, 'That was this particular language and that interpretation was very accurate.' I was amazed. You can say, 'This is really great. Let's do it again. But can you tell me what the message was?' It took time to learn not to be fascinated with those things, but to be fascinated with the Lord.

When we got over the fascination with the gifts, I think the danger was that of treating the spiritual gifts as commonplace. For instance, there's a simple prophecy which I've heard many times. It is, *'My people, I love you.'* People tend to miss this prophetic word and that's tragic. God loves you! That's the most common prophecy I ever heard all these years in the Charismatic Renewal. I think I've have heard it in almost every meeting I've ever attended. Don't ever think that this isn't a precious word from God. Do you know why He tells us that all the time? It's because we don't believe it. Don't disdain prophecy, even simple prophetic words.

God renewed our awareness of spiritual gifts because we needed to know about them to grow in our Christian lives.

They're not decorations or extra added attractions. If the apostles and Mary in the upper room needed spiritual gifts and discernment, I need them too. If you think you don't, what you're basically saying is, 'I am better than they are. Maybe Peter needed them, maybe Mary needed them, but I don't need them.' How silly could you be? They needed them. I need them. You need them.

In closing this testimony I want to say that it's important to look at the Charismatic Renewal as a work of God. That *doesn't* mean that everything that has occurred has been God's will. Thank God that he doesn't check out when we stray from him. He is very patient, very kind, very loving. We are all testimonies to that. It *does* mean that God is patiently leading us on, very gently, very lovingly. For this reason, we should not disdain what God has done, nor how he has done it.

I look back on the past and I treasure it, but we can't live in the past. We need to be in touch with God now, in the present moment. I value the things God did in the early days of the Charismatic Renewal, even though there were many painful lessons. I have no desire to go back, none whatsoever, not even a twinge. *The good old days are right now.* The good old days are when God *is* acting, not only when he acted before, but where he is acting now. God is a dynamic God, always on the move, and I want to be with him. I pledge myself to be with him.

In the final analysis, our criteria for evaluating the Charismatic Renewal is the same we use to evaluate anything: The two great commandments, love of God, and love of neighbour. Is the Charismatic Renewal helping you love God? Is it helping you love your neighbour? If it's doing those two things, then it's a smashing success. If it's not doing those things, it might have a lot of flash and dash, but it's not doing what God is about. I believe that this is what God is trying to build in us. He is trying to build a people that will love him and love each other. That's the way to win the world.

OUR GOD IS A CONSUMING FIRE

A TESTIMONY BY PAUL GRAY AND MARY ANN SPRINGEL

Mary Ann Springel was a senior at Duquesne University in 1967. Paul Gray, a Duquesne alumnus, was a graduate student in theology at Fordham University that year. Both Mary Ann and Paul were members of the Chi Rho Society throughout their years at Duquesne. Each of them gave a talk during the Duquesne Weekend. This testimony was originally published in New Covenant Magazine, February, 1973, and is reprinted here with permission. Photo, 1967

Mary Ann and I were puzzled by our friends as we sat at their kitchen table that night in late December, 1966. They obviously shared some secret that caused them to bubble with laughter even more than usual. Finally one of them responded to the question voiced only in our glances with another question: 'What if I were to tell you that the New Testament is true?' Again Mary Ann and 1 looked at each other. What was our friend intimating? We had come to know him when he taught us a theology course two years earlier. What initially attracted our attention had been his obvious commitment to and joyous participation in all that he taught. What was he now trying to say? What new depth had he discovered?... Because of him, I was going off to graduate school to pursue my master's degree in theology... That night we wanted to know what new source of joy our friends had discovered, but we didn't specifically ask, and they didn't specifically tell us.

A few weeks later, this theology instructor, Mary Ann and I, and several other students sat in the office of another Duquesne professor solidifying plans for the Spring Weekend of Renewal for the *Chi Rho Society. Chi Rho* was going through an identity crisis and hope for its survival hinged on the success of the retreat. Our best efforts to create Christian community and renew the world had failed. We had set out to add some meaning to the despair-filled alcoholics in Pittsburgh's Hill District ghetto, and had wound up questioning our own meaning. These two professors suggested a change in the theme of the retreat from *'The Beatitudes: or How To Act Like*

Christians' to *'The Acts of the Apostles: or How To Become Christians.'* Without fully realising the significance of this change, we all agreed.

I went off to graduate school in February more excited and more apprehensive about the Weekend of Renewal than about graduate studies. During those first weeks in February, I searched every commentary in the Manhattan College and Union Theological Seminary libraries in preparation for the talk I was to give on Acts 1. I wanted to return to Pittsburgh showing everyone how much I had learned in only three weeks of graduate theology. But as I flew out of LaGuardia on February 16, I had so many notes that there was no possibility of organising them into a clear talk.

After three weeks in New York City, it was good to arrive at the Ark and the Dove, where the retreat was to be held, for an entire weekend with Mary Ann and our friends from *Chi Rho*. But the unprepared talk hung over me like a dark cloud. At least it would all be over by Saturday morning, and then I could really enjoy the Weekend. I sat through Saturday breakfast unable to eat a thing as the scattered thoughts I was about to deliver raced through my mind.

As the others entered the room where the talk was to be given, I sat at the speaker's table more nervous than ever. We all stood and began to sing 'Come Holy Ghost'. The strangest experience in my life up to that time occurred as I felt my nerves calm and my hands grow warm. The hymn finished, and I began to speak.

I heard myself being not only calm, but coherent. I surprised myself as I heard statements that I hadn't found in any commentary and didn't have anywhere in my notes.

After the talk, the professors both told me I had really become a teacher. The very approval I had spent so many hours of research and anxiety hoping to gain for myself now was given by the two men from whom it meant the most. But now I knew that I didn't deserve the credit. Jesus did. I bowed my head and thanked Him.

The talk on Acts 2 was given Saturday afternoon by an Episcopalian woman who had experienced Pentecost in her life. We don't remember what she said, but she gave us a hunger for the reality of Pentecost in our lives. In the discussion following the talk, Dave Mangan summarised the attitude of the students by asking our chaplain if we could renew our Confirmation in the Sunday liturgy in order to experience something more than we had when first confirmed.

After 'quiet time' and while dinner was being prepared, Mary Ann and I went to our theology instructor friend and told him we wanted him to pray for us that we would experience whatever he had. The three of us went up to his room. Amidst sleeping bags and tossed pajamas, Mary Ann and I knelt on the floor while he laid his hands on each of our heads and prayed, first in English, then in tongues. It was the first time we had heard tongues and neither of us quite knew how to take it. We gave our lives to Jesus, and he gave us His Holy Spirit.

As he was praying, the tip of my tongue lifted and then began to move up and down, making a clicking sound as it hit against the roof of my mouth. Mary Ann felt a joy well up within her like a tremendous balloon that totally filled her and then settled in her throat; 'I just had to smile and smile and praise Jesus,' she recalls.

That joy very likely would have erupted into the gift of tongues if she had known how to co-operate with the Holy Spirit. Instead she got up somewhat bewildered. She had heard me begin to yield to tongues, but had not experienced the same thing herself. 'I thought I didn't have the Baptism in the Holy Spirit if it was what they had, yet I felt a bursting but inarticulate joy. I kept suppressing a holy laugh. It was as though I knew a wonderful secret though I wasn't sure what it was. Had someone asked, I probably would have told them I knew for sure that Jesus loved me. Since no one did ask, I kept quiet as we went down to dinner.'

As we were eating dinner, one of the nuns from the Ark and the Dove came in to tell us that there was no water in the well and that we would have to leave Saturday evening. One of the professors went to the chapel to pray. Mary Ann and I and a few others joined him. We all knelt on the chapel floor as he began to pray aloud. He asked the Father in Jesus' name for water; then he began thanking God for the water. He continued for some time singing about the water and praising the Lord for it.

Unlike the rest of us, he obviously believed God had provided the water. When we later asked how he could thank God for the water before it was evident, he explained that when Jesus said on the cross, *'It is finished'*, he meant not only his life, but his work. Jesus had completely obeyed the Father in everything and his kingdom was now established through the blood he had shed.

It was left for us to believe God for the specific manifestations of that kingdom. Knowing it was God's will that we experience Him on the Weekend, our theology instructor saw clearly that it was not of God that the well go dry at such a strategic time. The faith exercised turned Satan's obstacle into the Lord's miracle. Our faith was such that, after his somewhat lonely prayer, we were still resigned to going home that night.

We came together for an apparently final Bible vigil. When it was over, Dave Mangan went downstairs to get a drink. When he turned on the faucet, the water gushed out.

Mary Ann and I were just leaving the chapel when David came back in. He fell prostrate before the tabernacle; Mary Ann and I did also. God had all the time been close enough to hear that prayer for water, and now had shown that He was powerful enough to answer it.

Fear of the Lord welled up within us; a fearful awe kept us from looking up. He was personally present and we feared being loved too much. We worshipped him, knowing for the first time the meaning of worship. We knew a burning experience of the terrible reality and presence of the Lord that has since caused us to understand at first hand the images of Yahweh on Mt. Sinai as it rumbles and explodes with the fire of his Being, and the experience of Isaiah 6:1-5, and the statement that *our God is a consuming fire.* This holy fear was somehow the same as love or evoked love as we really beheld him. He was altogether lovely and beautiful, yet we saw no visual image. It was as though the splendorous, brilliant, personal God had come into the room and filled both it and us.

David, by this time was so in love with the Lord that he needed more room to show it and began rolling about. I knelt worshipping, as Mary Ann went to her room to write the outline for her talk on Acts 3.

Others were now coming into the chapel by twos and threes. Within a short time, almost all of the students were in the chapel, kneeling, holding hands, and worshipping the Lord. Mary Ann returned. The others, like us, were not accustomed to kneeling long or praying simply. Worship had meant standing up, reading poetry, playing guitars, singing and unfurling banners. Now we were totally occupied by saying nothing more than *'Jesus'* or *'Yes, Lord'* over and over, addressing the Lord who was there. *'I love you, Jesus'* came forth from kids whose faces shone with gladness.

The two faculty moderators went down the line of kneeling converts, praying for the Baptism in the Holy Spirit for each one. We have never since seen such a spontaneous and universal move of the Spirit. One of the professors said he felt as though fire was engulfing him. Some of the students were saying, 'It's getting brighter,' as he was saying, 'It's getting hotter'. The Holy Spirit, who appeared as tongues of fire on the first Pentecost, again manifested himself as a consuming fire. Singing and speaking in tongues could be heard as we knelt there loving Jesus and being loved by him until 3 a.m. when the good sense of the chaplain and the nuns sent us to bed.

When Mary Ann got to her room, all she could do was worry about the next day's talk. 'I had failed repeatedly before the weekend to find a worthwhile commentary on Acts 3.1 had been terribly concerned about giving a good talk, wanting very much to impress my peer group and Paul. I had spent hours planning what I would wear, and had arrived at the Ark and the Dove with a carefully chosen dress in my suitcase, but almost no talk in my hand or head,' she recalls.

'Even though I had just witnessed the Lord's glory, I didn't realise how able the Lord is. Since the others were speaking in tongues, I didn't realise I was even baptised in the Spirit. Knowing so little, I didn't recognise the joy, fear of the Lord, love, and the quickly outlined talk as manifestations of the Holy Spirit.' Patti Gallagher laid hands on Mary Ann, prayed for her, and then hung a note on the door saying 'Jesus loves you!' With that, Mary Ann fell asleep and awakened the next morning, her first thought being, 'Praise the Lord,' and her second, 'O my God - I have to give that talk.'

'I told the Lord I was proud, but though I confessed it, it seemed to remain. I was thinking of how good I wanted to look for Paul and began to get dressed. The dress seemed to epitomise my concern for myself. Then I saw the clothes I had thrown into the suitcase four hours earlier, wrinkled slacks and a very wrinkled blouse. I said 'Lord, I am proud inside; I can't seem to make that go away. I want to be different; I want to give that talk for you. When you look at me, Lord, know by these clothes that I don't want to be proud. The clothes are all I can change, Lord! You, please, change my spirit.' 'I dressed in the wrinkled clothes and, with only a few backward glances at the dress and heels, I met dressed-up friends and walked over to the big house with them for breakfast amid some curious looks. I knew the Lord's gaze was upon me, too, and my clothes were a constant plea for help.'

As in the matter of the well, Mary Ann had little faith in the matter of the talk. Her knees knocked both under the breakfast table and under the speaker's table.' As my brothers and sisters sang 'Come, Holy Ghost,' however, he did, sovereignly. I knew what it meant to be saved by grace! The cold, clammy fear faded; I felt warm all over and began to speak wisdom that was not mine.'

The talk was interrupted several times by prayer and praise, and was followed by a conspicuously long period of applause. 'That applause that I had so greatly desired no longer gratified anything inside. It would only touch off in me praise for my Father. I knew he did it. I opened my mouth to thank him while the applause (for him) continued; I began speaking in tongues, realising that I, too was a part of what God was doing. ...'

After I [Paul] returned to New York... I was led to Rev. Harald Bredesen, who immediately took an interest in my story of the Duquesne Weekend. Harald had me sharing my testimony everywhere he could. It was quite a new experience, standing in front of large groups of Protestants telling them what God was doing in the Catholic Church. The greatest surprise was the enthusiasm with which they received the news.

Meanwhile, Mary Ann was learning about charismatic prayer meetings and community with the other students in Pittsburgh. ...For three months [that summer], the Lord gave us the Kingdom experience of living in community with Harald and his family, six students from Duquesne, and a number of Spirit-filled Protestants.

There we experienced on a communal level what the Lord was desiring to do in us as individuals as he set about *'breaking down the dividing wall of hostility... that He might create one new man in place of the two by reconciling us both to God in one Body through the cross' as we both came to have 'access in one Spirit to the Father' (Eph. 2:14-18).* As we witnessed our Protestant brothers and sisters so willingly laying down their lives for us, giving up even their style of praying if it offended us, we learned the depth of love the Spirit gives through Jesus' Body.

To this day, as we continue to walk with him, the Lord continues to show us the depth of the love he first showed us when he called us to and for himself in 1967.

MAY THE PEACE OF CHRIST BE WITH YOU

A TESTIMONY BY MARYBETH MUTMANSKY GREENE[7]

Marybeth Mutmansky (Greene) graduated from Duquesne University with a B.A. in English in 1968. She lives in the Bronx, New York, where she and her husband serves as the Associate Directors of LAMP MINISTRIES. Testimony and photo, 1992.

The Duquesne Weekend took place during my junior year. As part of the committee of students and faculty from *Chi Rho* which planned this retreat weekend, I was aware that the group had been struggling to identify its focus. Some members wanted the group to be a social action/civil rights group; others encouraged action for liturgical renewal on campus; still others wanted to limit activity to daily prayer times; others wanted more of a communal life.

The faculty moderators had begun to attend prayer meetings. There they experienced the Holy Spirit in a way which convinced them that the focus of our weekend should be: the Holy Spirit.

To prepare for the Weekend, those attending were asked to read *The Cross and the Switchblade*, by Rev. David Wilkerson, and the first four chapters of the Acts of the Apostles. Also, several of us were asked to give meditations on women in Scripture who responded faithfully to God. The woman I was to meditate on was Mary, the Mother of Jesus.

I was deeply moved as I read the stories of the teenagers in Rev. Wilkerson's account of his ministry with New York street gangs. The night before the retreat weekend began, I knelt beside my bed and, for the first time in months, talked to God personally. I said something like this: 'I don't want to fight you. From now on, whatever you want in my life, I want too.'

The first night of the retreat, the thirty of us participated in a

Penance Service. At one point there was time for spontaneous prayer, and we began to confess our sins to one another. It seemed to me that walls within me and among the group were breaking down. Afterwards, the priest who was there offered to any individuals who desired it, the Sacrament of Reconciliation.

The next day, during the celebration of the Eucharist, the sense grew within me that I needed to take a step in faith and say, 'Yes, I believe that Jesus is the Son of God and is alive.' When it came time for the Sign of Peace before Communion, I knew it would imply a commitment to say aloud the name of Jesus, and I was afraid. I went around the chapel nodding my head as I shook hands. Then I came to a professor who said to me, 'Go on, you can say it!'

When I wished him the peace of Christ, the presence of Jesus in the Eucharist, in our midst, and in my heart became so real to me that I began to weep for joy! 'What's wrong?' my friends wanted to know as soon as Mass was over. 'It's not what's wrong,' I replied. 'It's what's right!'

That afternoon, when I shared with the group some thoughts about Mary saying 'yes' to God the Father's call, I could identify with her in a new way, a deeper way than ever before. She became someone I felt close to, not someone remote and unapproachable.

Saturday evening a birthday party was scheduled, but those present restlessly wandered in and out of the house. I felt a tug within me to return to the chapel. As I entered, I experienced the presence of the Holy Spirit filling the room. It was like a combination of water and light. For many hours that night we prayed spontaneously and praised God. We interceded for the Church. And we enjoyed the Lord's presence. I understood then that God - Father, Son, and Spirit - is family. I realised that the Spirit in our lives brings us into the heart of the Trinity.

On Sunday morning, after very little sleep but feeling like God had given me a cruise vacation, I became aware of gifts of the Holy Spirit active among us. In particular, when one of the people present abruptly and with agitation ran out of our gathering, I went out and prayed with the person for deliverance and peace, something I knew nothing about except that the Spirit gave me the words. The person then returned to the gathering, calm and peaceful. That left me in awe of God's power and holiness.

At the end of the weekend, I experienced the gift of tongues when friends prayed with me for this gift. Feelings of personal unworthiness in relation to a very holy God gave way to a deep peace and an awareness of God's personal love and acceptance of me.

The Lord's goodness was poured out in my life during that Duquesne Weekend and during the days and weeks that followed. Jesus was alive and his ways were attractive to me. I had an incredible hunger for God's presence through prayer, through reading his word, and through receiving the Eucharist.

My heart changed from cynicism to a love for the Church. Before the weekend I saw the weakness and failings within the Catholic Church, but did not grasp its essence. Suddenly the Church took on a whole new meaning. Through Jesus I saw that I was united in one body with the Universal Church, that together we are Church.

I saw that 'those who have gone before us,' the faithful of other ages, are our brothers and sisters, concerned for us and eager to help us when we ask. In particular, Mary, the Mother of Jesus, became a special helper and friend. I began to see that planning a career had no meaning for me. What did make sense was following the Holy Spirit as he led me toward Jesus and the Father.

If I were to state only two major blessings which God has given me in these years (there are so many), one significant blessing has been a special love for sharing God's word and his love with children and young people.

Another grace has been a desire to serve with and through the Catholic Church as a lay missionary. When my friends Tom and Lyn Scheuring shared with me their proposal to develop LAMP MINISTRIES, a lay missionary service of evangelisation with the materially poor in the metropolitan New York area, I was drawn to LAMP through prayer and the desires of my heart. I discovered that I had a desire to find Jesus in the poor and rejected of our society, those who bear most deeply in their lives the wounds of the crucified Jesus. For many years I have been a lay missionary with LAMP, serving as its associate director. Those who serve with us make a full-time commitment for a year to evangelise (and be evangelised) among the poor and homeless.

To God be the glory for the countless ways he has given his Spirit of love to me, and to all who have only to ask!

Al and Patti Mansfield with Marybeth Mutmansky Greene and her husband, taken inn 2002

The chapel at the Ark and the Dove, 1967

The chapel at the Ark and the Dove, 2015

Mary Ellen Belfiore (left) and Marybeth Mutmansky (right) at a Chi Rho picnic, 1966

Men from Chi Rho at a picnic, 1966

WATERFALL OF LIGHT

A Testimony by Karin Sefcik Treiber

Karin Sefcik Treiber graduated from Duquesne University with a B.A. in English in 1968. She held an M.A. in education from Michigan State University and a PhD. She was married to Bob Treiber and was mother of two sons, David and Paul and two grandchildren. She went home to the Lord on December 27, 2012 but she told me that she would be present at the Golden Jubilee celebration. Testimony and photo, 1992

Baptism in the Spirit was a phrase that came up at an organisational meeting for our student retreat weekend at Duquesne University in February, 1967. It was mentioned by one of our faculty members. Before long I glowed like him, because I, too, had been gifted richly in the *Baptism in the Holy Spirit*. I participated in the now famous Duquesne Weekend which marked the beginning of the Charismatic Renewal in the Catholic Church. It seems both such a short time ago and such a lifetime ago. What a beginning it was!

While a junior at Duquesne, I had come to a very low point in my life. Studies were going well, but emotionally I felt that everything I reached for or wanted was slipping through my fingers: A meaningful relationship came to an abrupt end and I wondered what I would do after graduation.

One group at the University that kept me going was the *Chi Rho Society*. I was secretary of *Chi Rho* at that time and Bill Deigan was president. At one point, Bill suggested we have a retreat to grow closer together as a group. He felt that we needed to learn what it meant to be a Christian. Bill suggested that we read the Beatitudes to prepare for the retreat. In early January, 1967, the officers of *Chi Rho* met with a faculty member in the History Department conference room to plan the retreat.

During that planning meeting, one of the faculty members looked different to me. His eyes shone and there was a conviction in his voice when he talked about the Lord. I remember thinking, *'Whatever he has, I want it, too.'* He asked us to do three things about the retreat: One: Scrap our original plan. Instead, we were to plan talks on the Acts 1-4. Two: Read the book *The Cross and the Switchblade*. Three: Pray for the retreat as we had never prayed before. He urged us to pray that we would leave the retreat changed, not having just undergone a pious exercise. I was surprised by this comment since I had never heard anything like it before. What an unusual mixture of instructions!

For the retreat, Bill Deigan had a schedule of events, some of which were times of prayer and reflection. I remember that the passage Bill shared was, *'Jesus Christ is the same yesterday, today, and forever' (Heb. 13:8)*. As we approached the retreat, a faculty member said we would sing a hymn to the Holy Spirit before each of the sessions. As I looked back on my minutes from the planning meeting, I saw this notation, *'We will pray to be baptised in the Holy Spirit.'* I honestly do not recall that anyone said that.

Well, we did what we were told. We prepared. My faith life at that point was characterised by faithful attendance at Sunday liturgies, rushed daily prayer, sacramental devotion to the Eucharist and occasional use of the Sacrament of Reconciliation. I was thrilled when Vatican II allowed the use of English. During high school I had gone through what seemed to me a crisis of faith. For years I had thought of serving God as a religious but had decided to finish college first at the suggestion of my favorite uncle, a priest. I majored in English in college and honestly had no plans during college as to what I would do upon completion of my studies.

As I prepared for the retreat by reading *The Cross and the Switchblade,* I remember thinking, 'I believe in Jesus. I'm a baptised Catholic. Why haven't things like I'm reading about here happened to me?' I prayed expectantly for a change in my own heart to happen during the retreat, but because I was part of the organising group, I was more concerned with others and their participation than I was aware of my own spiritual need.

On Friday, February 17, 1967, we arrived at the Ark and the Dove Retreat House. It was a very grey winter's day. Since I was part of the planning group, I remember doing some things to help people get settled, and I heard Patti Gallagher say *'I'm expecting a miracle!'* She also glowed from the moment we arrived. We had planned Friday as a time for setting a tone.

We began each session with a hymn to the Holy Spirit. On Saturday afternoon, an Episcopalian woman came to speak to us. When she spoke, she had an inner dynamism which was different from what I had observed in any other Christian or Catholic. She spoke about the Lord as if she walked closely with him and had just had a special, intimate, personal conversation with him that very morning. I had the same thought about her as I did about our faculty moderator - *'Whatever it is she has, I want it, too.'*

We had a social break Saturday afternoon. After supper, we were preparing to wash the spaghetti-dirtied dishes, but we learned that there was no water to complete our clean-up task. I remember thinking that we'd have to go home. It seemed odd to me that we would have to leave, yet I was willing to go if necessary. Someone directed us to go to the chapel to pray. As some of us prayed in the chapel, some sang, and some of us pleaded. Our faculty moderator smiled at the Lord's sense of humor. I remember someone, perhaps Dave Mangan, asking God for water, then thanking him for all types of water: bubbling brooks, sprinkling water, rain water, gushing water, waterfalls, etc., etc. I also remember Dave went to the faucet, touched it, and water came out. With the water supplied, we were able to stay on the retreat.

About mid-evening we had planned a party to lighten the mood. A young man I had met, Danny appeared on the retreat because he knew I would be there. I began to notice that fewer and fewer were in the living room where the party was supposed to be going on. Instead, people seemed to be going upstairs to the chapel. I, too, went upstairs and knelt along with the others (twenty or so of us). I remember one of the faculty members leading us in prayer for a number of intentions but I more vividly recall a golden glow in that room. I prayed intently for Tom Mangan, Dave's brother and a special friend of mine, who was with the Peace Corps in Turkey. I heard people praying for other intentions, too, and felt a real closeness to God. We were praying with an earnestness I had never experienced before. Although people began to leave the chapel after a while, I stayed a bit longer and remember seeing Dave Mangan prostrate on the floor. At one point his body seemed to move as if in response to a hand, an invisible one. By an insight which must have been divinely inspired and by what was perhaps the beginning of my

Baptism in the Spirit too, I thought, 'God is moving him.' Striking changes began to take place at the Ark and the Dove.

Later in the evening we were able to receive the Sacrament of Reconciliation if we chose. I remember slipping into the chapel alone and felt again a special presence of the Lord. It seemed to me that I heard one word in my mind... *'community.'* I resisted this word because I thought it meant I was to become a nun and at that moment such a notion was far from my plans. I realise now that God was showing me that he was dealing with us as a people, a community, not just as individuals. It was important for us to be *together* when the Holy Spirit came.

The next day, Sunday, I awoke and wondered if Danny would come back. He did. The experience the night before had touched him, too. The first thing I remember hearing was that one of the girls on retreat had left for some reason. I also felt a deep sense of sinfulness and rebelliousness in myself. I remember being in a large room on the first floor of the retreat house, standing in front of the picture window and looking out at the grey woods. I thought, *'Lord, I want to jump into your hands,'* yet I felt so ambivalent. Our chaplain for the retreat was nearby. I told him that I was afraid to give myself to God because I didn't want to be someone other than myself, a 'goody-two-shoes'. He simply said, 'The Lord only wants you to be more Karin.' His words and a gentle hand on my shoulder reassured me.

In the next moment I recall jumping into the Lord's hands, in my mind and heart. The amazing thing was that I felt caught and lifted instantly. Bill Deigan was standing nearby and through my tears I said something like, 'God is real.' Bill smiled and said something like, 'Of course.' Marybeth Mutmansky and Patti Gallagher came into the room, and as Patti laid her hands on my head she exclaimed, 'The Spirit of God is in you!' I knew it was so.

Moments later I joined the other students in an adjoining room as we began the next session. We sang a hymn just as we had at the beginning of each session. I closed my eyes as we sang and experienced what I can only describe as a waterfall of light, accompanied by a tremendous peace. I didn't know what else could be happening, but that the Holy Spirit had become real to me by entering my heart in a special way. As we prayed for a few moments longer, I felt my hands which are normally stone-cold during the winter, grow warm. I knew Someone was present to me in a real way. A deep peace filled me. As the session continued, I remember being asked to extend my hands to pray.

As we left the retreat house, I really did not know exactly how to talk about what had happened to me. I experienced a peace deep-down which remained with me. When we got back to university life on Monday, some of us talked with the faculty moderator about our weekend experiences. He explained to us that we had received the Baptism in the Holy Spirit.

After the weekend, several things became real to me right away. Scripture jumped off the page and spoke to me. When I prayed for assistance, a beautifully helpful passage was given. The discipline of daily Scripture reading seemed less of a chore, more of a joy, more of a kind of refreshment, challenge or prayer. Kathryn Kuhlmann's ministry, located in Pittsburgh where I had lived since birth, became meaningful and believable, though I never had the opportunity to attend one of her services. I wanted to pray and attend the Eucharist more often. The Mother of God became more special to me as I grew in my desire to be a better woman. Worries plagued me only briefly — until I cast my care literally on the Lord who has sustained me well.

My experience on the Duquesne Weekend deepened my concern for the renewal of the Catholic Church as well. My prayers began to include the pope, bishops, and specific priests more than before. I felt a closer link with the Church, a renewed concern for individuals in special need, a regenerated faith and confidence as I praised God for his goodness, his gifts and overflowing love.

The faculty moderator took several of us to a prayer meeting about a week after the retreat to show us the people who had led him into the Baptism in the Holy Spirit and who had prayed for our retreat. It was at that prayer meeting that I first heard prayer in tongues, and without an explanation, understood what it was — probably because of reading *The Cross and the Switchblade.*

I received the gift of tongues myself several months after the Duquesne Weekend. One day at lunch on campus, Marybeth

Mutmansky asked me if I had received the gift of tongues yet. I told her that I was content to pray in English and felt that my prayer in English had intensified. Marybeth beckoned me to join her in the 'upper room,' or 'oratory,' a very small chapel above the University chapel at Duquesne. There we knelt in simple prayer. Marybeth prayed for me, then instructed me how to 'yield' to the gift. For a while I had only two words. Gradually, I was given more.

Because I was a full-time student, I remember taking very seriously our faculty moderator's advice that our most important job was to finish the degrees we had begun. Perhaps because I was a commuter, I missed out on some of the 'action' on campus in the time following the Duquesne Weekend. I did attend prayer meetings. For a while we met at the home of our faculty moderator. Later we moved to David Mangan's apartment on Mt. Washington, and finally the prayer meeting moved to the Passionist Monastery in Pittsburgh. I also remember that we were encouraged to write down our experiences of what happened to us on the Weekend. Some of them were published in *Catholic Pentecostals* in 1969.

On June 2, 1968, I graduated from Duquesne. It was Pentecost Sunday! I felt 'launched' into God's vineyard! Since that day, I've done graduate studies in both education and theology and worked in a variety of jobs over the years. I have taken many risks but always felt the peace of God as I've accepted his will for my life.

Life with the Lord has taken me literally thousands of miles into numerous situations and relationships. One of those relationships blossomed into marriage after many years of waiting, praying and wondering. In time the Lord gave my husband and me two sons.

Throughout these years, I have had the opportunity to witness about our Duquesne experience, give talks at Charismatic Renewal meetings and conferences, facilitated women's groups, and served in covenant community roles. We remain very active within our Catholic parish. I have served for three years as a member of the Board of Education, one of these years as president of the group; I've also served as a Eucharistic minister in the parishes to which we have belonged in Minneapolis.

The Baptism in the Holy Spirit brought me into a personal relationship with Jesus Christ as my Lord, Saviour, Friend, Beloved, and all at a time when I was about to enter the adult world. I believe the *chief* benefits have been a desire to surrender myself to the Lord, a strong belief that the Lord will lead me, and a deep dedication to the Catholic Church and what I call Catholic orthodoxy - a belief structure which is not ultra-liberal nor reactionary but rooted in sacramental theology.

The teachings we had in the 'early days' of the Charismatic Renewal - expect God to act, read and listen to the Word of God and let it take root, remain faithful to the teachings of the bishops, seek God - have remained guiding forces in my life. Along the way I have learned so much from teachers like

Fr. Michael Scanlan, T.O.R., and also from Protestants. I deeply value the teachings I have encountered from people such as Basilea Schlink, Bob Mumford, James Dobson, and many others.

Like the faculty moderator on the Duquesne Weekend said, *'Without the Lord Jesus, my life makes no sense'*. Before I could mess up my life, the Lord sovereignly intervened and enabled me to respond to His Spirit. At times over the years I have wondered 'Who am I?' but have come to a fairly rapid answer. *'I am the servant, the handmaid of the Lord and will do what he says.'* This has given my life a sense of direction, although it may seem kaleidoscopic and unplanned to one who hasn't lived it. *The Baptism in the Holy Spirit has enabled me to open my heart more fully to Jesus, his Father and the Holy Spirit.*

In all the situations, challenges, relationships and turmoil of life after the Baptism in the Holy Spirit, I still hunger for more of the Lord and His Holy Spirit. I still long to spend more time with him in prayer. I still seek his word in my life. I still long for him to be even more truly the reason for my being, the strength of my life, the Lord of my life.

Karin Sefcik Treiber (centre) with A1 and Patti Mansfield, 1990

A SHEPHERD'S CARE

A TESTIMONY BY JOHN ROSSMILLER

John Rossmiller graduated from Duquesne University in 1967 with a B.A. in mathematics. John worked for many years as a senior systems engineer for Westinghouse. He and his wife, Christine, are parents of nine children and nine grandchildren. They live in Donegal, Pennsylvania. John and his wife continue to have a close relationship with the Carmelites. Testimony, 1992. Photo, 1985

I first knew I was called by God when I was in the sixth grade. During the Christmas holidays I volunteered to clean the Church and assist at Mass. During the consecration of the Mass one day, I became very much aware of God's presence and I was moved by what the Lord had done in my life. There were several things I felt grateful for: to be in a Catholic school, to have a brother in Heaven praying for me (my brother died shortly after Baptism), and to have the grace of the Sacraments of Baptism and Confirmation.

After this experience of turning to the Lord at the age of eleven, I began to think about religious life. I entered the Carmelite seminary in Niagara Falls, Ontario, right after grade school and remained in the seminary for the next seven years. Although I eventually left the seminary due to health problems, my years there were fruitful for me spiritually. They gave me a confidence about trying new things. I began to read the Bible for spiritual growth and I was deeply impressed by the Carmelite spirituality. Their motto, 'With zeal, I am zealous for the Lord, the God of Hosts' *(1 Kgs. 19:10)*, is still very meaningful in my life. Perhaps the most important thing that happened to me is that I learned to trust in the Lord.

One of the great graces in my life as I look back is that the Lord has always guided me. Anytime I've been in some sort of trouble, ready to take an initiative to do something, the Lord has been good enough to direct me to do the right thing. Many blessings have come to me because of the Lord's gentle guidance, inclining me toward things that would help me discover His will.

For instance, the first day of registration of my second year at Duquesne, I went to Mass in the chapel. After Mass I approached a student whom I recognised as having lectured the year before. I asked him if there was any kind of organisation with a Christian orientation on campus. In God's providence, it turned out that this young man was Ed Fahrmeier, who was active in leadership of the *Chi Rho* Society. He introduced me to *Chi Rho* members that very afternoon and I began forming very close friendships within the group. *Chi Rho* provided a real communal gathering which also had a spiritual benefit. Our parties were always good, clean fun too. Some of the strongest members of *Chi Rho* were commuters. We had the benefit of seeing each other over the summer and during school holidays. We'd have a Christmas party and a Paschal meal yearly.

As in any group, *Chi Rho* had divisions among the members and some cliques which led to certain tensions. In the early spring of 1966, I believe it was February or March, a Study Weekend was held for the men of *Chi Rho* in the ROTC building on campus. Both of our faculty advisors were *cursillistas* and they had invited some friends of theirs, Ralph Martin and Steve Clark, to give us a Study Weekend. In fact, the Study Weekend was modeled on the Cursillo. That's why the first one was given to men only. This is a Cursillo principle. There were about twenty men who made the Study Weekend including Paul Gray, Ed Fahrmeier, and Bob Meadows. After the Study Weekend, we even had follow-up group reunions among ourselves. Long-standing friendships resulted. The women in *Chi Rho* were anxious to have a co-ed retreat the following year.

There was a development in my own life around that time which also had an effect on the lives of other members of *Chi Rho*. It involved a ministry to alcoholics in the Hill District of Pittsburgh. Tom Verner, a Duquesne student, was working with St. Joseph's House of Hospitality which provided shelter for homeless men. At St. Joseph's, Tom met a man named Frank Fagan, a recovered alcoholic, who was working to help rehabilitate other alcoholics. Frank came to speak to some of us on Duquesne's campus during the summer of 1966. I volunteered to help Frank and during my last year on campus, I enlisted the help of many others from *Chi Rho*... painting, cleaning, and serving in a variety of ways. I moved out of my own apartment and slept on the floor in one of the houses Frank rented for alcoholics. It was another adventure in trusting in the Lord.

At one point, when Frank was in need of funds for his work with alcoholics, I gave him my savings. It was a step in faith for me because I knew he might not be able to pay me back. The next day I found out that I had won a scholarship which met my own financial need. The Lord rewarded my trust. One of the volunteers that fall was Christine Heller whom I started to date in December.

Then came an incident which was very significant for me. One of the men we were trying to help rehabilitate began to vandalise my clothes by cutting them with a razor blade. The third time occurred while I was at Sunday Mass, which left me with only the clothes I had on my back. Upon returning, I went to tell

Frank what had happened. He was meeting with a visitor at the time, who had come wanting to help in some way. Frank introduced me to the visitor and before I knew it, this gentleman and his friends had provided me with new clothes.

This was a concrete expression to me of how the Lord wanted to provide for me as I trusted him. I was very moved. Interestingly enough, the very day I received my new wardrobe happened to be February 17, 1967, the day the Duquesne Weekend began. I left for that retreat very much aware of how concretely the Lord was taking care of me.

As I look back, it's interesting that I brought a camera to the Duquesne Weekend and took a few photos. In three years of college I had only taken about one roll of film. Even today I forget to bring a camera to important events like my children's graduation ceremonies. I knew there was going to be a birthday party Saturday night of the retreat and I thought I would use the remaining four photos on the birthday party. The only thing I can remember about Friday night of the retreat is that I shared with the group the moving experience that I had just had with a new wardrobe being provided by strangers.

I have no recollection of the talks on Saturday. But in the evening, I stayed in chapel a good while, renewing my relationship with the Lord. Eventually I went downstairs to take part in the birthday party. That's when I took a photo of Marybeth Mutmansky, as well as Elaine Kersting and Annamarie Nacko for whom the birthday party was to be held.

However, the party just wasn't getting started. I wondered, 'Is this birthday party ever going to take place?' It seemed that some people were going up to the chapel, so I went up there too.

I was moved very deeply by the experience I had when I returned to the chapel that night. But for me it wasn't a totally new experience of the Lord. Rather, it was a re-affirmation of my relationship with Jesus which began in the sixth grade. It was a quiet and deep re-dedication of my life to God, not a first-time encounter as it was for some of the other students. Dave Mangan and Patti Gallagher were there in chapel along with a few others.

What I saw in the others who were praying in chapel that night was a very deep devotion and reverence for God. When people become aware of the Lord's presence, it shows in their faces. You can see they are experiencing him. Something important was happening for everybody. I knew it was a significant event. That's why I decided to save the last three photos for the next morning. I now have the only four photos of the Duquesne Weekend.

Not everyone came up into the chapel Saturday night. There were different groups of friends present within that *Chi Rho* retreat. Some of the people already felt very much a part of things. Other people were folks that the chaplain was trying to draw in. There were even a few girls there from La Roche College who just came during the day. I remember a guy from Scotland who was present on the weekend. The group of students who came at the chaplain's invitation never did come up to the chapel Saturday night and didn't experience what the rest of us did. This led to difficulties after the weekend and some divisions within *Chi Rho* itself.

I remember that on Sunday an Episcopalian woman who had spoken to us Saturday came back. I believe that she and our faculty advisors gave us some advice in a talk Sunday morning about what to expect in the future. Several readings from 1 Corinthians were shared including the passage about the primacy of love.

One of the girls from our group gave witness to the fact that at a certain point in the retreat, she just wanted to get as far away from that place as she could. She ran away and someone went after her to bring her back. She left again and was sought out again. Finally, she was prayed with and hands were laid on her. A tremendous peace came over her. This testimony was very moving to many of us and was one of the first times we ever heard someone give witness to a spiritual healing. Of course, many of us were very immature spiritually, and after the Duquesne Weekend this incident was sometimes recounted in a way that was not helpful.

After the Duquesne Weekend, Christine Heller and I grew in our relationship with each other. Prayer meetings were taking place during that time, but I was not very active with them. I remained in close contact with others from the Duquesne Weekend and I heard that a lot of things were happening in their lives. In their enthusiasm, some people did certain things that lacked spiritual maturity. There was not much wisdom as to how to deal with the intense spiritual experiences of those early days.

Christine and I were married in August of 1967. We kept in touch with some of the members of *Chi Rho* who were on the Duquesne Weekend. Chris and I both made a Cursillo and have attended charismatic prayer meetings sporadically over the years. We then moved to Donegal, about fifty miles outside Pittsburgh, where we are very committed to our parish church. Chris serves as Eucharistic minister and I serve on the parish council and as a lector.

Something that has concerned me over the years as I've watched the Charismatic Renewal grow, is its relationship to the Catholic Church. For me, the good in the Church did not just begin after Vatican II. It was always present. As a child and young man, I knew many holy people serving God in the Catholic Church. As others experienced the Baptism in the Spirit and began to discover the Word of God in Scripture, I was anxious for them to also discover the power of God in the sacraments and the truth of God in the teachings and devotions of the Catholic Church, including devotion to Our Lady.

In my life, the Duquesne Weekend was *one* of many significant moments with the Lord wherein I deepened my commitment to him. It has an equal importance with other spiritual encounters, and every one of these experiences has helped to strengthen me. Just because you've had a moving experience with the Lord is no guarantee that you'll be with him until the end. That's why every encounter with the Lord is important. I just pray that the Lord will keep tapping me on the shoulder; that the Hound of Heaven will keep after me. There's a continual need for repentance and renewal as we grow in union with him.

I work a sheep farm. The analogy of the Good Shepherd and his sheep from Scripture has really come alive for me. I see how much people are like sheep. They're so stubborn; they frighten easily and scatter. Sheep resist being driven anywhere, but a good shepherd *can* lead them. When separated from the flock, sheep become frantic. They need to be part of the flock, to be close to others.

Just as sheep need a shepherd to guide and protect them, so do we. We need someone to follow. It's important who that someone is. We need the Lord Jesus Christ to be our Shepherd. We need the Lord Jesus Christ to call us by name. I am very humbled as I recall the continual mercy and patience of the Lord toward me, one of his sheep, from the very earliest years of my life until now.

TO GOD BE THE GLORY

A TESTIMONY BY ANNAMARIE NACKO CAFARDI

Annamarie Nacko Cafardi graduated from Duquesne in 1969 with a B.A. in English. She and her husband Jerry have two children. In 1992 when she wrote this testimony they were living in Waterford, Pennsylvania. Photo, 1992

It is almost impossible to believe that so many years since the Duquesne Weekend. Many of the memories have faded, but there is a clear fact that cannot be altered: my life changed dramatically during that weekend in mid-February, 1967, and nothing has ever been the same.

In retrospect, it is now obvious to me that God was at work in my life long before then. I grew up in Pittsburgh and attended a Catholic grade school and high school. I wanted very much to attend college out of town and hoped to be able to win a scholarship. One of my best friends from high school, Elaine Kersting (Ransil), was a freshman at Duquesne, and mid-way through my senior year, she invited me to spend a day with her at school. I had already visited several other campuses and, even though Duquesne was not where I wanted to go, I agreed to go with her. I loved it and, more significantly, came away with an unexplainable sense that Duquesne was where I was supposed to be.

I enrolled in the fall of 1965 as an English major and almost immediately became involved with the group called *Chi Rho*. Elaine was a member of *Chi Rho* and I found the group to be an excellent source of social, spiritual, and intellectual activities. The people were genuine and friendly. I particularly enjoyed relating with guys and girls as friends, without the pressure of always pairing off.

My faith at the time was primarily intellectual. I was excited about what was going on in the Catholic Church because it seemed as though much significant and needed change was taking place. *Chi Rho* was involved in planning the daily liturgy and that provided an opportunity to participate in the Mass that I had not experienced in my home parish. The people in *Chi Rho* were intellectually exciting to be with also. We had a chaplain and two faculty members who were excellent leaders. Because of my involvement with *Chi Rho,* my freshman year at Duquesne was better than I could have hoped.

My involvement in *Chi Rho* deepened during my sophomore year and I became involved in planning for a weekend retreat that was scheduled for February, 1967. It was at this time that I began to notice something strange going on. Our two faculty advisors and a theology instructor, Pat Bourgeois, seemed to behave differently as we were gathering to work out details for the retreat. There were side comments and uncharacteristic giggling from those men as we discussed the topic for the retreat, the first four chapters of the Acts of the Apostles.

In addition to the Acts, those attending were asked to read David Wilkerson's book, The Cross and the Switchblade. This was very unsettling to me. I read the book and found it simplistic and somewhat bizarre. The type of experience detailed in *The Cross and the Switchblade* had no resemblance to the intellectual theology that I espoused. I began to become concerned that what I had found with *Chi Rho* was about to change.

This perception was enhanced by a chance meeting that Elaine and I had with Marybeth Mutmansky on a Saturday afternoon in the Duquesne library prior to the scheduled retreat. Marybeth was a *Chi Rho* member who frequently babysat for one of the faculty advisors and his wife. Marybeth told us that the night before, both our faculty advisors and Pat Bourgeois had gone to some kind of meeting. When they returned afterwards, Marybeth overheard them discussing the meeting. She sensed that there was some relationship between this meeting they attended, David Wilkerson's book, and our upcoming *Chi Rho* retreat. In fact, a woman from this meeting was scheduled to speak at our retreat.

I didn't like what I was hearing. I was comfortable with *Chi Rho* the way it was, and more than comfortable with my theology. I felt that life as I knew it was going to change in a major way.

As the weekend for the retreat approached, the concerns remained, but I also thought that socially it would provide an opportunity to be together with the people I had come to love. There was even a birthday party scheduled for Elaine, our chaplain and me on Saturday night, during the retreat. I entered the retreat with the sense that it would be fun.

On Friday night, after the opening talk, there was a Penance Service. At least up to this point, nothing had happened to cause me to think that it would not turn out to be a typical *Chi Rho* gathering after all.

But all that changed on Saturday. The talk on Saturday was

given by the woman from the meeting our advisors had attended, and it was on Chapter 2 of Acts. Her message was one of the most unsettling that I had ever heard. What amplified the problem, as I saw it, was that none of the leaders of the group seemed bothered by what she had said. She talked about speaking in tongues, healing, and miracles as occurrences that were part of her experience, not only events in the Bible. I knew that this was not an issue that *Chi Rho* members could simply agree to disagree with. Her words necessitated a response, and mine was *'no!'*

The rest of the afternoon passed with members of the group sharing with each other in unstructured ways how they felt about what they had heard. I was very concerned that many of them had a 'why not?' attitude of openness to the message. I had been spending time with Jerry Cafardi, a junior whom I had met the summer before. I knew I needed to talk with one of the leaders and Jerry was interested in coming with me. Working through some of my questions took priority over the birthday party that was scheduled to begin - even though the party was for me! Jerry and I approached one of the faculty advisors and I asked my questions and expressed my concerns to him. He listened, but did not offer answers or advice. He encouraged us to pray.

Prayer was not something that was foreign to me, yet the kind of praying that he was suggesting was different than what I was used to. My prayers were almost always of the request variety. What he was suggesting was that we pray for direction and a sense of what the Lord was saying to us through this. I remember that he spoke about God in a way that was more personal than what I had experienced, yet there was a peace and a gentleness about what he was saying. Even though I still did not have definitive answers to my questions, the turmoil and anxiety were gone and I knew that I wanted to pray.

I went to the chapel, sat down and *'just opened'* my Bible. It opened to Psalm 116 and for the first time in my experience, I knew that the Lord was speaking directly to me. *'I love the Lord, because he hears my voice and my supplications. Because he has inclined his ear to me, therefore I shall call upon him as long as I live.'* I had an assurance of God's personal hand on me and personal concern for me and my questions.

It was Saturday evening and from this point events unfolded rapidly. Patti Gallagher was in the chapel also and as I was praying, she stood up and said, *'God is real! God is real!'* I knew that reality, too. I also became aware of a problem with the well. People were praying that it would be fixed so that we could continue the retreat. It was clear to me that it would be. I knew that the Lord intended that we continue, so it did not surprise me when people began filtering into the chapel to thank and praise God for fixing the well.

Soon the chapel was nearly full, even though we were 'scheduled' to be having a birthday party, not a chapel service. Our two faculty advisors moved among us, laying hands on us and praying. Several people were praying in languages that I had never heard before. Others were worshipping and many were in tears. No one stopped to instruct us on how to receive the Baptism in the Holy Spirit or the gift of tongues. We were undergraduate students, graduate students and professors from a large urban Catholic university experiencing the presence and the power of God in a sovereign way. We were not people who were accustomed to expressing our faith in an emotional way, and yet something had happened to touch our lives.

My own experience puzzled me. I am usually outgoing and expressive, yet in this situation, I was not 'feeling' anything. We stayed in the chapel, praying and singing, for the rest of Saturday evening and into the morning hours of Sunday. No one wanted to leave, but at some point the leaders encouraged us to go to our cabins and go to bed.

Jerry walked me to the cabin where the girls were staying. As we were walking and discussing the evening's events, I began to cry the most peaceful, joyful and happy tears I had ever experienced. I really knew the Lord's presence and his love: my life has not been the same since. The girls spent several more hours talking and praying. It had been a truly remarkable night.

Sunday's schedule was revised to include more specific instruction about the Baptism in the Holy Spirit and practical advice about how to share what we had experienced. We learned from the beginning that the Baptism in the Holy Spirit is given to point to Jesus and the saving power of his love. It was an important lesson. We also learned that some of the people on the weekend had been very upset by what had happened. Not everyone on the retreat had shared in the experiences of the night before and it was a difficult situation for those in leadership.

My sense was that what I had experienced was God's sovereign power at work in my life. I had not come seeking spiritual experiences; on the contrary, I had been sceptical and wary of what I had read in *The Cross and the Switchblade* and heard from the woman who spoke on Acts 2. It was clear to me from the very beginning that, for whatever reason, God had chosen to act among this group of people at this time and in this place. The faith that I had practiced out of obedience and intellectual understanding had become real to me. God was a person, not a concept, and is love for me as an individual was now something that I knew in my heart as well as in my head.

There was a sense of excitement and apprehension as the events of Sunday drew the retreat to a close. We were told that we should not witness to our experiences, but to the Lord. Yet it was hard not to detail what had just happened. When I arrived home, I shared and prayed with my mom. She was a devout Catholic and her response was one of openness and interest. At school over the next several days, there was a mixed response. Even those who were intensely critical and skeptical could not dampen my enthusiasm. I knew that what had happened to me was not the result of emotionalism or someone manipulating a situation. God had touched my life.

Although many of my friends had experienced the gift of tongues on the Duquesne Weekend or in prayer shortly thereafter, I had not. There was no doubt in my mind that it was a valid experience and that I was open, even eager, to receive a prayer language. I also had a peace that this was not something that I needed to be anxious and concerned about. There was no pressure or frenzy. There were several small rooms above the Duquesne chapel that *Chi Rho* members often used for private or small group prayer. One afternoon, exactly a month after the Duquesne Weekend, while I was praying alone in one of those rooms, I began to pray in tongues. Since then, I have used my prayer language in worship and private devotions.

In the spring of 1967, a Protestant minister, Rev. Harald Bredesen came to Duquesne to meet with the group. Rev. Bredesen, who has a dynamic and exciting personality, had a desire to see Catholics and Protestants work together to present the Gospel of Jesus. He invited *Chi Rho* members to come to his church in Mt. Vernon, New York, to live and work among the people there. I did not have an inclination either to go or not to go, but I knew I felt a responsibility to pray and ask the Lord for guidance. As I prayed it was clear to me, not by voices or visions but through an inner peace,that I was to go to Mt. Vernon that summer. It was one of the most exciting and difficult summers of my life.

Even though I was a firm believer in ecumenism and the need for Protestants and Catholics to lay down their differences for the sake of those who had no faith, the working out of that belief was far more difficult than I could have ever imagined. Several of us lived in the Bredesen home that summer, worked at jobs in the city, and spent evenings working with the people of Mt. Vernon. It was my first experience of street witnessing and I saw the power and the love of God at work in the lives of many who had deep spiritual needs. I also watched the Lord gradually break down walls that had built up over centuries among denominations. That summer experience convinced me that what had happened on the Duquesne Weekend was part of God's plan to renew and revitalise his whole church, not just one group or denomination.

When we returned to school in the fall, we were meeting on Friday nights for prayer and worship in Pat Bourgeois' apartment. The meetings at Pat's drew other students who had not been part of *Chi Rho* before and also many non-students who had heard about what the Lord was doing among us. The meetings provided times of prayer, Bible study, and ministry to one another. They were also times of real growth for me. I was drawn to personal prayer and daily reading of God's word. God's presence and love in my life were real to me on a daily basis.

I graduated from Duquesne in June, 1969, and in August, 1969, Jerry Cafardi and I were married in the Duquesne Chapel. We both accepted teaching jobs in the Pittsburgh area; I began teaching English at a Catholic high school and Jerry began a job in special education at a suburban public high school. We have both been involved in education over the years since then. Our lives also continued to be intertwined with friends from *Chi Rho*.

After all these years, it is nearly impossible to express fully the significance of the Baptism in the Holy Spirit in my life. Clearly, the events of February, 1967, mark a turning point like no other. Even though I had always taken religion and God seriously, what happened on the Duquesne Weekend moved my faith from the intellectual level to the level of daily experience.

I now know Jesus Christ personally and love him with all my heart. I have a desire to serve him and to live my life for him every day. I want to tell others about him and about what he can do for them. I am drawn to prayer and study of his word, the Bible, and I know a lack and emptiness when I do not take time for daily devotions. I have been able to draw strength from the Lord in difficult circumstances.

Jerry and I suffered through nine years of infertility before our son, John, was born, and God's help and strength were there for us in tangible and intangible ways. I know that God cares for the large and small issues of my life and that I can go to him in prayer anytime for anything.

When I wrote my testimony for *New Covenant* magazine for the sixth anniversary of the Duquesne Weekend in 1973,1 used Romans 11:33-36. These words still express my feelings as I reflect on what God has done.

> Oh, the depth of the riches both of the wisdom and knowledge of God! How unsearchable are his judgments and unfathomable his ways! For who has known the mind

of the Lord, or who became his counsellor? Or who has first given to him that it might be paid back to him again? For from him and through him and to him are all things. To him be the glory forever. Amen.

GOD HAS BEEN THERE AT EVERY TURN

A TESTIMONY BY JERRY CAFARDI

Jerry Cafardi graduated from Duquesne University in January,1969, with a B.S. in special education and secondary education degree in history. He and his wife Annamarie were both members of Chi Rho. Testimony and photo, 1992

I was attracted to the *Chi Rho* group because it provided me with an opportunity to meet with some nice kids who shared similar social and religious experiences. Besides, I ran out of excuses for not attending the meetings. Karin Sefcik (Treiber), the only female in my 201 English class, persisted in inviting me to *Chi Rho* meetings. My primary reason for being part of the group was social. The religious experience, though significant, was secondary.

I remember little about the *Chi Rho* meetings prior to the Duquesne Weekend, but one impression (certainly not representative of *all* the meetings) sticks vividly in my mind. While *Chi Rho* met in the old Philosophy Building, sometimes the discussion turned to philosophical questions. I was amazed that seven to ten people could all be speaking English, yet I had no idea what they were talking about! However I didn't let that stop me from giving a knowing nod or furrowing my brow every once in a while, just to let them know I was alive. Intellectuals usually made me nervous, but one of our faculty advisors for *Chi Rho* seemed different in that he was warm and accepting.

Prior to the Duquesne Weekend, I lived with a strong religious sense that my parents, school, and Church fostered in me. The Catholic Church provided the basis and structure for that faith. I served as an altar boy and then as a lector in my parish, Sacred Heart, in Pittsburgh, Pennsylvania. I am grateful for that! I entered Duquesne with a strong faith in a God who was *out there*. I began my studies at Duquesne as a history major in liberal arts. By my junior year, I had switched to special education.

During the Duquesne Weekend, I remember that a water shortage developed which threatened to cut the retreat short. I know there was prayer, that a plumber was called by the Ladies of Bethany, and that the water shortage ended. In 1972, while visiting the Ladies of Bethany at the Ark and the Dove, the Ladies contended that the problem was solved by the plumber.

The Duquesne Weekend provided for me an awareness of and a sensitivity to a living God—alive in me. I felt compelled to pray and read Scripture. Although my experience was more of a gradual sense of the Lord and his power becoming real to me, I know something happened to me on the Duquesne Weekend when one of the leaders laid hands on me and prayed for me in the chapel Saturday night. One concrete immediate manifestation of this was that when the Word of God was preached and Communion was shared, I had an assurance of God's presence.

Regarding spiritual gifts in general and tongues in particular, I was at first frustrated and then bitter... frustrated because I had apparently been 'left out'; bitter because of the way the gifts were used as a 'badge of holiness' - which was my perception at the time. It may have been three to four years after the Duquesne Weekend that I experienced any of the charismatic gifts. Expressing the gift of tongues seemed to 'open the door' for prophetic words that came afterwards.

When Rev. Harald Bredesen came to visit us after the Duquesne Weekend, I remember he pointed to the Duquesne University logo and motto on the wall behind him. He commented on how appropriate it was that the Spirit would be poured out at the University whose motto was *'Spiritus Est Qui Vivificat' - 'It is the Spirit Who gives life!'*

The Baptism in the Holy Spirit has turned my life right side up! Having met God in a personal way through his Spirit, I can never be the same. Jesus is the Rock—He doesn't change. Knowing him enables me to grow and change without fear of 'losing my identity'. After all these years I have my own history of peaks and valleys. *God has been there at every turn.* That has made for some exciting living and provided a hope for the future.

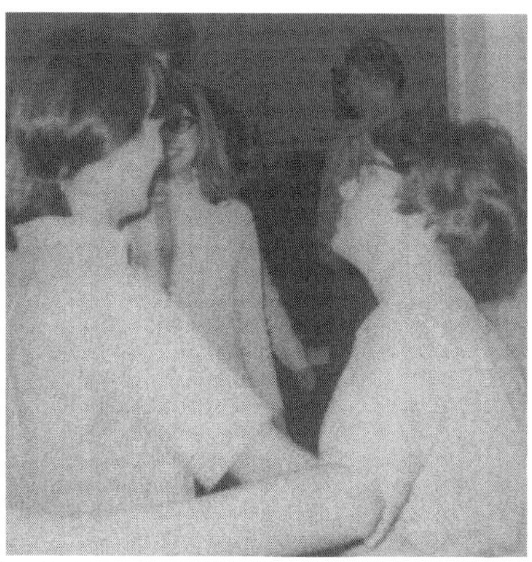

Two of the birthday girls, Annamarie Nacko (left) and Elaine Kersting (facing front), being embraced by Marybeth Mutmansky at the birthday party, Saturday, February 18, 1967, just before the sovereign outpouring of the Holy Spirit

Gina Steinmetz Scanlon with her daughter Lori. 1967. She was pregnant with Lori on the Duquesne Weekend

AMAZING GRACE

A TESTIMONY BY ELAINE KERSTING RANSIL

Elaine Kersting Ransil, graduated from Duquesne University with a B.A. in English Literature in 1968. She and her husband, Lenny, have four children. Testimony and photo, 1992

I came from a very religious Catholic family and always attended Catholic schools. As assistant church organist, I spent many hours in church. Unfortunately my religion was very much of a 'head' thing - I knew plenty of doctrine and dogma but had no idea of any possibility of a living, personal relationship with Jesus.

I knew that God was real but he seemed very distant and he had certain standards of performance that he expected me to meet. I didn't do very well with that part. I alternated between bursts of intense spiritual effort, trying hard to 'be good' but inevitably failing, and other times when it all seemed impossible.

I believed God performed miracles for the saints and at special places like Lourdes but it didn't seem like he was available to ordinary people like me. When I was confirmed, I had hopes that something would happen and I would somehow be different afterward. But, although I observed myself very closely, as far as I could tell, nothing changed.

My major at Duquesne was English Literature and my plans were vague. I was too idealistic to even think of a career in business or anything practical. I just wanted to do something to 'help the world'.

I thank God I sat next to Marybeth Mutmansky in my first freshman chemistry class and through her learned about *Chi Rho*. I joined immediately and gladly in 1964. I think we did the Gospel of John that year. Responsibility for preparing an exegesis of the passage rotated among members of the group. Some of us relied pretty heavily on the explanatory notes, while others had more original insights. Paul Gray and Mary Ann Springel were in my group and I was impressed with what they had to say. Since I didn't know the Bible very well, it was all new and interesting to me. Yet, as I recall it now, it seems we were doing so much by our own minds and our own efforts instead of looking to Jesus.

By definition, the group was comprised of students who were interested in talking about theology and philosophy. Many were majoring in those subjects. There was also a very strong orientation of idealism - wanting to help the world - whether by teaching, serving in the Peace Corps, or fixing up a house in the Hill district of Pittsburgh for alcoholics. I used to hang out at the 'chaplain's house' on campus since it provided a sort of home base for many of us who were commuters. Besides being a place for meeting people informally, we also held some of the regular meetings there. For me, *Chi Rho* was not just a club or a sideline - it was the foundation or the thread that tied everything else together at Duquesne.

During much of my time at college I was in a lot of emotional pain. There were two difficult relationships that didn't work out. It seems to me that there were others in the *Chi Rho* group who were struggling too. We wanted to help people, to help each other, but were coming up empty. And that was maybe the worst thing of all - seeing the whole world struggling and having no strength and no answers. What are we here for, anyway? What's it all about? It sounds kind of crazy as I'm trying to describe it now, but I can remember being extremely depressed about the condition of the world. Nothing made any sense.

During my sophomore year, as I was casting around for some satisfying answers, I began to read some of Alan Watts' books and got interested in Zen Buddhism. While I wasn't ready to leave my Catholicism behind and fully plunge into the Eastern way, I thought a synthesis of the two might offer some benefit. I wrote a psychology paper about the possibilities of Zen Buddhism and found that the professor was also interested in exploring Zen. When I shared my thoughts about it in a *Chi Rho* meeting, one of our faculty advisors said very firmly that if you are a disciple of someone, you follow only that person and don't start adding in other things. Being a disciple of Jesus means not mixing in Zen Buddhism or anything else that isn't in the Gospel. I should have remembered that later on in my life.

February 17-19, 1967, *Chi Rho* sponsored a Study Weekend and I went primarily anticipating a good time with a group of friends. I was especially looking forward to spending time with John Rosenbaum, since we had just starting dating. I suppose I also expected a temporary religious 'lift', but experience had taught me that such bursts of renewed fervor always proved to be transitory.

What impressed me from the first talk on Friday night was the idea that God can be as real, powerful and present to us today as he was to his disciples. What Jesus was, he is; what he said, he says; what he did, he does. And the kingdom of Heaven does not consist in talk but in power. God wants to answer our prayers but he is limited by our unbelief. After the talk, we all went up to the chapel for an intercessory prayer service. After each prayer request, everyone sang, *'God the Father, hear our prayer, hear us, God the Son; Holy Spirit, hear our prayer, mercy on your people, Lord.'* It seemed like all of us were gripped with the significance of being able to influence events through believing prayer, because we prayed on for hours. But it didn't seem long because we were into it so intensely.

I think the talks on Saturday were about receiving power from the Holy Spirit to live the Christian life. We looked at the book of Acts, at the changes the disciples experienced when the Holy Spirit came upon them. Most of us had received the Sacrament of Confirmation. Why didn't we experience the charismatic gifts, then? Because the Holy Spirit doesn't take us over by force but awaits our invitation. We already 'had' the Holy Spirit — much as we might have a gift-wrapped birthday present — but what we needed was a release of the Spirit, or taking the present out of the package and putting it to use. Were we willing to have God's power released in us?

The question that cut me to the heart was, *'Who really is in charge of your life?'* The Lord showed me that my sinfulness was not the catalogue of bad things I had done but the whole orientation of my life. All my life I had been the one calling the shots and I had to admit I had done a pretty lousy job. For maybe the first time, 1 was able to drop the phony mask of self-sufficiency because I finally realised that I had been trying to carry burdens that were just too heavy for me. My sinfulness lay in my prideful efforts to do it myself rather than turn everything over to the Lord and let Him handle it his way.

At the first opportunity, in late morning or early afternoon, I took my Bible and my box of Kleenex and went to the chapel. As God showed me the reality of my sins, I couldn't stop crying. But the tears were good; it felt cleansing. Every place I turned in my Bible seemed to speak directly to me. No wonder I had been so miserable and depressed: I had been carrying burdens for myself, my friends, and the rest of the world as well. Now I felt released. I didn't have to be my own savior, much less the saviour of the world - that's what Jesus came for. O, Hallelujah!

I knew that God had begun something significant in me, and I also knew he wasn't finished yet. I resented having to waste time on something so mundane as eating dinner. I remember thinking that others seemed to be feeling the same lack of interest in food.

On Saturday afternoon I heard that there was a serious problem with the water supply to the house. The well was dry, there was no water, and without water, we would all have to go home. Well, we had just been talking about the power of God and about praying in faith, believing that we received what we asked for. I knew that God wasn't finished with us yet. We prayed, believed God would act and thanked him in advance for what he would do. It was an immediate life application of what we had been talking about. As far as I know, there is no natural explanation for what happened, but by early evening, the water we needed was there in abundance. I was grateful - awed - but not really surprised.

I was so absorbed in what God was showing me that I had avoided spending any time with John. Naturally, he was wondering what was wrong, so we talked for a while. I tried to explain that it was nothing personal against him, but I just needed to be able to spend time with God.

After John and I talked Saturday evening, we went to the downstairs front room of the main building. Chris Strasser and a girl named Tracy were there, and they seemed disgruntled that there was supposed to be a party going on and no one else was interested in partying. Since my birthday is February 21, I was one of the people whose birthday was supposed to be celebrated that night. I didn't care. It all seemed irrelevant in the face of what God was doing. The only place I wanted to be was in the chapel and that's where I headed. I had a sense that God was in the process of doing something momentous and it seemed natural to just wait on him there.

When I got to the chapel, about 8:00 p.m., there were already many others praying. I knelt there with them, thinking, *'I don't understand all of this, but whatever you have for me, Lord, I want it. I believe, Lord, help my unbelief!'* After a while, we were holding hands as we knelt around the altar. Paul Gray was on one side of me. Suddenly it felt like an electric current was flowing from his hand into mine and surging through my whole body. I was crying again in sheer joy as I realised for the first time in my life the overpowering reality of God. Somehow I found myself prostrate before the altar, with only one joyful thought in my mind, *'Praise, God! Praise God! Praise God!'* I had no sense of time or of other people around me. I was enraptured in the presence of God.

Sometime after midnight, maybe 1:00 or 2:00 a.m., I was dragged unwillingly back to earth. Our chaplain made me get up. He said we couldn't stay in the chapel all night; we all had to go to bed. How strange! What I had just experienced was so wonderful, but the priest seemed distressed. I was so high, so full of joy that I didn't see how I could possibly get to sleep, but I went over to the little house anyway where I met Annamarie and Marybeth. We asked each other, 'You too?' And we jumped up and down together for joy.

The next day, the joy was still there. I felt like the dry bones in Ezekiel 37 who were raised up to life again. I wanted to dance, I wanted to sing. The Spirit-filled Episcopalian woman who had spoken to us the day before on Acts 2 had cautioned us that the Baptism in the Holy Spirit does not equal instant holiness, but somehow that was hard to grasp. Before we left to go home, we came together and people shared what God had done in them that Weekend. It seemed like most of us had experienced God touching us in powerful ways. I had hoped that everyone would feel drawn to be with the Lord — how could they resist? I've always wondered how anyone could have come away from that weekend untouched. But I think some did. Before the Duquesne

Weekend, I had been very good friends with our campus chaplain. But on the Duquesne Weekend, I had the sense that he was frightened by the dramatic manifestations of the outpouring of the Spirit.

Strangely enough, I did not receive - or at least, did not manifest - the gift of tongues on the weekend. What I did experience was a transforming sense of the presence of God, followed by a bubbling joy. In the next few weeks I sought the gift of tongues with some frustration. My only problem was that I didn't understand that I had to speak in order to speak in tongues. I expected God to just take over and have it pour out, and of course, that didn't happen. It was about three weeks later, in the midst of praying over a visiting priest in a prayer meeting on campus, that I realised that I wasn't praying in English. After that, I had no problem speaking in tongues. Sometimes I seemed to be saying the same things over and over again; other times it just flowed on and on. It wasn't always the same.

The joy and euphoria of the Duquesne Weekend lasted for a long time afterward. I had a tremendous hunger for Scripture and prayer. God seemed to be talking directly to me when I read his word. I carried my Bible with me everywhere (the big four-inch-thick Jerusalem Bible!). It wasn't unusual to spend several hours a day praying and reading the Word. I couldn't get enough! God was real. I knew what salvation meant, and that was exciting news worth sharing. So I witnessed to anyone who would hold still and listen. I knew that the power wasn't in me, but was available to me. I could really believe that God cared about all the details of my life and that I could go to him with any request, great or small. I was still a student at that time (midway through my junior year). Unfortunately, I was so excited about all of the wonderful things that God was doing, I was always willing to cut a class in order to witness. It was exciting to do things because I felt *'led by the Spirit'*, but what I needed was to develop more discipline in my life. I was more than a little flaky in those days, as I remember it.

When I shared with my parents what had happened on the weekend, they thought I had totally flipped out. It sounded altogether weird to them. They eventually decided it was okay for me - although not for themselves. One of my brothers and my sister did come to be baptised in the Spirit and involved in the Renewal, but that was several years later. Interestingly, years later, many of my aunts and uncles and cousins became involved in the Charismatic Renewal, but not through any direct personal witness on my part.

The reactions from my classmates were mixed. Some embraced this new dimension with enthusiasm, others politely declined. I specifically remember Marybeth Mutmansky and I sharing with Dr. and Mrs. Pausen, both teachers of philosophy. It didn't go over real well, to say the least. Fr. Anton Morganroth, C.S.Sp., remained uninvolved but tolerant, in a distant sort of way.

As far as the chaplain's office was concerned, there was a distinct pulling away after the Duquense Weekend. The chaplain wanted nothing to do with it. For the rest of the time I was at Duquesne, it was very difficult for any of us Spirit-baptised people to work together with the others from the chaplain's office. We now had a different vision. One of the major news magazines, I think it was *Time,* heard about the Duquesne Weekend and wanted to do a story on it. They contacted our chaplain. But that was the last thing he wanted, and the story was never done. As far as I can recall, what God was doing through the Baptism in the Holy Spirit was never received by Duquesne University or nurtured there in any way.

In terms of spiritual gifts, I remember a lot of weird physical sensations - burning in the palms of the hands, for example. It seemed like I was 'discerning spirits' in things and in other people, and I have no idea how much, if any of it, was legitimate. There were 'impressions' or 'leadings' to do this or that. We shared our experiences with each other and tried to figure out what was for real and what wasn't. Ultimately, we realised that the Scripture was the standard and that anything else had to be judged according to the Word.

The earliest 'spiritual warfare' experience I remember was the testimony of the girl who received prayer for deliverance on the weekend itself. Later I got involved in some intense deliverance prayer for some of Mary Ann Springel's high school students who were very involved in witchcraft. It was clear that the Baptism in the Holy Spirit also stirred up Satan to counter-attack, but God had equipped us for that warfare.

After the weekend, we did not continue to hold prayer meetings at Duquesne for long. Almost immediately, prayer meetings were held at one of our faculty advisor's homes on Friday nights but I couldn't usually go because I had to play the organ at church on the other side of the city. I was able to get there maybe once or twice.

The thing that amazes me as I look back is the prayer meetings. It just seemed the most obvious thing in the world to continue to meet together in prayer. But the meetings were totally unstructured. There was no planned program, no music ministry. During the time I attended, there wasn't even anybody who played guitar. Anyone could lead out in a song, read a Scripture, share a testimony or an insight that the Lord had given them. We usually ended by praying for the Baptism in the Holy Spirit for anyone who was interested or for any other needs. Meetings tended to last for many hours, yet the time seemed to go very fast. In those days, I thought that if I could only get someone to come to a prayer meeting and experience it for themselves, they would automatically want to give their lives to Jesus and be baptised in the Holy Spirit.

Shortly after the weekend, John Rosenbaum left for Naval Officers Training School. We stayed in touch for a while but broke off the relationship in the fall of 1967. At a Christmas party at Karin Sefcik's, God brought me together with Lenny Ransil. We started seeing each other regularly and in August, 1968 we were married. Lenny was friends with several *Chi Rho* people, and had even given some of them a ride out to the Ark and the

Dove Retreat Centre in February, 1967. He had been unable to attend the retreat himself because he played sax in a combo on weekends. Although he came to one prayer meeting at Duquesne afterward, he was turned off by all the 'emotionalism'. An ex-seminarian and a good Catholic, he felt no need for that.

Since Lenny wasn't interested in going to prayer meetings, I had the choice of going alone or spending Friday nights with him. I chose to spend the time with him. This wasn't a matter of intentionally rejecting God or the pentecostal experience, but in spite of my good intentions I soon found myself drifting away. I had not established the habit of praying even when I didn't feel like it or when it wasn't convenient. I stopped going to prayer meetings in early 1968, and we moved away in September, 1969.

Occasionally in the following years, I had opportunities to talk to someone about the weekend and I would realise again what an important and powerful experience it had been. But I was also forced to recognise that while my ideas were considerably different as a result, my way of life hadn't really changed at all. And because I wasn't following through with prayer and walking in the Spirit, the experience now seemed far away.

In our early married life, Lenny and I both became interested in Oriental philosophy, health foods and vegetarianism, psychic channeling, astrology, meditation and other occult practices. We were spiritually hungry, and because we were not rooted deeply in a life of prayer and walking in the Spirit of Jesus, we sank deeper and deeper into the quicksand of occultism.

Through all of this, we never made a conscious decision to turn away from Christianity. We just kept mixing other things in. But we didn't realise how insidious Satan is - he truly disguises himself as an *'angel of light'*. We thought we could discern good from evil because we were intelligent people and we would surely recognise evil when we saw it. Wrong! The only way we can discern evil is by the standard given in the Word of God. If I had been judging the value of these psychic studies according to the Scripture, I would never have gotten into them.

On the other hand, my experience of God on the Duquesne Weekend was so powerful that it served as a sort of touchstone in some respects. I *knew* that God was a person not an impersonal 'force'. I knew, too, that God heard and answered prayer. And ultimately that was what made the difference for us.

Through the prayers of our Christian friends and relatives, the Holy Spirit penetrated our confusion, leading us to pray, *'Lord, show us your truth, whatever the cost. If we're wrong we want to change.'* And the Lord showed us. By March, 1972, Lenny was convinced not only that there were no answers in Edgar Cayce but that there was, after all, something for him in the Baptism in the Holy Spirit, although he expressed one concern: What if God's plan for his life was different from the plan he had worked out so carefully? The day after Lenny prayed to receive the Baptism in the Spirit two things happened: He woke up praising God, and he found out that a major problem was brewing at the Montessori school where he taught that ultimately cost him his job. But through all the turmoil of the following weeks, God gave Lenny peace and a recognition that He was in charge of all that was happening.

To tell of all that God has done for us in the past years that followed would take a book in itself, so I will just say that the Baptism in the Holy Spirit was truly the pivotal point in my life. I came to know the Lord Jesus Christ and nothing has ever been the same.

I have seen the hand of God on my life in so many specific ways: healing from cancer, renewed hope and purpose instead of paralysing depression, renewed commitment to marriage instead of divorce that seemed imminent, kids who are committed to Jesus instead of messed up in the world's emptiness, a job I really enjoy with a great company. I know that God has a purpose for my life. I gave myself to him, he took me and he won't let go. Even when I am unfaithful, he is always faithful.

God has done great things and I never did anything to deserve it. It's all grace. I am reminded of the Scripture, *'He gives me beauty for ashes, the oil of joy for mourning, the garment of praise for the spirit of heaviness' (cf. Is. 61:3)*. He really does.

Flo Dodge and her mother at the entrance to their townhouse in Chapel Hill, 1967

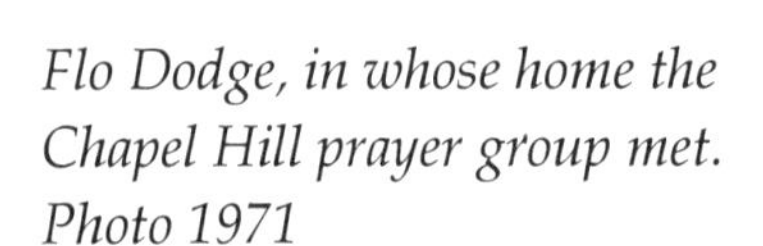

Flo Dodge, in whose home the Chapel Hill prayer group met. Photo 1971

THE PROMISE IS TO YOU AND TO YOUR CHILDREN

A TESTIMONY BY GINA STEINMETZ SCANLON

Gina Steinmetz Scanlon and her husband, Pat, graduated from Duquesne in 1968 and were members of Chi Rho. The Scanlons are parents of three children. Gina has been a teacher and Pat is an attorney in private practice. Testimony, 1992. Photo 1966

My husband Pat and I are natives of Pittsburgh and were students at Duquesne. I was a psychology major and Pat had been in the seminary for several years in Cincinnati. As a young girl, I had considered religious life for a while and even had dreams of going to Africa as a missionary sister. When I got to Duquesne and joined *Chi Rho,* it helped me realise that I could serve God as a laywoman too. When Pat got to campus in 1965, he also joined *Chi Rho.*

Many members of *Chi Rho* were active with another group on campus called the Council of Interracial Friendship, or COIF. We had a great concern for social justice and racial equality. Sometimes we'd sing at church services of different denominations with black men and women. We wanted to promote racial friendship. The concerns of COIF flowed into *Chi Rho,* and vice versa, since so many of us participated in both organisations.

I joined *Chi Rho* as a freshman and it had a great impact on my life and formed the basis for many friendships. *Chi Rho* helped forge a real bond of community among us. At Easter we'd celebrate a Passover meal, which was a real highlight.

In September, 1966, Pat and I were married. By the time of the retreat weekend in February, 1967, I was already pregnant with our first child. It was an extremely busy time in my life and one of great adjustments. I was tutoring in the Hill district, still a full-time student, newly married and pregnant. I wasn't feeling well around the time of the retreat weekend and I really don't remember any special preparations we were asked to make.

On Saturday, February 18, 1967, after the evening meal at the Ark and the Dove Retreat House, I felt so tired that I went to bed early. Not until the next day did I realise what had happened in the chapel while I was sleeping. On Sunday, many of the other *Chi Rho* members told of how they had stayed up praying until the early morning hours. People seemed so excited about what had happened and what was happening. I felt confused by the whole thing. I had been very active in *Chi Rho* up until that point, but I wasn't sure if I believed all this or not.

On Sunday, people were praying over one another with the laying on of hands. I just felt like I wanted to leave. Then, one of the girls came up and laid her hands on my stomach to pray for my baby. Even though I was afraid of all of this at the time, over the years since then, I've often reflected that the child I was carrying during the Duquesne Weekend has been especially blessed by the Holy Spirit. I've wondered if this was a result of the prayer she received while she was still in my womb.

As I reflect on my reaction during the Duquesne Weekend and in the weeks and months thereafter, I remember asking myself a basic question: 'If a person really believes the Gospel and believes in the validity of the experiences in the early Church, then what happened on the Duquesne Weekend would be natural.' Yet I wasn't sure I could believe it for myself.

The Duquesne Weekend precipitated a kind of crisis of faith in me. It was a difficult time. I kept saying, 'Either you believe this or you don't. If you do, you have to make a commitment to change the way you're living.' I could see others from the weekend making changes in their lives, but I didn't feel ready. I knew that, to some extent, if I embraced this new experience of the Holy Spirit, it would mean looking foolish. I wasn't sure I could do that. It wouldn't have been easy considering my circumstances at the time. My husband, Pat, wasn't particularly interested in the prayer meetings that grew out of the Duquesne Weekend.

For a few months I kept looking at the *Chi Rho* prayer group and thinking over whether I could make the commitment and accept this new work of the Holy Spirit. Finally, I backed away from it and slowly dropped out of *Chi Rho* completely.

Someone asked me recently if I would say that the Duquesne Weekend had no impact on my spiritual life, since I did not become active in the Charismatic Renewal afterwards. I would have to say that the Duquesne Weekend was a landmark for me, because up until that time I had always seen myself as being very committed to my beliefs. After the Duquesne Weekend, I felt as though my faith commitment was limited, because I wasn't willing to take that further step like other members of *Chi Rho* had.

Pat and I both graduated from Duquesne in 1968. Pat taught African history in a predominantly black college for a while, and I worked part-time as a social worker. In 1970, I earned a Master's degree in special education and eventually Pat received his law degree. We are both still practicing Catholics, but we're not as deeply involved with Church activities as we were during our early days in *Chi Rho*.

A DEEPENING MOMENT

A TESTIMONY BY BILL DEIGAN

Bill Deigan graduated from Duquesne in 1968 with a B.A. in psychology and holds an M.A. in industrial relations from the University of Minnesota. He was president of Chi Rho at the time of the Duquesne Weekend. He and his wife have two sons and live in Florida. Testimony and photo,1992

I began attending *Chi Rho* meetings in 1966 after my initial contact with the group at a Paschal meal. The chaplain at Duquesne University wanted someone to step forth in leadership and I was elected as president of the organisation. Our meetings seemed to focus on the question of our identity at that time. We were asking, 'What's the purpose of *Chi Rho*? What are we about?'

The officers had a planning session to determine what to do on our retreat which was to be held in February, 1967. Our faculty moderators seemed to have a special enthusiasm about them as we talked. They suggested a new direction for the weekend retreat and asked us to read *The Cross and the Switchblade*. We later found out they had attended a prayer group and their experience in the group accounted for their new enthusiasm and the change in plans.

My faith was important in my life. I attended daily Mass and taught catechism in the Hill district while at Duquesne. Members of *Chi Rho* met for prayer and served at the daily Mass in the chapel. We also had social functions.

I have a vague recollection of the Saturday talks and discussions on the retreat. When I went upstairs to the chapel, I seem to remember one woman praying in tongues and another one prostrate. There was a feeling of an 'in group' and an 'out group'. Some people were having an intense spiritual experience while others, like myself, seemed more like observers. My experience on the Duquesne Weekend could be described as a deepening moment to stop and think about God rather than an initial conversion experience.

After the retreat, I wanted to keep the experience of the weekend *in balance.* Others seemed to be committing so much time and energy to the events and meetings that followed the retreat. I didn't feel comfortable with this approach. I saw the need to keep up my studies and pursue a degree. Much of what was happening among certain members of *Chi Rho* seemed very emotional to me. I tried to express my cautions at the time. Perhaps the different responses among the participants were due to different personalities. Some people were more expressive than others.

After the Duquesne Weekend I attended some of the prayer meetings held in private homes where there were spiritual gifts manifested. During the summer of 1967, *Chi Rho* members continued to meet for Scripture study and prayer. In August, another representative from Duquesne and I attended a meeting at University of Notre Dame where twenty to thirty people gathered who were involved in the early prayer meetings on various campuses.

After the Duquesne Weekend, the chaplain on campus met with some of the students to try and give them direction, but before long he distanced himself from the prayer group. He did not pursue involvement in the Charismatic Renewal. As the movement grew, I also had questions about what I saw happening, much of which seemed emotional. After a while, I also distanced myself and lost contact with what developed into the Charismatic Renewal movement.

My involvement in the Catholic Church remains strong through service in the parish. Over the years I have served in parish council work, taught catechism, lectured and led the parish liturgy committee. In the future or upon retirement, I'd like to use my background in organisational psychology and my experiences as Director of Human Resources at Union Carbide to assist Church organisations in defining their mission, strategy, organisational structure and roles.

PART THREE
WE TOO HAVE SEEN HIM

'Today I would like to extend this invitation
to everyone: let us rediscover,
dear brothers and sisters,
the beauty of being baptised in the Spirit.'

Pope Benedict XVI
Regina Caeli Message, Pentecost Sunday,
May 11, 2008

NOT BY MIGHT NOR BY POWER BUT BY MY SPIRIT

A TESTIMONY BY PETER COLLINS

Peter Collins graduated from University of Notre Dame in 1966 with a B.A. in liberal studies. He holds an M.S. in resource ecology from the University of Michigan. Peter, a native of Toronto, Canada, now lives in Ann Arbor, Michigan, with his wife, Linda. They have two daughters. Testimony and photo, 1992

This account concerns events of 1966 and 1967 in which I directly participated. While written years after the events occurred, it is, I'm convinced, quite accurate. While memory certainly gets weaker with the passing of time, I remember these events as though they had just occurred last month. That this could be so is borne out, I think, by the nature of the events themselves. They immediately influenced my whole life direction profoundly, and even today continue to shape my life. Moreover, I recognised as early as 1968 that these events were very special because of the tremendous release of the Spirit of Jesus throughout the Roman Catholic Church that stemmed in part from them. So, like many, many followers of Jesus through the last 2,000 years, I *'treasured these things in my heart.'*

What exactly were those events? They were encounters and sharings with other Christians - encounters filled with a feeling that we had good news for each other. The good news was about what the Holy Spirit wanted to do in our lives and about how the gifts of the Holy Spirit were designed to create Christian community. All of this was very exciting - exciting enough to change the direction of my life and friends' lives. For me, life-changing experiences like these are not easily forgotten. Even after all these years, details of conversations, the rooms in which they took place, what was generally said and done remain quite clear to me. But let the readers as well as the serious students of history decide for themselves.

In June of 1966 I returned to Toronto, Ontario, after graduating from the University of Notre Dame. I also returned to my summer job in the Traffic Engineering Department, City of Toronto. This was my second summer of working as an analyst of city traffic counts. This summer, however, I planned to work only six to eight weeks because in late July, I was to begin work as a volunteer in the Extension Society of the Catholic Church.

Michael Fitzgerald, a classmate from Notre Dame, and I had been accepted by the Extension Society in Chicago as Lay Volunteers. We had requested an assignment together as campus workers. As of our graduation in June, all we knew was that we were to attend several weeks of orientation in San Antonio, Texas, and that our assignment would be the University of Colorado in Boulder. We also knew one other thing about orientation: part of the program would be presented by Steve Clark and Ralph Martin, two men Michael and I knew from Notre Dame and esteemed as older brothers in the Lord.

My summer job was going to be the epitome of routine - routine bordering on boredom. I really expected nothing but badly needed paychecks! Soon after beginning work, however, something happened which made it impossible for me to ever forget that summer.

One day Bruce Robertson, who managed the automated traffic counts program, took me and another summer worker out to check some traffic counters. He had planned the work so that we could eat our sack lunches down by the Canadian National Exhibition grounds, right at the waterfront.

At lunchtime, traffic moved more slowly as we got close to the park. This was mostly due to an outdoor convention of Jehovah's Witnesses which filled the stadium at the Exhibition grounds. We found a place in the park to eat lunch, and soon the conversation turned to the convention nearby.

The other summer worker, who attended a college in Indiana, began criticizing the Jehovah's Witnesses for some of their practices and beliefs. He particularly scorned the position of the Witnesses with respect to military service: Jehovah's Witnesses claimed they all qualified for the ministerial deferment from the draft for the U.S. Armed Services. Since the Vietnam War was rapidly escalating, this was a big issue to him, and for him the Witnesses' belief was just a cop-out.

I explained to him that many Christians read portions of the New Testament to mean that all Jesus' followers were entrusted with some share of ministry work, and so to me, a Christian, the Witnesses' position about their religion made a certain amount of sense. If one's religion is as important as one claims, I said, then it's logical that it would take a lot of one's time in organised service and promotion work.

He disagreed vigorously, and after lunch, walked down to the water's edge. Nonetheless, in a sense, the explanation I gave worked. As a result of it, Bruce knew that, like himself, I was a Christian. So right away he began to ask me about my belief in Jesus. As we returned to work, he invited me to join him and his wife at church on Sunday.

I think that Bruce noticed I was a Roman Catholic Christian, had certainly accepted Jesus as my Lord and Saviour, and because of this was going to serve in campus ministry, doing evangelism and building Christian community. This was not what he had come to expect of Catholics. Bruce, moreover, thought that his church, The Stone Church on Davenport Road, had something that I might be interested in.

That Sunday the spirited worship, especially the singing, impressed me greatly. And the sermon was very good - clear and focused on the power of God in our lives. What particularly impressed me was an inscription on the white wood arch separating the sanctuary from the congregation - the Scripture from Zechariah 4:6 - *'Not by might nor by power, but by my Spirit, says the Lord.'* At the end of the service, the minister invited one man in the congregation to close the service with a prayer, and a brief, but fervent prayer came forth loud, confident and clear.

My impression then was that the level of involvement of everyone present in the service was very high. This was evident in the faces of those listening to the sermon, the strong, practiced singing from everyone in the congregation (to a Roman Catholic, it sounded so heartfelt, so good) and the obvious experience with public prayer displayed by the minister and others in the service. These were things that renewal groups - the liturgical movement, Cursillo, for example - were trying to instill in Catholics. To me, the Scripture on the arch captured what I experienced there.

After the service, Bruce and I talked with Pastor Vaters, and as we left the church he gave me a book that, he said, had just come out. Bruce added that he himself had not read it yet. He put *They Speak with Other Tongues* by John Sherrill in my hands. I remember that my reaction - no enthusiasm, faint curiosity - gave way to an interior admonition: 'Be gracious, accept it politely!'

Around ten p.m. that same Sunday night, however, I was bored, but there wasn't anything in the house to read that interested me. Then I remembered the book by Sherrill. I wondered what it was about; it seemed to me it couldn't be any heavyweight because it was just a small paperback. So I found it and began reading it.

Like many others who started *They Speak with Other Tongues,* I found I couldn't put it down. After just a few chapters, I had to admit that there were many Christians - alive today - who were experiencing the gifts of the Holy Spirit, and they were in every conceivable Christian church, communion or sect. And all this was brand new to me.

By midnight, mild curiosity had given way to excitement. This book told how God changed people's lives, how his Spirit was making Jesus' disciples effective apostles, pastors, evangelists, and servants in his church - and in a manner unknown to me by either reading or personal experience. Although no theologian, I couldn't find any reasoning in the book at variance with what I knew of Catholic teaching. After all, most of it was simply the direct testimony of people experiencing the Holy Spirit in their lives. I finally finished the book sometime between two and three a.m. and drifted off to sleep, my mind still turning over and over Sherrill's exciting story.

I got to work Monday morning and right away told Bruce I had finished the book. At coffee break we shared with each other our understanding of the gifts of the Spirit. I remember he put the question to me, *'Is this something you might want for yourself?'* I told him 'yes'.

However, by this time I only had two to three weeks left in Toronto before I went to San Antonio, Texas, for training. During that time I attended the Stone Church once more. It was, I learned, part of the Pentecostal Assemblies of Canada. Just before leaving Toronto I attended a Wednesday night church picnic in a city park. Two things I remember about that night: Bruce, his wife, Pastor Vaters, and I earnestly discussing life in the Holy Spirit, and my realisation that I really wanted what they had.

So in late July, 1966, I was headed for San Antonio, Texas, filled with excitement at starting Extension Volunteer training, and knowing for myself that campus ministry was the place where I wanted to serve. I also had *They Speak with Other Tongues* with me. I aimed to give it to Steve Clark and Ralph Martin when we met in San Antonio. I wanted them to know about it, and I wondered what they would think about it all.

Shortly after Steve and Ralph arrived in San Antonio, Michael Fitzgerald and I found ourselves in Steve's dormitory room at the college where training was held. We had lots to catch up on, and Michael and I were very interested in the experiences he and Ralph had in campus ministry at Michigan State University in East Lansing. I brought *They Speak with Other Tongues* up to his room.

Steve had a book for me and Michael, too. When I gave him *They Speak with Other Tongues,* he handed me *The Cross and the Switchblade.* At once we noticed that both books were by the same author. Michael latched onto *The Cross and the Switchblade,* and we brought the book with us to Boulder, Colorado, at the end of Extension Volunteers training.

At Boulder, we immersed ourselves in the campus ministry at Newman Center and time flew for us. Soon it was mid-April, 1967. We received a letter from Steve Clark who never wrote without a very good reason. I recall the letter: typed, on a little sheet of white paper, only a few sentences. Steve wrote that he and others had been baptised in the Holy Spirit! He signed the letter 'Alleluia, Steve.'

Michael and I wondered: what were Steve and Ralph involved in? But I thought I knew, because it sounded like events described in *They Speak with Other Tongues*. Even so, we both wondered.

Within a few days I learned that Pastor Larry Christenson was to speak on Pentecost Sunday at a local Lutheran church. By that time I knew that he was involved in the renewal movement centered on experience of the Baptism in the Holy Spirit. When I learned that he would speak on campus on that Sunday evening, I resolved right away to hear him.

The evening of Pentecost Sunday, May 15th, 1967, came quickly. I went alone to hear Larry Christenson because Michael couldn't attend. That night for the first time I heard a basic theology of the Baptism in the Holy Spirit. It sounded so logical, and something so desirable. After Larry Christenson's talk I stayed to listen to his answers to questions from the audience. Eventually everybody left, and the two of us discussed the Baptism in the Holy Spirit. He asked me if I wanted him to pray that I would be baptised in the Holy Spirit, and I said 'yes'.

Immediately upon Larry Christenson's prayer for me, I had an intense awareness of God. It could be described as being in awe of him, but with a sense of delight, too. It was marked by an awareness of greater personal knowledge of him, greater power from him and reverence for him. After praying for me, Larry Christenson asked what I experienced, and I told him. He then asked me if I felt like praying in tongues, and I said I wasn't sure. So he suggested I begin by just repeating phrases that he prayed.

I was too self-conscious, however, for this to work. Larry then suggested that I just go outside into an adjacent walled courtyard and pray there. I went outside and, still very aware of God's presence, looked up. It was a very clear night, the stars were visible, and under their canopy was a perfect place to pray. A torrent of sounds, syllables, words which I didn't understand, but nevertheless wanted to say, came out! I prayed outside for a while, and then went back inside to see Larry Christenson. After some parting advice and counsel from Larry, we said our goodbyes, and I left for the apartment.

In the next few days, Michael and I talked about what had happened that night. He knew that I had had an experience of God that night - for me it was turning into a compelling, continuing awareness of his presence. He asked whether I had prayed in tongues, and I said that I had.

Michael was moved deeply by the sense of prayer and praise in the gift of tongues. Michael began to pray for the gift and a couple of weeks later he spontaneously received tongues during a time of prayer for me. Michael, in turn, shared his experience over lunch with a student Ardell Bell (Fitzgerald) whom he married the next year. Immediately after their conversation, Ardell received the gift of tongues while driving to class!

These events, together with reflection and discussion of them, convinced Michael and me that we had to speak to students directly about the power of the Holy Spirit, and make them aware of God's gift for them. However, the school year was about to end, and we were headed for training in Chicago for the second year of work in Boulder. We were looking forward to seeing firsthand what friends in Chicago and East Lansing were experiencing, and to telling them about events in Colorado.

Thus the summer of 1967 was the first time the two of us had an opportunity to share this experience with other Catholics. Some of them had considerably more theological formation and practical experience in pastoral work, and so we learned much from them. So it was that by September, 1967, Michael and I had developed an awareness of our work and goals that had changed greatly in a mere twelve months!

Of course, this is not the end. It's just a portion of a much bigger story - the story about renewal of Roman Catholics throughout the world. That part of the story I leave to others to tell.

AN OVERWHELMING FLOOD OF GOD'S LOVE AND MERCY

A Testimony by Ralph Martin

Ralph Martin graduated from University of Notre Dame in 1964 with a degree in philosophy. He holds a Doctorate of Sacred Theology from the Angelicum in Rome. Ralph is President of Renewal Ministries, an evangelistic outreach around the world and is host of 'The Choices We Face' television programme. He has authored numerous books and is on the faculty of Sacred Heart Seminary in Detroit, Michigan. Testimony, 2015. Photo, 1992

The Cursillo Movement was a significant factor in my own life and in some ways became the seed-bed out of which the Charismatic Renewal blossomed. While a student at Notre Dame in the sixties, despite a solid Catholic upbringing in New Jersey, I got caught up in the intellectual and moral confusion of the times. It wasn't until three months before graduating that things turned around. A friend invited me to make Cursillo No. 2 in South Bend, Indiana, held at Fatima Retreat House on the campus of the University of Notre Dame. Very reluctantly and sceptically, I went.

There I heard impressive presentations that forced me to think about the purpose of life and reconsider the beauty and truth of Christianity. There also I encountered in prayer, in the Word, in the Blessed Sacrament, in the community, and in the silence of my soul, the gentle but clear invitation from Jesus himself to recognise him for who he was and surrender my life to him. It was a struggle, but thanks be to God, I was able to respond to the grace to recommit my life to Christ and make a firm decision to follow him. At the very end of the Cursillo, I experienced an overwhelming flood of God's love and mercy entering my soul and igniting in me a fervent desire to love him and help others love him. I got up to testify to that publicly and that is what I have tried to live out to this very day. I think I was actually baptised in the Spirit at that point and a month later I found myself making strange sounds in prayer that worried me, so I stopped. I think that was the beginning of speaking in tongues; although, not having any concepts to understand it at the time, I stopped.

It was relationships through the Cursillo Movement that led to our first visit to Duquesne University in 1966. Steve Clark and I were working together in East Lansing, Michigan, for the National Cursillo Office and also doing campus ministry at St. John's Student Parish at Michigan State University. We received an invitation from some theology professors at Duquesne, who were also involved in the Cursillo Movement, to lead a retreat there, which we did. It was the following year that the famous retreat took place, led also by the same theology professors, that was the start of the Charismatic Renewal in the Catholic Church.

A short time after the Renewal broke out in Pittsburgh, we went to visit to see what was happening. It was there that I met some who have become lifelong friends and companions in the Gospel, Patti Gallagher Mansfield and Dave Mangan. It was there also that I received prayer for more of the Holy Spirit, and recognised that what I had experienced at the end of that Cursillo a few years previously was the same experience that was now becoming widespread through what has come to be known as Charismatic Renewal. The visit to Duquesne also gave me confidence to trust what I had experienced, and provided an environment and theological and scriptural understanding that enabled me to proceed with confidence sharing this great grace with everyone I could.

Upon returning to Michigan State, we started a student prayer group where many of the students experienced the grace of this Renewal. That Spring a whole group of us went down to University of Notre Dame, where the Renewal had also broken out, to share together in what came to be known as the First International Conference of the Catholic Charismatic Renewal (a nun from Canada made it international!).

But the early days of the renewal were not without controversy and misunderstandings. In our work with the Cursillo Movement we had developed and were conducting leadership training weekends for Cursillo leaders all over the country, and were receiving requests to pray for many of these leaders for what has come to be called 'baptism in the Spirit'. This is most properly understood, I think, as a release of the graces of Christian initiation, or a 'renewal' of sacramental baptism in the Spirit. Eventually the Cursillo Movement decided that it wanted to remain separate from this grace, even though some in the Cursillo Movement spontaneously experienced it through the Movement, as I had. This led to Steve and me being 'let go' from the National Cursillo Office.

Because of the enthusiasm of many of the Michigan State University students as a result of their encounter with the Lord and openness to the Holy Spirit, our presence at the student parish became controversial and we were suddenly fired. The Catholic student parish in Ann Arbor, St. Mary's Student Chapel, heard that we were available and since nothing seemed to be working there at the time, those in charge decided to take a chance on us getting something started. They invited us to be on the staff of the student center at the University of Michigan.

Then in the summer and fall of 1967 we were joined in Ann

Arbor by two friends from the University of Notre Dame, Jim Cavnar (now head of Cross International, a large aid organisation to third world countries), and Gerry Rauch, (now an instructor in pastoral counseling at the seminary where I teach, Sacred Heart Major Seminary in the Archdiocese of Detroit), and by none other than Patti Gallagher (Mansfield) and Nan Nader.

Eventually, so many students were coming to the prayer meetings at St. Mary's that some felt it was overwhelming the parish, and we were 'let go' again. This led to the formation of the Word of God Community, *New Covenant* Magazine, the International Communication Center, National Leaders Conferences, as well as many various committees. In the early 1970s we were visited by a mysterious Belgian priest, Fr. Michel Dubois, and his Irish assistant, who had come to discern if this Renewal was really from the Lord or not. At the end of the visit he revealed publicly his true identity: Cardinal Leo Joseph Suenens, Primate of the Catholic Church in Belgium, and one of the most significant leaders of Vatican Council II as one of its four Moderators. He decided to give me his first public interview endorsing the Renewal for *New Covenant* magazine.

This meeting with Cardinal Suenens led to other significant events: for example, our first International Leaders' Conference held in Rome in 1973, wherein Pope Paul VI met with a small group of us; it also led to the first truly International General Conference in Rome in 1975, wherein the closing liturgy was held in St. Peter's Basilica. It was here that Pope Paul VI addressed the 10,000 people in the Basilica after the Mass and gave his famous address calling the Renewal a 'chance for the Church'.

And then, down through the years, there were many meetings with Pope Saint John Paul II; there was Patti Mansfield addressing Benedict XVI at a world meeting of movements in Rome in 2006; and then there was the wonderful encounter with Pope Francis at the conference in Rome's Olympic Stadium in 2014, in which both Patti and I were speakers. And the story goes on and on. I don't want to say that so much has happened that all the books in the world couldn't contain all the marvellous individual stories of encounters with God's grace these past 50 years. But the showering of graces, of salvation, of healing, of deliverance, of vocation, are truly wonderful... overwhelming really. And all this of course has taken place in the midst of weakness, failure, problems, disappointments – just as it's always been.

What a privilege to have been touched so many years ago by the Spirit and launched into a worldwide movement of mercy and salvation through that Duquesne Weekend! Can we ever thank and praise God enough?

IT WAS THE TIME AND PLACE

A TESTIMONY BY STEPHEN B. CLARK

Stephen B. Clark holds a B.A. in History from Yale University (1962) and an M.A. in Philosophy from the University of Notre Dame. He has served in leadership in the Cursillo Movement, the Catholic Charismatic Renewal, as International President of the Sword of the Spirit, and as a member of the Board of Directors of Servant Publications. He presently resides in Chelsea, Michigan. Testimony, 2015. Photo, 1992

The Duquesne Weekend is often spoken about as the beginning of the Charismatic Renewal, and that has some truth to it. As someone put it, the weekend kick-started the Charismatic Renewal. Not having been on the weekend, I have no personal testimony about the weekend itself, but I was involved in the events that led up to it and what happened afterwards.

My first acquaintance with charismatic things began with reading *The Cross and the Switchblade*, a very influential book in the beginnings of the Renewal. Paradoxically enough, it was given to me by a Campus Crusade staff member who also worked at Michigan State University. At that time Campus Crusade was negative on 'Pentecostalism' (the word that was used for charismatic movements), but the staff member did not seem to realise that she was in fact promoting Pentecostalism by passing on the book. Like her, I was impressed with what I could read about what happened to people when they were baptised in the Spirit. I was even more impressed, because I had worked with young people in a New York neighbourhood like the one described in *The Cross and the Switchblade* and knew how hard it was to get them to change for the better.

That event has a certain symbolism. It is symbolic first of how many have been impressed with the effects of being baptised in the Spirit. It is also symbolic of the ecumenical origins of the Charismatic Renewal and of the Duquesne Weekend itself. Some have described the Duquesne Weekend as if it was a Catholic devotional experience - a group of Catholics praying to renew their Baptism and Confirmation or a group of Catholics praying before the Blessed Sacrament and experiencing grace. However, those who were there make it clear that the Duquesne Weekend would not have happened without the input of various non-Catholic Pentecostals, and of the Pentecostal movement as a whole, and without the message of baptism in the Spirit, in whatever terminology it was presented. We Catholics should be grateful to the Pentecostals, as Pope Francis recently said.

History also makes something else clear - the Charismatic Renewal and the Duquesne Weekend did not humanly come out of nowhere, but it began with a group of people who were seeking to serve the Lord and who were working together to evangelise and bring renewal to the church. That group had grown out of the Cursillo Movement, at that time somewhat new in the United States. Its origin was at Notre Dame University in the early sixties and many of those involved in it worked on the Antioch Weekend movement, an offshoot of the Cursillo. The first Antioch Weekend held at Duquesne was something of a pre-cursor of the Duquesne Weekend. The group that worked on the Antioch Weekend and in the Cursillo Movement was not a formal organisation, but there was a conscious bond among them that came from working together.

Some have said that the Charismatic Renewal did not have a founder as other movements have. That is partly accurate. But it did have a founding group that provided the leadership for the beginnings of the Charismatic Renewal, including the Duquesne Weekend and its follow-up. It included many of those who have added their testimonies to this book, *As By A New Pentecost*: Ralph Martin, Jim Cavnar, Peter Collins and Bert Ghezzi.

Those us who had worked in the endeavors of that group had seen some real success, but we were also aware that we were not seeing something up to the standard of what we could read about in the Acts of the Apostles. More could be possible. We were ready for the understanding that the Charismatic (Pentecostal) experience could provide the spiritual power that would make something much more effective happen. *The Cross and the Switchblade* and *They Speak with Other Tongues* circulated rapidly among this group, and it oriented many among us to look to the Pentecostal experience for the answer to a felt need. The folk at Duquesne were the ones who took the key step.

Here then is the main point I would make about the Duquesne Weekend. It was put together to get people baptised in the Spirit. But the result was something different than any old programme that might be effective in bringing people into a charismatic experience. It was the time and place when God met people who were looking for the power to advance his kingdom, not just those who were on the weekend at the time (most of them were not) but also those in the broader movement. They in turn quickly received the testimony of those on the weekend and entered into the charismatic experience themselves. It was the initial action of God that began something that could be described as a revival, and whose rapid and successful spread surprised those involved with it.

Most spiritual renewal movements have begun much the same way. They have grown out of a group of people seeking the Lord and seeking to serve him. His grace then meets them, and equips them for something beyond their ability.

I would put the next most important single event in the launching of the Charismatic Renewal to be the First International Conference in the summer of 1967. Much had happened before then. Those who had been on the Duquesne Weekend, especially the two professors, immediately began to talk about what had happened to them. Their word spread among those who had worked together at Notre Dame and in the Cursillo and Antioch Weekend movements. Most of those entered quickly into the charismatic experience. But they also began to spread the word and spread the Baptism in the Spirit.

In two important places prayer meetings developed that created groups of charismatics, mainly at first of students: Notre Dame and Michigan State University. The latter group also began regular Days of Renewal that soon attracted people from throughout Michigan. The Notre Dame people decided to hold a conference in the summer. The Michigan State people joined them. This conference became the event which fostered and maintained the existence of the Charismatic Renewal in a self-conscious way and was named in retrospect the First International Conference.

It is perhaps this conference and related activities that established the Duquesne Weekend as in a certain way the founding event of the Charismatic Renewal. We referred back to it as the origin of something new and a testimony to God providing a new grace. Since then the Duquesne Weekend has been considered central to the origin of the Charismatic Renewal, even though many have entered into the charismatic experience without any direct or indirect connection with the Duquesne Weekend.

The international conference was held every year for a number of years thereafter. In 1969 the leaders who gathered at the Third International Conference agreed to set up a communications office for the Charismatic Renewal and a service committee, the Catholic Charismatic Renewal Service Committee. That was done in June 1970 and the services provided by the communities at Notre Dame and now Ann Arbor, Michigan were unified under that committee. Most of the members of the committee came from the group that had prepared the way for the Duquesne Weekend. The basic principles of the organisation were derived from the Cursillo Movement.

The Duquesne Weekend was an important event. I described it as the kick-start for the Charismatic Renewal. It did not, however, stand alone. It was prepared for and carried on by many other efforts for spiritual renewal of the churches and of many Christians. We all would say that the success of the Charismatic Renewal was something God did. But we also should say that it was effective because of the dedication of early members of the movement and from those outside who helped them. Finally, the Charismatic Renewal benefitted greatly from the wisdom that predecessor movements, especially the Cursillo, could teach us.

ONE SNOWY DAY

A TESTIMONY BY DEACON KEVIN M. RANAGHAN

Kevin M. Ranaghan holds a doctorate in liturgy from the University of Notre Dame and is a founding member of the People of Praise, a covenant community, based in South Bend, Indiana. He has served the Catholic Charismatic Renewal in many and varied leadership capacities, both nationally and internationally. He has represented the Catholic Charismatic Renewal on ecumenical committees and was the Chairman of the historic ecumenical charismatic Conference held in Kansas City in 1977. He is a permanent deacon. Testimony, 2015. Photo,1990s

One snowy day in January 1967, my wife Dorothy and I met our friend, Bert Ghezzi, outside the Notre Dame library. Bert told us the surprising story of some of our mutual friends who were faculty members at Duquesne University in Pittsburgh. They had just prayed to receive a Baptism in the Holy Spirit at a home prayer meeting, whose members were, for the most part, Episcopalians and Presbyterians. Prior to that they had been studying and praying about the stories of Pentecostal and charismatic Christians, also baptised in the Spirit, who experienced spiritual gifts such as healing, prophecy, praying in tongues and others. As Bert told us the story, we heard of their increases in faith, the growth in their prayer and understanding of Scripture, and the effectiveness of their witness.

Two things about this story turned us off. The introduction of some kind of new baptism was a non-starter. I knew enough of the Catholic theological tradition and especially about the sacraments of initiation to know when and how we had received the Holy Spirit. I understood how the graces of baptism and confirmation could grow in our lives. The notion of some second baptism was foreign. Secondly, while I was committed to ecumenism, including learning from our Protestant brothers and sisters in Christ, Pentecostalism had never entered my mind. All I knew of Pentecostals came from the popular impression that they were poorly educated 'holy rollers', whose religion was one hundred percent emotional. Thus their supposed use of spiritual gifts, especially tongues, was highly suspect.

However, we could not completely reject what Bert was telling us. We knew these men well. They were colleagues, scholars in theology, church history, and philosophy. They were trusted friends and brothers in Christ. And they were saying that their lives had been profoundly changed by this Baptism in the Holy Spirit and by the exercise of these spiritual gifts. We could not ignore the weight of their testimonies.

Dorothy and I then embarked on a six week journey of prayer, study and questioning. Could these stories be true? Did they have a basis in Scripture and the tradition of the Church? What, if anything, did the Second Vatican Council have to say on the subject? Could this Pentecostal–charismatic thing be part of the renewal of the Catholic Church? Could it have a place in our own lives? Over the course of these weeks we came to a number of conclusions. Here are some of them.

The New Testament is replete with examples of visions, spiritual dreams, miraculous healings, prophecies, speaking in tongues, casting out of evil spirits, inspired preaching, etc. This is true in the life of Jesus and in the church life recorded in Acts. In fact, Jesus said that the things he did we also would do. These spiritual gifts continued throughout church history at different times and places and with different people. The Church understands that the presence, action and grace of the Holy Spirit is not limited to the sacraments. Pope St. John XXIII had the whole church pray explicitly for a renewal of the wonders of Pentecost in our day. Finally, the Second Vatican Council's dogmatic constitution on the Church taught that the charismatic gifts of the Spirit, ordinary and extraordinary, are to be expected and encouraged as part of the normal life of the Church.

At the same time we were beginning to learn that this Pentecostal spirituality was not strictly speaking limited to Pentecostals. Since the early 1960's, hundreds of Episcopalians, Methodists, Presbyterians, Lutherans and many others had been baptised in the Holy Spirit and had begun using the spiritual gifts. In terms of religious culture and practice, they were much closer to us than the still mysterious Pentecostals. This quelled our fears that we might be moving towards the edge of a spiritual cliff.

Meanwhile, we were in regular phone contact with our friends at Duquesne. They had been involved with a student club, the *Chi Rho* Society, for some time. Dorothy and Bert had been founding members of this club several years before when they were Duquesne students. The club was focused on Church renewal, liturgical prayer and Christian social life. The club had planned a retreat for February at a retreat house called the Ark and the Dove. Our friends were quite cautious about their own new experience and simply organised the retreat around the first four chapters of the Acts of the Apostles. The story of this retreat has been told elsewhere by first-hand witnesses. What we heard was that many of the attendees had been baptised in the Holy Spirit and had begun using the spiritual gifts during the retreat. This news gave a final push to Dorothy and me.

At the beginning of March 1967, one of the Duquesne professors came to South Bend for a few days. He had work to do at Notre Dame. On March 4, I invited him to speak at a prayer gathering in our home. I was teaching theology at Saint Mary's College at the time and I invited many of my students who were interested in Church renewal. There were also some students from Notre Dame. I think there were about 30 there altogether. Everyone listened respectfully; some seemed deeply interested. We invited those who would like to pray to be baptised in the Holy Spirit to get together the next evening at Bert's apartment.

The next night there were nine of us sitting around Bert's living room and the professor from Duquesne was there to pray with us. After a bit of prayer and conversation, he began to pray with us individually, moving around the room and placing his hands on our heads as he did do. Dorothy and I were sitting side by side, and holding hands, at least part of the time. As we waited for him to come to us, I remember praying along these lines: Lord, I want to have as much of your Spirit as you want me to have so I can be and do what you want. Lord, I know I have your Holy Spirit, but if there is more of your Holy Spirit that you want me to have, then Lord send your Spirit and fill me.

When he came to us he placed one hand on each of our heads. So we were really being prayed with together. He prayed with us for several minutes. My experience was this. I noticed that the top of my head and my hands were very warm and very tingly. But that was completely overshadowed by the new and powerful experience I had of the actual presence of Jesus with me. Of course I knew the presence of Jesus in the Church, in the reception of Holy Communion, in the Blessed Sacrament reserved in the tabernacle. I had many moments of realising his presence. But this was different. It was intense and deeply personal. The image I had was of Jesus standing right next to me, on my left, and very close to me. This was not visual but I really knew he was there. I experienced him loving me and I could talk with him, silently as I recall. In his presence I knew joy, peace, faith and praise all at once. It was exhilarating but quite calm. I thought: the Holy Spirit is enabling me to know and relate to Jesus in a new way. He is not distant, he is not far away, he is right here with me.

That night I heard no speaking in tongues or prophecy, I saw no charismatic gifts. But everything had changed in the sense that my whole life, and faith, and relationships, and work, I now lived in the ongoing experience of the presence of Jesus. Every day over the next week I felt the Spirit leading me throughout the day, what to read, what to say, what to pray for, how to pray, and what to believe God could do.

Interested in learning more about the charismatic gifts, we contacted the president of the local chapter of the Full Gospel Businessmen and asked to meet him. Ray Bullard invited us to his home where we met him and a number of Pentecostal pastors eager to meet these Catholics who said they were baptised in the Holy Spirit. They would later say they were somewhat sceptical, but after some conversation they began to pray with us with the laying on of hands. Within just a minute of two, almost all of the nine of us there that night were praying in tongues. Some of us prayed loudly, some of us softly. It was just wonderful. And again, the experience that had begun for me the week before, and that had endured, was intensified. Jesus was with me.

Praying in tongues was a terrific new way of praise, worship and intercession. It also served as a gateway to other gifts, showing us in the next weeks how to step out into prophecy or prayer for healing. Some of our new Pentecostal friends urged us to leave the Catholic Church and join a Pentecostal church. That thought had never occurred to us. What we were doing we did as Catholics committed to the church. But wiser Pentecostal heads entered the same conversations saying: 'You stay right where you are. Who knows what the Lord wants to do in the Catholic Church?'

Soon our home and campus charismatic prayer meetings began. People came by the tens, scores and hundreds. Within a year Notre Dame had become a major center of the spread of baptism in the Spirit in the Catholic Church worldwide. Figures vary, but at least 120 million Roman Catholics have been baptised in the Holy Spirit. Recently, Pope Francis challenged us all: 'I expect from you that you share with all, within the Church, the grace of the Baptism in the Holy Spirit.' And so I recall the wise words of an old Pentecostal friend: Who knows what the Lord wants to do in the Catholic Church!

Kevin and Dorothy Ranaghan with their first child

RENEW YOUR WONDERS IN THIS OUR TIME

A TESTIMONY BY DOROTHY GARRITY RANAGHAN

Dorothy Ranaghan is a native of Pittsburgh, Pennsylvania, and was a founding member of the Chi Rho Society when she was an undergraduate at Duquesne University. She holds an M.A. in Theology from University of Notre Dame. Dorothy is an author, a former member of the National Service Committee of the Catholic Charismatic Renewal and a founding member of the People of Praise, an ecumenical, charismatic covenant community. She has six children and fifteen grandchildren. Testimony, 2015. Photo, 1990s

Those of you who know me now may not realise that my nickname in high school and most of college was 'the quiet one'. That changed on March 5, 1967, when I was baptised in the Holy Spirit. In 2 Timothy 1:7 it says, 'For the Spirit God gave us does not make us timid, but gives us power.' I will always be an introvert, but timidity is pushed aside by the Spirit.

Initially, I was quite the sceptic. Our friends from Pittsburgh talked of a whole new faith and power to live the Christian life. But I knew I had already been baptised and confirmed and received the Holy Spirit, so I really didn't understand what they were talking about. Eventually, my husband and I decided that if there was more of the Spirit that we wanted that and so a group of us gathered with our friends from Pittsburgh to pray. I experienced peace and joy but no discernible gifts. Very soon after, a group of us sought out a group of Pentecostals with whom to pray and that night everyone started to pray in tongues... everyone, that is, but me. I don't think it was my scepticism as much as distraction that held me back. The distraction was my husband of just seven months who was sitting in a chair next to me and quite literally preaching in what sounded like Hebrew. Whoa!

The next day I went to the high school at which I was teaching, and went into the chapel there and shut the door. I was alone. The students had all gone to lunch and the hallway was finally quiet. The stained-glass windows in the chapel sent rainbows around the altar. I closed my eyes and said 'Lord, if anything that happened last night was real, let it happen now, here, alone with you.' Slowly, haltingly, it came, the rhythm of a language I did not know. It was the 'morning after the night before', but I dared to speak in faith new strange and haunting syllables of praise. With each word my last faint doubts were gone. A flag of faith was planted there that said Jesus is here, and I am his. He is with me, of whom shall I be afraid?

Yes, I had received the Holy Spirit in Baptism and in Confirmation, but for me as for many of us it is as if we received a birthday present beautifully wrapped and tied with a bow that was then put on a shelf in our closet... unopened. Being baptised in the Holy Spirit opens that gift for each of us, gifts meant to be used to build up the body of Christ so that we can renew the face of the earth. There is always more to the life of the Spirit... much more!

In 1962, Pope John XXIII prayed for 'a new Pentecost'. In preparation for the Second Vatican Council, he prayed, 'Renew your wonders in our time, as by a new Pentecost.' The Council was the first answer to this prayer and the Pentecostal /charismatic renewal was another. Now, almost 50 years after the beginning of the charismatic renewal, we sense it is time for the Lord to renew his wonders in OUR time for the sake of the Church, for the sake of the world. Come Holy Spirit!

DRENCHED WITH DELIGHT

A TESTIMONY BY BERT GHEZZI

Bert Ghezzi graduated from Duquesne University in 1963 and was the founding President of Chi Rho several years before the Duquesne Weekend. He obtained his Ph.D. in history in 1969 from the University of Notre Dame and has held many leadership positions in the Charismatic Renewal. Bert was editor of New Covenant magazine and editorial director for Servant Publications. He is a prolific author and lives in Winter Park, Florida. This testimony originally appeared in Charisma magazine, March, 1987. Photo is from that era.

The Catholic Charismatic Renewal has been called 'a surprise of the Holy Spirit'.... I was among the first to be surprised. My wife, Mary Lou, and I were part of the original group of students who were baptised in the Holy Spirit in March, 1967, at the University of Notre Dame.

The excitement of those days is as fresh in my mind as was the new-fallen snow that crunched underfoot. Kevin and Dorothy Ranaghan and I received a letter that told us how some 20 students and teachers at Duquesne University in Pittsburgh had been sovereignly baptised in the Spirit during a now-famous weekend retreat. We might have dismissed the whole event with a patronising 'tsk-tsk' had not some very close friends been involved. Instead, our faith expanded and we began to expect the Holy Spirit to do the same for us.

We didn't have to wait long. The first week of March, 1967, one of the Duquesne professors who had been baptised in the Spirit, visited Notre Dame. At an open prayer meeting on the evening of March 4, he read the description of spiritual gifts from 1 Corinthians 12 and declared that he no longer had to believe in the power of Pentecost because it was now a part of his personal experience. Most of his hearers seemed to miss what he said or regarded it as strange. However, with heightened anticipation, nine of us arranged to meet with him the following evening at my apartment.

That night Kevin and Dorothy Ranaghan, Jim Cavnar, Gerry Rauch and three others joined Mary Lou and me in our tiny living room. We listened intently as he spoke about the marvellous, life-changing events that were unfolding among our Pittsburgh friends. In the background my second son, Paul - only a week old - cried sporadically, distracting us occasionally. When our friend finished speaking there was an uncharacteristically brief discussion and only a few questions before we asked him to pray for us. He went from person to person, laying on hands, commanding evil spirits to go and asking Jesus to baptise us in the Holy Spirit.

And he did, although much more quietly and with much more decorum than I had anticipated. That night several people, including Kevin, Jim, Gerry and Mary Lou, experienced the Holy Spirit in dramatic personal ways. My own baptism in the Holy Spirit came more haltingly. So little happened for me at first that I would have been left behind had my professor friend not encouraged me the next day to expect the Holy Spirit to do something in areas where I felt the most personal need. Within a week, however, the Lord had cut the roots of my long-standing bout with low self-esteem and depression, and I knew with the others that the Holy Spirit was working in me in a new way.

That first week all of us were expecting to experience spiritual gifts, but we didn't know what we were looking for. Before that time none of us had ever heard of praying in tongues, let alone even dream that we might do it ourselves. So we turned to Pentecostals for help.

We phoned Ray Bullard, the president of the South Bend chapter of the Full Gospel Business Men's Fellowship International and a deacon at Calvary Temple. We explained that some Notre Dame students, including graduate students in theology, had been baptised in the Spirit and wanted to learn about spiritual gifts. Without hesitation Bullard invited us to come to his house.

When we arrived on the evening of March 13, 1967, we were greeted by 11 Pentecostal ministers and their wives from all over Indiana. Bullard was not about to deal alone with us Catholic intellectuals. He told us later that he had prayed for Notre Dame students for many years. He also said he believed the Lord had him remodel his basement room just for our visit. That night his prayers were answered, and his room was well-used.

For several hours we discussed speaking in tongues. We knew we were baptised in the Spirit and were open to spiritual gifts; the ministers wanted us to receive the gift of tongues because they believed that would be evidence of our being baptised in the Spirit. The debate ended in a draw: We were open to receiving the gift of tongues if we could understand it our own way; the ministers wanted to pray for us and they would understand it their own way.

So at about midnight we prayed. The Catholics lined up at one side of the room. One of the ministers gave some explanation about how to yield to the gift of tongues, and then the ministers lined up facing us, about 10 feet away. As we all turned to the Lord, the ministers began walking toward us, stretching out their arms and praying in tongues. The sound struck me as wonderfully strange. Before our new Pentecostal friends were halfway across the room, we began to pray in tongues. My wife, Mary Lou, began to sing in an oriental chant and Kevin Ranaghan burst into a fluent guttural sounding language. I stammered a few syllables that began 'ab ba la....'

Sometimes I smile at the humorous touches in this event, but at the time I was awestruck. Here we were, a handful of Roman Catholics in the 20th century, praying in tongues just as the disciples had done at Pentecost!

As we were about to leave Ray Bullard's home in the wee hours of the morning, one of the ministers' wives asked us when we would be joining the Pentecostal church. I was puzzled by her question and asked what she meant. She explained that in her experience when Catholics were baptised in the Spirit they had to leave the church. Had she not raised the question, the thought would never have crossed my mind. No, I said politely, we would not be leaving the Catholic Church. I was sure at the outset that our experience of the Holy Spirit not only did not contradict Catholic orthodoxy but was at the very heart of it.

That night at Ray Bullard's was a paradigm of the mutually beneficial relations that would develop generally between Catholics and Pentecostals. We came seeking and received spiritual gifts, which we brought back and helped distribute to our Catholic brothers and sisters. Our hosts learned about Catholics, were impressed by our loyalty and inspired by the way the Holy Spirit worked among us. Later, when they shared the news with their brothers and sisters, it sparked new life among them.

When Mary Lou and I got home from the Bullard's, I sat for a long time in my rocking chair, praying in tongues. I was drenched with delight. A marvellous power was coursing through me, an energy I knew somehow would be with me for my lifetime. I had worshipped the Lord since I was a boy, but never like this. Being baptised in the Spirit closed the distance between the Lord and me - I was adoring Someone I knew intimately.

Recently I asked six Catholic Charismatic Renewal leaders from across the United States what that movement's main contribution has been. Each one said it was enabling Catholics to know Jesus in a personal way. What had happened for us Catholic Pentecostal pioneers has happened for countless others. Looking back over the years of Catholic Charismatic Renewal, which has seen millions baptised in the Spirit, I appreciate what a privilege it was to have been a part of its beginnings.

'SEEK ME,' SAYS THE LORD

A TESTIMONY BY JIM CAVNAR

Jim Cavnar graduated from the University of Notre Dame in 1967. He has served in leadership in the Catholic Charismatic Renewal from its inception and was one of the first worship leaders and musicians in Ann Arbor. Jim presently works as President of Cross International, an outreach to the poor. Jim and his wife, Betsy, have five children. Testimony and photo, 1992

When I first heard of the now-historic Duquesne Weekend, I was a senior at the University of Notre Dame only four months away from graduating with a degree in theology. I hoped that I would soon be engaged in a full-time career devoted to evangelisation. I would never have suspected that events hundreds of miles away were about to make this dream a reality, yet a reality unlike any I could ever have imagined.

It was surprising enough that I was about to depart Notre Dame with any faith at all, let alone with a faith that had become the central reality of my life. Only two years before, I would have described myself as an agnostic who had cast off the veneer of Catholicism in the conviction that it added nothing of consequence to common sense humanism.

I had come to Notre Dame from a Catholic family and twelve years of Catholic education. I had chosen the school precisely because it was a Catholic institution. I came expecting that Christianity would continue to be top priority. But as I became wrapped up in the social movements of the early 1960's, I was plagued by a fundamental question: 'Is there a difference between a Christian and a humanist?' In the Civil Rights Movement I encountered both Christians and non-Christians who seemed to share the same convictions and act in the same ways. Did being a 'Christian' really add anything more than an alternative terminology to progressive humanism? More often than not, when I raised the question, even to nuns and priests, I was told it did not. Eventually I dropped the label 'Christian.'

At first this step seemed liberating, like a ship that has slipped its moorings and is free to sail unimpeded toward a limitless horizon. But eventually this lack of an anchorage produced an oppressive despair - if there is no longer some ultimate truth and meaning then there seems no longer to be any ultimate purpose to life. I hurled myself into a whirlwind of academic work and student politics. But, beneath the busyness, an insidious emptiness was stealing away my life. The visible symptom was an uncompromising cynicism.

Then, toward the end of my second year at Notre Dame, a friend invited me to attend a Cursillo. All I knew about the Cursillo was that people claimed the weekend experience had changed their lives. That was all the challenge I needed - I would take on the Cursillo and prove its claims hollow. Nothing would change my life!

During the three days of the Cursillo I listened to laymen from the local area talk about the Christian life and about their own lives. Almost from the first moment of the weekend my heart was captivated by the vision they conveyed. At first I couldn't explain it. But in the course of the weekend I suddenly saw, in a compelling and life-shattering way, what it was that made a Christian different. It was Christ!

To be a Christian meant having a personal relationship with another person - Jesus Christ himself. It meant living in union with him and in union with others who shared that relationship. What Christianity offered, that no other philosophy could, was not an ideal, ethic, or doctrine, but the living Jesus of Nazareth.

My life was radically changed overnight. Despair vanished before the joy and purposefulness of knowing Christ. I began praying daily, reading Scripture, and taking every opportunity to share Christ with others. I linked up with others on the campus who had had a similar experience and together we worked to bring others to a deeper relationship with the Lord. After much prayer and counsel with my deans, I changed my major from physics to theology to prepare myself for what I hoped would be a life devoted to the Christian apostolate.

Despite this dramatic re-orientation, when I first heard about the Duquesne Weekend and the Baptism in the Holy Spirit in March of my senior year at Notre Dame, I wanted nothing to do with it. This may seem a strange reaction from someone so eager to serve God who was already involved in a then unconventional renewal movement. It seems doubly so when I recall that I had previously welcomed news of the new Pentecostal Movement then beginning to sweep through the mainline Protestant churches.

In the previous summer of 1966, I lived with Steve Clark and Ralph Martin in East Lansing, Michigan. Steve and Ralph were on the staff of the National Cursillo Secretariat headquartered nearby. Both had been students at Notre Dame and I knew them through the Cursillo Movement. They served on the staff of the local university student parish and I hoped to work with them after graduation.

That summer Steve visited with another Notre Dame alumnus and *cursillista,* Peter Collins. Peter described his remarkable encounter that summer with a small Pentecostal church in Toronto. He excitedly described his visits to the church where he had witnessed lively worship and heard stories of miraculous healings. In his suitcase he carried an eye-opening book, *They Speak with Other Tongues.*

We read the book quickly, our doubt and scepticism restrained by the first-hand accounts of a trusted friend corroborating the tales in the book. Such things had happened in the lives of the saints, I reasoned, why not now? It seemed possible, even likely, that these accounts were real. I was prepared to accept them and hoped that someone (else!) would investigate.

For a life-long Catholic with a theological degree, the prospect of visiting a Pentecostal church was intimidating. I had heard tales of 'holy rollers' from my father's boyhood. How could I find a way of making contact with this newly-discovered world without getting entangled in some bizarre cult? I hoped someone would investigate and let me know what they found. Within a few months it happened.

At the national Cursillo convention that August, 1966, Steve and Ralph gave copies of the book to two professors from Duquesne University. They were more daring than we. After reading the book they made contact with a prayer group in Pittsburgh attended by Presbyterians and other mainline Protestants. They attended for a while and then asked to be prayed with to be baptised in the Spirit.

Soon word had filtered back to us at Notre Dame through mutual friends that something dramatic had happened to them through their contact with the group. We got wind of remarkable happenings at a retreat they had led at Duquesne. In a letter, one of them wrote, 'I hope all this doesn't sound too enigmatic, but the whole experience has been rather like having all our suspicions about the truth of Christianity confirmed.' We were intrigued. One of the men was coming to our campus shortly, he said, so he would tell us the whole story then.

When he arrived, about twenty of us gathered in the living room of Kevin and Dorothy Ranaghan, not far from the Notre Dame campus. There we sat in amazement as we heard stories of the extraordinary events of the Duquesne Weekend. Students had been baptised in the Spirit. Some had spoken in tongues. They had prayed for hours, even days, in fervent ardor. Healings had taken place and even miraculous answers to prayer. The man who related these events was obviously himself 'on fire'with the Spirit and bold in faith.

I sat on the carpet across the room from him and thought to myself, 'This is really true.' My next thought was, 'Get me out of here!' I didn't want anything to do with it. I sat in stony silence. I was gripped by an intense struggle. I believed what I was hearing and longed to share the faith and power being described for us. At the same time I felt an immense resistance. It wasn't a resistance provoked by this encounter, I realised. It had been dogging me for months.

In fact, for the previous two months I had felt an increasing burden of discouragement and dryness in my Christian life. Though I had persevered in my efforts at daily prayer and evangelisation, I confessed to my spiritual director that I felt helpless to overcome this interior obstacle. Now I wrestled with it again as I felt both inspired and repelled by the visitor's vivid account of the Duquesne Weekend. At the end of the evening he closed with a prayer for us. As he began I was struck by the power and conviction of his prayer. 'Here,' I thought, 'is a man who speaks with authority. This must have been the quality people saw in Jesus.' I struggled to respond.

As he prayed I repeated each word in my mind slowly and deliberately. He prayed for two things: first, that we would all be free from the influence of Satan, and, second, that we would be filled with the Holy Spirit. It couldn't have taken more than two minutes.

I awoke the next morning feeling like a different person. The strain of the last two months was entirely gone. I felt cheerful and buoyant, full of faith in God. The conflicting feelings of the night before had fled and I was eager to pursue further this experience of the Holy Spirit. Above all, I felt that a change had taken place in me through some action of God. Later that evening I found out what had happened.

Nine of us gathered again with the Duquesne professor to ask for prayer. He went around the room to each person, laying hands on each one and praying briefly for each to be filled with the Holy Spirit. No one said a word. Each seemed to sink into silent and deep prayer. There was no other sound except for his voice. I was the last.

He stopped in front of me and, as he had done eight times previously, commanded in the name of Jesus that any evil spirit should depart from me. A shudder went through my body and I briefly smelled the distinctive odor of burning sulphur. I recognised it immediately from my experience of chemistry lab. I knew instantly it was a sign from God that through this man's prayer I had been freed from the oppression of an evil spirit. This was the obstacle I wrestled with in vain for so long. I felt a great sense of relief and gratitude.

When he laid his hands on my head and prayed for me to be filled with the Holy Spirit, I tried to concentrate on having faith in God. I didn't speak in tongues or experience any other sensation. But I wasn't concerned. I had understood that the key to the Baptism in the Spirit was asking in faith and that not everyone had a dramatic reaction. Besides, the exorcism experience was startling enough.

We concluded by talking briefly about what we had experienced. None had prayed in tongues but all seemed to believe that God had done something. We would wait to see what the effect would be. As we went outside that early March evening, it was cold and crisp. The night was clear and there was still a bit of snow on the ground. Some people started climbing up in the trees and swinging from the branches, throwing snowballs at one another and generally acting like a bunch of intoxicated college students. We laughed as we piled into the cars and joked about the disciples at the first Pentecost. Hadn't they also behaved as if they were 'drunk with new wine?'

In the days that followed we checked in with one another frequently. 'Did anything happen to you? Did you hear from anyone else in the group?' I awoke one morning to find Gerry Rauch, my roommate, sitting on the edge of the bed in his pajamas reading the Bible. 'Wow!' he said. 'This is fantastic! I'm going to read this whole thing.' Within a few weeks he did.

Others reported the same phenomenon. Scripture seemed to come alive. They couldn't get enough of it. The same with prayer. 'Did you hear that Tom has been praying in the chapel for five hours?' I was asked. 'He doesn't want to leave.' I had the same experience when I went to pray. Hours flew by. The sense of God's presence was overwhelming. A visitor to the chapel would have wondered what was wrong with that guy on the back pew who just seemed to sit there for so long with the big smile on his face. I ran into Bert Ghezzi at the snack bar in the basement of the library. 'Did you experience anything?' he asked. 'No,' I said, 'but I feel like my whole life has changed.'

Most striking to me was the experience of talking with some of my friends whom I had been trying to evangelise all year. We had often talked long into the night about their doubts about Christianity. Now I was startled to find myself witnessing to them confidently and seeming to have exactly the right thing to say. We ended up praying together - an inconceivable outcome just a few days ago. Didn't Jesus say not to worry about what to say, the Holy Spirit would give us the words? Others were having the same experience.

A week later we would meet a group of Pentecostals and have our first experience of praying in tongues. Soon we would offer our first prophecies and later see healings. But for now it was clear - the Holy Spirit had indeed come in answer to our prayers. Our hearts were on fire, our lives transformed.

Both then, and now, so many years later, it seemed to me that the most significant transformation in our lives brought about by Baptism in the Holy Spirit was a fundamental shift in dynamism. Prior to this experience of the Holy Spirit I would say that our Christian lives were characterised by a dynamic of dedication and idealism. God had touched us through the Cursillo and our shared apostolates and we had grasped a great vision of his call. We did our best to dedicate our lives to fulfilling it. The down side of such an approach is that it is susceptible to the temptation to self-reliance. One can easily slip into the unconscious attitude that we must 'work like everything depends on us *and* pray like everything depends on us.'

With Baptism in the Spirit a revolution took place. Suddenly we were experiencing God's action as the primary dynamic. We were now in the position of trying to cooperate and respond. Steve Clark once compared this shift to the experience of trying to push a car uphill. As long as you kept pushing, the car would keep moving. But as soon as you let up for a moment the car would roll back down to the starting point. Such was much of our experience of Christian ministry. The forward momentum seemed dependent on our own continual effort. Now, it seemed, the car was rolling downhill with a momentum of its own, gathering speed as it moved. We were no longer pushing, we were being carried along at an accelerating pace, hanging on for dear life. The Holy Spirit was now the source of dynamism beyond anything we had experienced before.

In fact, it quickly became clear that we had much to learn about yielding to the Holy Spirit instead of just pursuing our own vision and agenda. I vividly recall an early lesson from the Lord that impressed this new principle upon me. Steve, Ralph, Gerry Rauch, and I spent the summer of 1967 together in East Lansing. We had been baptised in the Spirit less than three months but our coming together had been planned for two years. Our intention was to work together in campus ministry. Our problem was being without a campus to work on. In addition to spending the summer in prayer and various writing projects, we had one major agenda item - to figure out where to go in the fall.

Early on we prayed together and asked the Lord which campus he wanted to lead us to. There was a prophecy, 'Seek me. Put me first in all things. Set aside every concern and seek me above all things.' For five minutes we all would pray fervently, trying to 'seek the Lord.' Then again we would pray for guidance. And again the Lord would say 'Seek me. Put me first.'

A week or so later we tried again. 'Lord, where do you want us to go? What's the next step? We can't stay here forever. The lease on our apartment runs out at the end of the summer. Where are we going to go?' And the Lord would respond, 'Seek me.'

Finally we began to understand the message. We tended to look at seeking God, drawing close to God in prayer, as the means by which we would find out what to do. But God was saying that the most important thing to do was to draw close to him. This wasn't just a means to another end. We began to take the Lord seriously and concentrated on putting our relationship with him first and our service to him second.

When summer ended we still had made no decision for the future. The lease ran out, we packed our bags, and drove to Notre Dame to conduct a conference on campus ministry. When the weekend conference ended, we helped others load up their cars and waved as they drove off. When everyone had left we locked the door of the retreat centre, put our bags in the car, and then stopped short. 'Hey, wait a minute! Where are we going?' It dawned on us that we didn't have a place to live, didn't have a plan, *and* didn't have a key to the retreat centre. We climbed through a window to find a place to sit down and pray.

'Lord,' we said with greater earnestness, 'where should we go?' Again came a prophetic word, 'Seek me first. Don't worry about that. Just seek me.' This approach was creating a crisis!

We went to visit with some friends in Michigan for the next week. In return for room and board, we helped them excavate a new sewer line. We continued our discussions and prayers throughout the week, finally culminating in an all-night vigil on the last night.

Dawn came as we sat together on the floor talking about what God wanted for us. It was becoming clear at last. He was saying, 'It's okay to accept the invitation to go the University of Michigan campus in Ann Arbor. That is a good place to go. But it doesn't matter so much where you go. What matters most of all is that you seek me above all. That you put me first, above your work, above your decision, above your future.'

I began to understand that God wasn't just giving us a word for a brief period of time. He was giving us a command for our lives. In the experience of Baptism in the Holy Spirit we had seen how powerfully God could work. We had also seen how little could be accomplished by human effort alone, even dedicated and idealistic effort, if God did not empower it by his Holy Spirit.

No human action could produce the Holy Spirit. We could receive him and his power only by drawing near to God himself. In fact, when we fell into the temptation of relying on our own efforts and power, God would allow us to experience failure and frustration until we would turn again to him and seek to yield to his Spirit.

In the years that followed the Duquesne Weekend and the outpouring of the Spirit at Notre Dame, a worldwide movement developed. I travelled throughout the country witnessing to God's action and introducing others to Baptism in the Holy Spirit. The 'career' that I had hoped for in college - to devote myself to evangelisation - materialised in the form of ministries that grew out of the Charismatic Renewal movement.

I met my wife through a charismatic group and my entire adult life has been shaped by the profound experience of the Holy Spirit that began in 1967. And, yes, I still wrestle with the tendency to 'take the ball and run with it' instead of following the guidance of the Holy Spirit and relying on his power.

Shortly after my initial encounter with the Holy Spirit and spiritual gifts, I found a way to describe to others the enormous impact this had had on my Christian faith. I used to say then, and still would today, 'I no longer just *believe* in Pentecost. I've *seen* it.'

MY LIFE WAS NO LONGER IN MY OWN HANDS

A TESTIMONY BY GERRY RAUCH

Gerry Rauch is a 1967 graduate of University of Notre Dame. He and his wife Marla live in Ypsilanti, Michigan. He has six children and ten grandchildren. Gerry is a member of the Pauline Holy Family Institute, and works in the formation of future priests at three Catholic seminaries. He is also President of Annunciation Institute, a non-profit organisation that provides resources for ministry of the word and for growth in the theological and cardinal virtues. Testimony and photo, 2015

God was at work in my life from the very beginning. In so many ways, he let me know himself and his love, and made me want to love him in return. I grew up in a wonderful Catholic family, and attended Catholic schools from kindergarten through college. I have great memories of the sisters of St. Francis, St. Joseph and St Dominic, and of many diocesan priests – and at the University of Notre Dame, priests of the Holy Cross. They all taught me about Christ, the history of the Church, and the lives of the saints. I wanted to live my life in the same way as the saints, but that possibility seemed to be reserved for other places far off, and for times long ago.

A new door opened, however, near the end of my freshman year at Notre Dame. A friend invited me to go with him to a Mass attended by people who had come together through the Cursillo Movement. These people were different – as a group I mean. Their faith was more obvious, more definite, more expectant, more woven into their everyday lives. If I had encountered them one by one in other settings, I don't think anything would have seemed unusual or remarkable. Here and now at this Mass, however, the way they were together was a manifestation of something I knew my heart wanted.

I attended a Cursillo weekend that summer, and during the following school year, continued to go to the meetings of the movement at Notre Dame, slowly growing in my understanding that it was Christ himself, alive today, who was working in my life.

At one of the Cursillo meetings, a speaker said, 'When you pray, don't just speak to God; also listen Him.' That seemed far fetched – that God would directly speak to me. During the next summer break, one day alone in my apartment, I decided to put what he had said to the test, fully convinced I would not hear a thing. I knelt down, telling myself, 'I will wait five minutes in silence. Nothing will happen and that will show he was wrong.' As soon as I put everything else out of my mind, to do nothing but listen, I was startled because I immediately knew Christ was present in person. He was standing across the room with arms outstretched, the way he died on the cross. There were tears running down his face and he said to me, 'Come to me.' I could not comprehend what that might mean. 'But, Lord, I have been with you all my life.' He repeated, 'Come to me.' Then I understood what he meant –it was the stance I was taking toward him that was the problem. Instead of expecting him to recognise me as 'a good Catholic kid,' I needed to be repentantly and gratefully at his feet, for all he had forgiven, and for all he done for me. That was the beginning of my understanding that God acted not only long ago and far away.

Fast forward to senior year at Notre Dame. I had continued to be more and more active in the Cursillo group, when some friends from Duquesne University wrote and told us about their experiences with the Holy Spirit during an event we eventually called 'the Duquesne Weekend.' The report was dramatic and riveting: our mysterious and transcendent God again coming to people today, people we knew. As the letter was being read, I remember becoming afraid. In my imagination, this all could mean I should immediately leave school and become a street preacher, standing like some wild eccentric on a soapbox, haranguing people that 'Jesus Saves'. I did not want to be like that. In the end, that's not what happened, but I was sensing something accurately – that this news meant my life was no longer going to be in my own hands.

Those feelings of fear were real, but thankfully short-lived. The person reading the letter, told us that someone from the Duquesne weekend happened to be visiting Notre Dame in a few days. Relief! Before doing anything radical, I could wait to find out more from a sane university person.

We gathered to meet him at Bert Ghezzi's apartment and he told us about the Duquesne experiences in detail. We were eager for the same things to happen to us, and asked him to pray with us to be 'baptised in the Holy Spirit'. How many were present that night? Others might remember more accurately. Twelve? In any case, he prayed over us, at first seemingly without result. I felt no changes, no presence of God, nothing spiritual. Outwardly, it seemed like others present were also unmoved – although later they explained that they were experiencing dramatic interior workings of God.

By the next day I was too. The biggest change for me had to do with reading scripture. Every word of the Bible was now full of power. I found it hard to stop reading and pay attention to anything else. Other parts of life also began to unfold in new ways. Visitors came at every time of day and night, wanting to talk about what was going on. Reporters interviewed us, and usually got the story distressingly wrong. Still their reports brought out more people who wanted to hear. And we were experiencing plenty to share: praying in tongues, interpretation of tongues, physical healings, deliverance from evil spirits – true 'Acts of the Apostles' scenarios.

My new gift to read the scriptures as words of life and power has remained with me over a lifetime, and turned out to be key to my eventual career – with charismatic covenant communities and Catholic media; with Cardinal Suenens in Belgium and at the Vatican; with three seminaries, teaching future priests how to use the scriptures in ministry. It did turn out to be true that my life was no longer in my own hands, but that meant it was full of marvels, not something odd-ball and eccentric.

Over the years, I have to say growing in Christ came slowly in the ways that matter most. I thank God though, because the Charismatic Renewal also meant that 'he gave marvellous comrades to me' to help me along the way – from those earliest days of the renewal Steve Clark, Jim Cavnar, Ralph Martin, Fr. Charles Harris, Bruce Yocum, and my eventual wife, Marla Olmsted. She came to the Charismatic Renewal by her own path of the wondrous deeds of God, and wanted to love him in return as much as I did. Over the years, so many others have been dear and supportive friends in Christ.

In fact, that is what I would emphasise the most. I encountered a new way of life first at that Cursillo Mass. Then we experienced the beginnings of the Charismatic Renewal together. Which one of us, if any, would have ventured on such a history alone? How could this have happened without God bringing us together first, to be ready to receive these graces of the Holy Spirit? Having ventured out, we saw the Renewal become a worldwide phenomenon with spiritual benefits no one could number. We have continued in it together, with the Holy Spirit crying out in our hearts, 'Come, Lord Jesus!'

A RENEWAL OF CHARISMATIC GIFTS

A TESTIMONY BY FR. EDWARD O'CONNOR, C.S.C.

Fr. Edward O'Connor, C.S.C., is a pioneer in the Catholic Charismatic Renewal and author of one of the first books on the Renewal entitled The Pentecostal Movement in the Catholic Church (Ave Maria, 1971). His theological expertise lent great credibility to the Renewal in its early years. He provided much appreciated guidance for students at University of Notre Dame throughout the formative years of the Renewal. This article is reprinted with permission from Pentecost Today, Vol. 40, Number 1, Winter, 2015. Photo, 2015.

The name 'Charismatic Renewal' comes from the 'charisms' of the Holy Spirit, of which St. Paul speaks in several texts, especially in I Corinthians 12: the gifts of tongues, prophecy and healing, the power to work miracles, discernment of spirits and others. Judging from the way St. Paul speaks, these gifts seem to have been a common part of the life of the early Church, so that the apostle had to give his readers regulations on how to use them. Over the first few centuries, however, they largely disappeared, occurring only in the lives of exceptional mystics.

The charisms reappeared at the beginning of the twentieth century in some Protestant churches in Kansas and California. Most Protestants rejected them, with the result that a new type of church, called 'Pentecostal', was formed. The Pentecostals soon became the fastest growing denomination in the world

.

In 1967, the Pentecostal movement penetrated into the Catholic Church at Duquesne University in Pittsburgh. The first people involved were two young theology professors, both former students of mine at Notre Dame. While preparing for a retreat which they had organised for students, the two of them both had a profound experience of the presence of the Holy Spirit through prayer to be baptised in the Holy Spirit. This led them to focus the retreat on the Holy Spirit. It was attended by about twenty-five students and two professors, and climaxed with a dramatic experience of the Holy Spirit by many who were present. Most of them found themselves speaking 'in tongues,' and several received other gifts.

The two professors visited Notre Dame shortly thereafter, told about their experience, and prayed over some of our students. This was the beginning of the Renewal at Notre Dame. From here, as well as from Ann Arbor, it spread across the country and around the world.

The Catholic bishops were somewhat uneasy about this movement at first, but after interviewing several of the leaders, they accepted it. Pope Paul VI was also very concerned about this movement, but Cardinal Suenens from Belgium reassured him. The present Pope, when archbishop of Buenos Aires, had been very sceptical about the charismatics, but later accepted them wholeheartedly. 'They are a grace of the Spirit' *(The World Seen from Rome, Zenit 130729).*

The most famous charism is also the one most misunderstood. *Glossalalia* (praying or speaking in tongues) does not mean the ability to converse in a language one has never learned, though there are instances of such over the centuries. It is primarily a gift of prayer, in which a person finds himself speaking words he himself does not understand. He senses the presence of the Holy Spirit speaking through him. It is also, as Paul makes clear, like prophecy when spoken in a group and accompanied by the charism of interpretation.

Prophecy, however, is also misunderstood. It doesn't necessarily mean prediction of future events, although it includes that. Essentially, prophecy is a message God gives one person to be communicated to another or group. Obviously, the crucial question is whether the message really comes from God or is the work of imagination; but often there are very convincing signs that it is genuine. In group settings it is the discernment of the body that confirms it as God's word. There is much more to the gift of tongues and prophecy than can be addressed here.

In any case, these charisms are only the external manifestations of the movement. More important is the *Renewal* brought about in the lives of the participants: the peace, joy and love they experience, which makes them eager to praise the God who has so deeply touched their lives.

In Spiritu Sancto

A Testimony by Léon-Joseph Cardinal Suenens

Cardinal Suenens of Belgium, one of the four moderators of the Second Vatican Council, was one of the first champions of the Charismatic Renewal in the Catholic Church and was given special pastoral responsibility for it by Pope Paul VI and Saint Pope John Paul II. Although he was not involved until the early seventies, his article is included here because he played such an important role in the development and protection of the Renewal. This article is reprinted with permission from Goodnews magazine, March, 1992 . Photo, 1990s

'I Have Come To Bring Fire To The Earth And How I Wish It Were Blazing Already.' Luke 12:49

When I was consecrated a bishop I chose as a motto *'In Spiritu Sancto'* (in the Holy Spirit) symbolised by a silver dove taking off from an azure ground which was a symbol of Mary. This was 'in a nutshell' my entire programme of life: profound union with Mary's fiat in order to welcome the grace and force of the Holy Spirit. On the ecclesial plane it was the expression of my desire to be at the service, not of an administrative or canonical church, but of a church open to unforeseen graces and the Holy Spirit's surprises.

The Second Vatican Council marked an important ecumenical opening-up, both because certain important and positive texts in this direction were accepted by vote, and also because there were present about a hundred observers, Orthodox, Anglican, and Protestants of many persuasions. The Council allowed for many frank and friendly contacts and, when it was over, a new apostolic field opened up to me in the United States, as I was invited by some of the non-Catholic observers to prolong our dialogue in their respective churches and universities.

During my visits to the United States I heard a lot of talk about an astonishing religious renewal which had started at the beginning of the century. Little by little it was accepted by the traditional Protestant churches and in 1967 manifested itself in the Catholic Church. This spiritual renewal affected universities and the most diverse religious communities and parishes.

At that time I was writing a book already heralded under the title, *The Holy Spirit, our Hope*. I stopped writing, saying to myself that if the Holy Spirit was a work, even on the other side of the world, I had to go and see what was happening. And all the more so, because there was talk of a revival of charisms, for the cause of which I had pleaded at the Council.

I went to some of the principal centres, namely Ann Arbor and South Bend. There I met a French group conducted by Pierre Goursat, the future founder of the Emmanuel community in Paris, who was on sabbatical leave abroad. The unexpected meeting in America attested to our common wish to hear and eventually to understand what 'The Spirit is saying to the Churches.'

When I came into contact with these first Catholic charismatic communities, in university circles, I understood that Pentecostal grace was at work, and that it was not a question of a movement – there was no founder, no rule, no precise structure – but the breath of the Spirit which was vital for many aspects of life and indeed for all movements, whatever they are.

I informed Pope Paul VI of this current which was spreading with prodigious speed in the five continents and which affected the most diverse areas. On the occasion of the Holy Year in 1975 I had suggested that the Catholic leaders of this Renewal come on pilgrimage to Rome with a view of witnessing to their faith and their faithfulness to the Church.

Some prominent Protestants were invited to take part as well and came to Rome for the feast of Pentecost, which thus took on a moving ecumenical dimension. Paul VI welcomed warmly the ten thousand pilgrims coming from the most diverse countries and in his homily the Holy Father called the Renewal 'the good fortune for the Church and the world' (this phrase is sometimes translated 'a chance for the Church').

Here Pope Paul asked me to oversee the integration of the Catholic Renewal into the heart of the Church. I accepted this mission and, among other things, undertook to publish a series of Malines Documents of which the first – a collective work done by a highly qualified international group – forms a kind of doctrinal and pastoral charter for Catholic Charismatic Renewal.

It was a question of freeing the Catholic Renewal from all 'Pentecostal' ambiguity, and to immunise it against the temptation that has recurred ceaselessly through the ages, to bring Christians together outside their churches in a 'Super Church of the Holy Spirit'. Such a church was closely analysed by Cardinal de Lubac in his book on Joachim of Fiora.

I invited Ralph Martin and Steve Clark, the best known of the American pioneers, to come with a whole group to live in Brussels in order to follow up the dialogue and help with this integration of the Renewal in the Church.

With the passing of time the phrase of Paul VI on the Renewal as 'good fortune' (or 'a chance') for the Church remains a wish only partially fulfilled, because this grace was not grasped at the very level of the Church or taken to its heart.

To interpret the Renewal as a 'movement' among other movements is to misunderstand its nature; it is a movement of the Spirit offered to the entire Church and destined to rejuvenate every facet of the Church's life.

The soul of Renewal – Baptism in the Spirit – is a grace of Pentecostal refreshment offered to all Christians.

- Would that our theologians, who have experienced themselves the outpouring of the Spirit, would analyse it and put it in context.

- Would that our pastors would reflect on this baptism as being a possibility to Christianise in depth our Catholics, who are already baptised and confirmed sacramentally.

- Would that all Christians would express their faith externally in a joy which speaks and sings – even in tongues – not foreign ones, but in complete freedom of word in deep union with the Holy Spirit, who prays in us by sighs beyond all words (Rom. 8:26).

For my friends in Renewal all over the world, I should like to say that the Renewal is destined for the entire Church, and that their constant preoccupation should be that the waters of the river flow into the sea in loyalty to their source.

A Christian is not fully a Christian unless he is the maker of Christians. The cenacle is the place where Christians allow themselves – in welcoming the Holy Spirit – to be transformed by prayer. But it is also the place from which one goes out to bring the fire of Pentecost to one's brothers. The tongues of fire are there to remind us to conquer our silence, our fears and our mutism.

AN EXPERIENCE OF THE HOLY SPIRIT

A TESTIMONY BY PATRICK BOURGEOIS

Dr. Patrick L. Bourgeois was one of the Duquesne faculty members who received the Baptism in the Spirit at the Chapel Hill prayer meeting in January, 1967, immediately preceding the Duquesne Weekend. He received his B.A. in philosophy and his M.A. in religion from Notre Dame Seminary in New Orleans, Louisiana. He received a second M.A. in liturgical theology from Notre Dame and a Ph.D. from Duquesne. Dr. Bourgeois was a professor of philosophy at Loyola University in New Orleans for many years. He and his wife, Mary have two children. Testimony and photo, 1992

At the end of 1966 I made a Cursillo. This was an enriching experience of Christian community, but for me it was one step on the way to further growth. Shortly after that, a colleague and close friend prevailed upon me to read two books: *The Cross and the Switchblade* by David Wilkerson and *They Speak with Other Tongues* by John Sherrill. I found the depth of personal and expectant faith expressed in these books of great interest.

When I had completed the books, this same colleague and another friend invited me to accompany them to a charismatic prayer meeting at Miss Flo Dodge's home in the North Hills of Pittsburgh. They had met one of its members and had been invited to attend. I went to the first meeting, in spite of an extremely tight schedule as a full-time instructor of theology and full-time graduate student in philosophy, because I sensed that somehow this could be the occasion for something important and I was not going to miss out on it. I remember sensing this importance in talking to these two colleagues. On attending the first meeting, I found it quite interesting. I had some minimal experience with spontaneous prayer gatherings some time before at Notre Dame, and was deeply impressed with that experience.

This first visit to the North Hills group left me with the awareness that these people had tasted something unique in the Christian life. It was hard to focus precisely on what it was, but it seemed to be akin to something in David Wilkerson's book. I do not recall anything spectacular during the first meeting in the North Hills, but I remember talking to one of the colleagues at his house for a couple of hours afterward and then throughout the week before the next meeting. His experience with Protestants in his youth became something of a psychological obstacle to be overcome before he could return to the meeting the next week. Since I had come from a strictly Catholic background, this was not a problem for me. Once we worked through his reservations, we were both more receptive for the meeting the following week.

The main thing which stood out in the next meeting, to which only two of the four of us returned, was our request for the Baptism in the Spirit. The members of the prayer group prayed avidly over us. That intense prayer by a strong fellowship community elicited an intense inner response. The effect of this event for this colleague and myself is now well-known.

The main immediate effect was not too noticeable, but I noticed a somewhat 'fixating' experience which emerged from the depth of my being, gradually, over the next few days. I was quite aware that it would be superficial to call this an emotional experience, unless by that some profoundly personal, spiritual emotion is meant.

It was a good experience of the total unity of the depth of my being, drawn to the sublime. I knew that some naturalistic psychologists might have ready explanations for this experience, but I was also aware that they would have great difficulty in 'explaining' its origin. At any rate, one of the results was that if

I picked up Scripture to read, or began to pray, it was difficult to stop.

Two reflections stand out, even after all these years. First, this was an inter-denominational prayer group. When something of an anti-intellectual character emerged at one of the two first meetings which we attended, someone gently but firmly squelched it as improper. Further, one of the theological points which has always impressed me from the very beginning is that the intense experience of quickening, or of releasing the Spirit, occurs within lived experience in such a way as not to be limited to one theology. This has always struck me as extremely important since it shows that, within certain limits, this experience allows for a pluralism of theologies on a second level of reflection. To me this indicates that the experience does not unequivocally lead to a fundamentalistic theology. One could say the level of this experience is pre-theological, but no one, even on the basic and pre-theoretical level, is without theological assumptions, even if they are totally implicit and subliminal. The fact is that *the experience happens within differing theological assumptions,* and on this basic pre-theological level.

The second point of note indicated above is the role of this colleague, who at first had so much difficulty overcoming emotional resistance to his background with non-Catholics. He obviously became the anointed leader of the Pittsburgh group of Catholics for half a year until he left for further graduate studies. After the Duquesne Weekend, we attended more prayer meetings in the North Hills. Then, in response to some obvious need, this colleague began holding prayer meetings at his house every Friday evening until he left town. His role in my life, in the lives of the Duquesne community, and in the Charismatic Renewal in the Catholic tradition, was of central significance.

Perhaps it should be explicitly mentioned that I did not attend the Duquesne Weekend. While I recall feeling earlier that I 'had' to attend the meeting in North Hills, my position as a full-time teacher and full-time graduate student did not allow much spare time. I didn't feel that I should take the time to go. Further, I was not as involved with the students of *Chi Rho* as the two colleagues referred to previously. However, I became very involved with the group after we began our own Friday evening home prayer meetings, which for us took the place of the weekly North Hills meeting.

In fact, my involvement became such that, as a serious student and aspirant scholar, I was keenly aware of the need to step back and reassess my commitments and priorities. Should I continue my studies, turn to this work of the Holy Spirit, or continue trying to juggle them together? I was not the kind to give a half-hearted commitment. And it was impossible to continue scholarship and be so involved. I was willing to give up my studies, but all the signs seemed to point to continuing them. I returned to New Orleans to study and later took a position at Loyola University. Thus, in the ensuing years, the signs that I should be a scholar have been continually confirmed.

The Lord has continued to work in my life and in my family. I can rejoice that I heard his call then, as I can rejoice that each day he calls more and more to enter with him in that work.

VISITED BY THE HOLY SPIRIT

A TESTIMONY BY EILEEN KARL

Eileen Karl, sister of Fr. Edward O'Connor, C.S.C., was actively involved along with her husband in the Christian Family Movement and Cursillo in the Pittsburgh area before the Charismatic Renewal began. She shares here about contact with the people from Duquesne which led to her Baptism in the Spirit. Testimony and photo, 1992

My husband and I met another Pittsburgh couple in the late fifties who had a deep impact on our lives.

The man was a professor of history at Duquesne University and his wife was busy raising their family. We were involved in CFM (Christian Family Movement) together. Our professor friend encouraged us and other couples from CFM to read books on the liturgy. He also persuaded my husband and some of the other men from our group to make a Cursillo. Out of this nucleus of couples, along with other people and priests from the area, plans were made to begin holding Cursillos in Pittsburgh.

I was rector of the first women's Cursillo in Pittsburgh. I remember how my professor friend told me about the Duquesne Weekend which had just taken place one week before our Cursillo. He and I were driving to the Cursillo as he described the Weekend. He said he thought I should know all this, just in case 'anything happened' at the Cursillo.

I was thrilled to hear about it, because a few months earlier I had been 'visited by the Holy Spirit'. I was bursting to talk to someone about it, but didn't know whom to approach. I wasn't absolutely certain he and I were talking about the same thing, so I asked to be prayed over with the laying on of hands some time later. That's when I received the gift of tongues. But the experience of the Spirit, the overwhelming thrill of the Holy Spirit, came during an established half hour prayer time that I kept while my children were either asleep or at school.

Nevertheless, I associate this grace of the Baptism in the Holy Spirit with our professor friend from Duquesne, because he somehow inspired all of us in the group. It was his inspiration, or that of the books and people he led us to, that caused me to do the things I did - the things which prepared me to receive the Holy Spirit. I am enormously grateful to him, as many people in Pittsburgh and South Bend must be.

Frequently on Sunday mornings, our friends from Duquesne were seated in front of us at Mass. As I looked at the backs of their heads, I prayed on several consecutive Sundays for my professor friend to be filled with the Holy Spirit. In our group discussions, his desire for the Spirit was apparent. I even hoped that it would be in a visible way for the whole church community to see, like a tongue of fire. I was enormously delighted to hear of his Baptism in the Spirit, especially because it overflowed into so many other lives.

Eileen Karl with Patti Mansfield and Maura McDowell

NEVER TOO OLD, NEVER TOO LATE

A TESTIMONY BY MAURA MCDOWELL

Maura McDowell graduated from Duquesne University with a BS in Education in 1967. She also holds a M.Ed. and certifications in Montessori and Good Shepherd education. She is married to Dan Malinowski and they have three children and five grandchildren. Testimony, 2015. Photo, 2004

At the recommendation of a family friend, I joined *Chi Rho* during my freshman year at Duquesne University. It wasn't a surprise to be asked as a senior, along with Gerry Higgins and Bill Gailey, to accept some responsibility for the group. Primarily we would help with arrangements of locations, times, for some of the gatherings that year of 1966-1967. This was done with and through the faculty advisor.

Sometime during the school year of 1966-67, he began a routine of meeting for 'Morning Praise' in the History Department that he chaired. Connecting with him was easier after that. There were several places on campus that *Chi Rho* gathered but 'off campus' became a little more problematic considering how many of us were commuters. Some meetings were even in the homes of the local students.

Several of us were teaching CCD at a catechetical center in the north side of Pittsburgh. The program was run by the Ladies of Bethany, a group of nuns living and working in the Diocese of Pittsburgh. These sisters were also in charge of a retreat center called The Ark and The Dove. When two of the professors involved with Chi Rho were looking at locations for a retreat, the Ark and the Dove was the choice. Miss Jacinta Van Winkle, Superior of the order, spoke with Gerry Higgins and me after CCD sessions one Saturday to go over a few points. Additionally, she made one more contact with me to ask me to remind our professors that the number of students attending had to be limited because the well's water supply might run short.

The faculty advisors required that all who attended should be present from the beginning to the end of the retreat. Since this was my Student Teaching semester and I could not make the beginning of the retreat, I counted myself out.

The Tuesday following the retreat, I was on campus for a seminar and saw Marybeth Mutmansky and Karin Sefcik. They were so excited about what happened on that weekend, they began to talk a mile a minute. It didn't make sense to me. Eventually, I heard the entire story from some others and though the stories were the same, I was very puzzled by what they said.

Because I spent the rest of the semester off campus, I had limited contact with the *Chi Rho* group. When I did join them for a few gatherings, their new behavior in prayer was so different from any other experience I had had, I felt very removed.

After graduation my separation from *Chi Rho* became more complete with two exceptions: Gerry Higgins and Tom Mangan. Tom returned from a year in the Peace Corps and visited with Gerry and me, asking a lot of questions about the weekend. Tom's brother, Dave, had been on the retreat weekend, so he had first- hand information. Our contact with Tom ended shortly thereafter.

Over the next years when we would hear of a former *Chi Rho* member, one of us would tell the other. We each worked, married, and raised our families without too much more information.

That changed for me in 1995 while I was volunteering as a Eucharistic Minister at a local hospital. At an earlier time I had told the Duquesne story to the Sister of St. Joseph who was Chaplain. When my niece Karen (semi-comatose for 19 years) developed cancer, I asked Sister to pray for her and although Sister agreed, she suggested to me that I attend a Charismatic Mass for healing. Reluctantly, I attended. I witnessed some vaguely familiar activity during and after the Mass which reminded me of the Duquesne students who had attended the retreat in 1967.

Several months later, Sister invited me to a Life in the Spirit Seminar at St. Richard's Church in Gibsonia, Pennsylvania, telling me that it would help me understand the Duquesne Weekend. My husband encouraged me to attend so that I would have 'closure' on the Duquesne experience. To my surprise, one of the speakers was Tom Mangan! We spoke briefly for the first time in twenty-eight years and he encouraged me to finish the Life in the Spirit Seminar.

I was baptised in the Spirit, not in 1967 but in 1995! Closure? Not really, but a new beginning. Never too old, never too late. God is so faithful.

MY ALL IN ALL

A Testimony by Christine Heller Rossmiller

Christine Heller Rossmiller was a student at Duquesne University and a member of Chi Rho. She received the Baptism in the Holy Spirit the day after the Duquesne Weekend and was part of the beginnings of the Catholic Charismatic Renewal on campus. She is married to John Rossmiller and has nine children and nine grandchildren. Testimony, 1992, Photo, 1985

'*Apart from me you can do nothing'* (Jn. 15:5). That's the bottom line. It's taken me a long time to learn this. Like many young Catholics who were raised in the fifties and sixties, I received the sacraments and tried to love God. There was a reverence for Father God and a tenderness and love for Jesus Christ. The Holy Spirit was to me the unknown Person of the Blessed Trinity. I was trying to follow the Lord in my life.

During high school, my desire to follow Christ grew. God was good to me. However, during my sophomore year I suffered a trauma that left an emotional and physical 'thorn' in me and an abiding fear.

When I started my studies at Duquesne University, I was a journalism major. As time went by, I became quite interested in Montessori teaching and might have changed majors had I stayed to graduate.

While at Duquesne, I went to Mass a few times a week but didn't really have a life of personal prayer. During my second year at Duquesne, I joined the *Chi Rho* Society. I was still a newcomer at the time of the Duquesne Weekend in February, 1967.1 didn't attend the retreat myself, but I heard all about it when my friends from *Chi Rho* returned.

The Monday after the retreat, February 20, Patti Gallagher told me about the gifts of the Holy Spirit that were poured out upon the group over the course of the Weekend. Patti and I were talking together in a little kitchenette off of the recreation room in St. Ann's dormitory. She began to explain a little about praying for this fullness or Baptism in the Holy Spirit and how to yield to the gift of tongues. She laid her hands on me and the Holy Spirit graced me with great peace, joy and a growing awareness of God's personal love for me - the same love he desires to manifest to all his children. I also received the gift of tongues right there in the kitchenette of the dorm recreation room! Patti herself had not yet prayed in tongues.

There were noticeable changes in the *Chi Rho* members who were baptised in the Holy Spirit. They were HAPPY! There seemed to be among them a shared secret, a joy, smiles, mirth. One of the girls referred to us as the *'O.S.G.'* or *'Order of the Silly Grin'* because we all beamed with a special kind of happiness. We enjoyed *living, reading the Bible, loving God.* That says it best. *WE ENJOYED LOVING GOD!* Small wonder. That's what we were created for.

If my memory serves me correctly, I think we were advised by some members of the clergy not to talk about our experience. I got the impression that the Holy Ghost Fathers at Duquesne didn't fully embrace this sovereign work of God. There were also members of *Chi Rho* who had not felt personally touched by this grace of the Baptism in the Holy Spirit. However, since I was a newcomer, I was not much aware of their misgivings.

After the Duquesne Weekend, I dropped out of college. My relationship with John Rossmiller was getting more serious and we were thinking of marriage. John would be graduating in December and was looking for a job. In the time following the Duquesne Weekend I became very interested in Scripture. In fact, I read the Bible *a lot* and really enjoyed it. Prayer was no longer an effort. It came easily, naturally and regularly - like breathing.

Once when a friend told me some good news, I burst out in tongues. Otherwise, the gift of tongues was more controllable. We didn't worry much about discerning the authenticity of the gifts. It all seemed to be a grand adventure with God and we trusted Him. Prayer meetings were a special time to use the gifts of the Holy Spirit. Mass became more meaningful as I listened to the prayers of the liturgy and understood in a deeper way the meaning of the sacrifice of Jesus on the altar.

After spending several weeks with Rev. Harald Bredesen in Mt. Vernon, New York, John and I got married in August, 1967. We lived in Pittsburgh until the following June. At that time, we moved to Canonsburg for six years where we made a Cursillo, and taught catechism. I attended Catholic charismatic prayer meetings occasionally, usually with a nursing baby in tow. With nine children, there was usually one baby by my side.

At one point, we moved back to Pittsburgh and formed a covenant community with other couples and single people who were involved in the Catholic Charismatic Renewal. The community eventually disbanded and the prayer meetings ended.

We now live in the country again where both John and I are active in our parish. I'm a Eucharistic minister and John has taught catechism and he lectors. Much of my personal energy has been devoted to working our sheep farm and raising our large family who are a great challenge and a great blessing to us.

The Lord has shown me, in raising our children, the preciousness of his little ones - creeping, smiling, patting - so vulnerable. He's shown me the endearing thoughtfulness of teenagers as they search for meaning in their lives, evaluating the world we live in and pondering how they can make a difference. They delight and tickle me with their humor, even as they exasperate me with their messy rooms. I have deep satisfaction as my children take their place in the world as Christians - far better than I am! We can fast and pray for our families, seeking God's healing and guidance. Sometimes He answers dramatically to show himself to them.

There will always be trials and troubles in life. Children can break your heart at times. The Lord's peace doesn't depend on what kind of day I've had. When I'm at Mass or at prayer, everything comes into perspective - the eternal perspective. Sometimes I gaze at the tabernacle and pray silently with every fiber of my being, *'It's you. It's you. You are all in all.'*

If I could state what change has taken place in my life because of the Baptism in the Holy Spirit I would say this: God has taught me to be dependent on him, not on my own strengths.

They couldn't help me anyway. But he *has* helped me. He truly is our warrior, our provision, our shield, and the only truly worthwhile one we have. Money, talent, skills, status and even hard work can't satisfy the soul with that deep-down, lasting peace that a personal relationship with our loving Father can. They all end sooner or later anyway.

The Baptism in the Holy Spirit is a release of power, not just joy and peace and God's love. Real power. It's power to drive the darkness out of our lives and replace it with God's own glorious light... steady, enduring and true. Jesus is my deepest, dearest friend. Many, many times he has consoled me. He is always at my side - unless I have left him. He is no weak and powerless friend, either, as we pray in Lauds, *'the only Son of the most high Thunderer and Son of a pure virgin.'* He guides and nudges. He slays (or so we think at the time!) and gives life.

He is more of an enigma, a paradox, a mystery to me than ever as I ponder the cross. He is a beauty inviting challenge. I shrink from those challenges as often as I surrender to them. He has healed the darkness in my life. Sometime in past, he pulled 'the thorn' from my side. He freed me from the fear of it after all this time.

What can I say so many years after the Duquesne Weekend? *Whatever the cost of coming to know Jesus more deeply, he is worth the price.* He doesn't want a one-time sacrifice. He wants everything! Each day is a deeper call, inviting a more total surrender. He showed us how to make that surrender, and he will never abandon us.

LAVISH GRACE

A TESTIMONY BY IRENE PRIMEAU

Irene Primeau graduated from Duquesne in 1968 with a B.A. in philosophy. She was a member of Chi Rho and received the Baptism of the Holy Spirit after the Duquesne Weekend. Irene lived in Bristol, Rhode Island. She has served the Charismatic Renewal in a variety of capacities over the years. Her primary apostolate has been education. Testimony, 1992. Photo, 1967

As a child I had experiences of God's love. In third or fourth grade I became aware that I was a child of God, which was a wonderful discovery. I'd go to daily Mass with my mother while I was in elementary school, even during the summer. After school, I'd usually make a visit to church just to talk to God. As I was leaving church, I'd still be aware of God's presence. I knew he was always with me. As a result of all of this, I had a tremendous attraction to what was good.

When I was in seventh grade, I had an experience in which I heard the Lord speak to me. This was the only time during my childhood that I recall hearing the Lord in a specific way. One of the sisters at school accused me of cheating and I was innocent. I was very indignant and embarrassed. Since she accused me in front of the whole class, I was very upset about it. After school, I went running off to church as usual and told the Lord what this nun had done, what a terrible person she was, and how she had broken all these commandments. Besides all this, she was one of his! I'll never forget what I sensed the Lord say to me. 'Would I ever let you go through something you couldn't handle?' I was so taken aback by that. I never forgot it. This word stayed with me in later life as well. The Lord always sustains us no matter what we have to face.

In ninth grade I was aware of the fact that the Lord was calling me more deeply to himself. But like many Catholic school girls, I was afraid that he might want me to be a nun. So, I started backing off. Even though I still attended daily Mass, emotionally I began slowly to separate myself from the Lord. At first it started out with my claiming one thing or another as my own.

I'd say, 'This is mine. That is mine,' and so on. What started out as a little wedge between me and the Lord grew to be a huge chasm. So the experiential giftedness I once had of the Lord's presence just gradually faded away.

After two years at Anna Maria College, I transferred to Duquesne with a major in philosophy and a minor in theology. I didn't have a very active relationship with the Lord, but I did attend daily Mass. I was a member of *Chi Rho* during my junior and senior years. Because I had just made a retreat, I didn't attend the Duquesne Weekend, February 17-19, 1967. When I heard the witnesses of the people who were baptised in the Spirit, I realised that they were talking about the kind of relationship with God that I had had as a child.

Patti Gallagher and some of the other *Chi Rho* members shared with me what had happened on the Duquesne Weekend. I decided to renew my Confirmation. When I recommitted myself to the Lord, the intimacy with him from my childhood days all came back. As soon as I turned back to him, I began to experience his presence with me again.

After I was baptised in the Spirit I had many experiences of God's love. One experience I remember is when I was opening up my mailbox. Over the intercom the song 'Cherish' was being played. I heard the Lord say to me, 'I cherish you'. It might seem like a small thing, but it's a word that I've never forgotten. I knew I was precious to God.

During that year I took a theology course on Orthodoxy. It was another experience of God's love coming into my life. As I attended this course I felt like the Lord was feeding me. The beautiful theology of the Holy Spirit presented there helped new life to stir within me. It was a memorable experience.

There were tremendous changes in my life after the Baptism in the Holy Spirit. My prayer deepened. I rediscovered an intimacy with Jesus. I was aware of the fact that it was through the grace of the Holy Spirit that I could relate to Jesus this way. I used Scripture much more than before and daily Mass was a rich experience. A group of us met nightly at St. Ann's dorm to pray the Divine Office and support one another. Although I didn't receive any charismatic gifts such as the gift of tongues until sometime later, the Baptism in the Holy Spirit definitely revitalised my relationship with God.

I attended the weekly charismatic prayer meetings that were held after the Duquesne Weekend. But we were not permitted to remain on campus for long. As I remember it, there were faculty members, some in the philosophy department, who had problems with the charismatic dimension taking over *Chi Rho.* There was a big 'to do' over this experience of the Baptism in the Holy Spirit. As an organisation, *Chi Rho* was split right in two. I recall that we received criticism and there was some hostility against us. Our prayer meetings had to be held in someone's apartment.

I am very grateful for my time at Duquesne. I can't even begin to tell of all the graces God lavished on me. I had a daily experience of God's love. It was like I was this empty vessel and he just filled me up. My primary memory is one of the lavish outpouring of God's grace. It wasn't just an occasional experience of his love. But day in and day out, week in and week out, month in and month out, he was showing me his love.

I had no special plans after graduation. I wrote to Fr. John Randall, a priest I knew from Providence, Rhode Island, and told him about what had happened to us at Duquesne. Fr. Randall wrote back telling me about David Wilkerson's book *The Cross and the Switchblade.* He too had been led into the charismatic dimension. After I left Duquesne I worked for a summer in the lay apostolate in the inner city in Providence. In the fall of 1968, I began teaching in the public school system for a year. Then a group of us who was baptised in the Spirit moved to Federal Hill to work full-time in Charismatic Renewal. I continued to be involved for many years at St. Patrick's School as a teacher. My primary work has been in the field of education and I've developed some materials concerning the media and children.

If I had to identify the chief benefit of the Baptism in the Holy Spirit after all these years, I'd say that it brought me into an adult commitment of my life to Jesus. He has lavished ihs grace on me. To know the Lord, to have a sense of intimacy with him, Father, Son and Holy Spirit, is an extraordinary gift. I am very grateful for all that the grace of God has given me throughout my life. I will never forget all that Jesus did for me at Duquesne. Never. And I can never thank him enough for all he's done for me since. Even through trials and difficulties, the Lord has always sustained me. He is faithful.

PRAYER TO THE HOLY SPIRIT

Heavenly King, Comforter, Spirit of truth.
Who are everywhere present and fill all things,
Treasury of blessings and Giver of life,
come and dwell within us,
cleanse us of all stain,
and save our souls,
O gracious Lord

Byzantine Liturgy

LIVING WATER

A TESTIMONY BY FR. JIM SPONTAK

Fr. Jim Spontak graduated from Duquesne University in 1971 with a B.A. in theology. He was ordained a priest of the Byzantine Catholic Church in 1975 and holds an S.T.L.(1984) in Biblical Theology from Angelicum in Rome. Fr. Spontak is pastor of Saints Peter and Paul Byzantine Catholic Church in Portage, Pennsylvania. Testimony, 1992. Photo, 2015

'I give thanks to my God at every remembrance of you, praying always with joy in my every prayer for all of you because of your partnership in the gospel from the first day until now' (Phil. 1:3).

I offer this prayer because the people who formed the *Chi Rho* Society at Duquesne really were partners in the gospel coming to me and I continue to be grateful to them. When I arrived at Duquesne in September of 1967, it was an exciting time in my life. I had contact with the campus ministry staff and attended liturgies on campus. I was already discerning my vocation to the priesthood, so I was interested in becoming involved in programs sponsored by campus ministry. I found out about an Antioch Weekend which was being given December 1-3, 1967. To this day I have notes from the talks that I had heard on that Weekend. In fact, that Antioch Weekend was a watershed moment in my life. It allowed me to encounter the Lord in a way that has been very basic to my whole Christian experience.

The people who were a part of the team giving the Antioch Weekend were folks who had attended the Duquesne Weekend in February, 1967. Because of that, I felt that participants in our Antioch Weekend were only one step removed from the initial Weekend. All the team members showed evidence that they had had a deep experience of the Lord. Although they didn't speak about it specifically, it was evident that there was a special grace which all the team members shared. Only later did I begin to know more about that.

The Antioch Weekend team included Pat Bourgeois, Marybeth Mutmansky, Jerry Cafardi, David Mangan, Patti Gallagher, Tom Verner, Karin Sefcik and our campus chaplain. There was an intensity to that Antioch Weekend and a way in which Jesus became very personal to me. At times the word of God became tangible, concrete, and personal in a way that has never again been equaled in my life. It was a unique moment of grace. Each of the talks had an impact on me. Pat Bourgeois, one of the instructors at Duquesne, gave a presentation which contained basic insights that have formed important elements in my own spirituality. Of course, these initial insights from the Antioch Weekend had to be fine-tuned, balanced, and clarified, but they still help me respond to God's call.

There was one talk given by Marybeth Mutmansky, which was the most significant and gripping for me. It left me feeling face to face with the Lord in a way that was awesome, holy, joyful, and scary all at the same time.

The talk given by Patti Gallagher also helped put me in the Lord's presence. She told a story about a family who was taking a voyage on an ocean liner. They didn't realise that meals were included in the price of the voyage, so they brought their own sandwiches. They remained in a little cabin eating sandwiches, not realising that there was a marvellous seven-course banquet that they were entitled to every day. They were trying to content themselves with their own provisions until one of the children learned about the banquet. He said, 'Let's go up there and eat. After all, we're entitled to all of this food.' I often use this story to illustrate how we hover around our own provisions when God has provided much more bountifully for us. There's a depth of life in the Spirit he makes available to us; it's already been purchased; it's waiting for us. But because we don't realise it, we're deprived. It's amazing how this story from the Antioch Weekend has stayed with me all these years.

More important than any insights gained from the talks, was the experience of being face to face with the Lord. The culmination for me was on Saturday evening when I felt a very deep need and desire to pray in the chapel with an intensity, attentiveness and awareness that was quite profound. Many of the team stayed there in prayer until the wee hours of the morning. I remember an awesome feeling of wanting to offer myself to the Lord, which is what I did. I turned to Psalm 37 and the words went through me. That psalm has become a cornerstone of my spirituality... an expression of my own sense of following the Lord. 'Trust in the Lord, and do good so you will dwell in the land, and enjoy security. Take delight in the Lord, and He will give you the desires of your heart… Wait for the Lord, and keep to His way... ' (Ps. 37:3-4, 34).

After the Antioch Weekend, I began to attend the charismatic prayer meetings on a regular basis and I became more aware of the Baptism in the Holy Spirit. It was an overwhelming time in my life... a time of a new-found joy and enthusiasm for Christ, for prayer and Scripture. It was also a time of an unusual measure of struggle. I was becoming more aware of God's presence in my life and the prayer meetings helped me learn about the experience of the Baptism in the Spirit.

As I look back, I would have appreciated some help in balancing out all the various elements in my life. I needed direction and guidance to help me to maintain a perspective that I wasn't able to keep on my own. I only continued attending prayer meetings until the fall of 1968, but I did keep in contact with people in the prayer group. As time went on, the experience of the Baptism in the Spirit began to grow in my life. I also began to discover that there was something very important in my own background as a Catholic who grew up in the Byzantine Church. This was a very important part of my spirituality and my whole experience of Church and of worship. Much of my last few years in college were spent trying to get in touch with that, and to better integrate what I had experienced earlier in the Antioch Weekend and charismatic prayer group. It was not an easy integration for me to make. In some ways, making that integration has been an ongoing process over these past years.

I'd like to close by making use of one of the gospel stories which is read in the Byzantine Church on the Fourth Sunday after Easter. It's the gospel of the Samaritan woman. I see it as a marvellous story of evangelisation. I also find in it something which helps me to identify and express the experience of that retreat, the prayer meetings and all the experiences of that first year at Duquesne.

Jesus spoke about worshipping the Father in spirit and truth and that the Father seeks such people to worship Him. The experience I had with the participants of the Duquesne Week-end helped me to know what it means to worship the Father in spirit and in truth. The story of the Samaritan woman is a story of evangelisation, of sharing the Word. I see two parallel scenes.

I see the disciples going into the town and coming back to Jesus with bread, provisions, food. Even when Jesus tries to tell them about *'something more'*, they remain preoccupied with bread. Parallel to that, I see the Samaritan woman going into the town and coming back to Jesus with disciples... women and men who come to know him and understand him. Then these new disciples continue on their own to find out about the *'something more...'* the new life Jesus came to bring.

These two contrasting images help the Evangelist say something about the Church in his own day. He may have wanted to remind people that as they are about the work of the Church, they sometimes fail to appreciate what it is that Jesus *really* hungers and thirsts for. Sometimes it's the least likely people who, in responding to Jesus, discover what He is really after. This kind of contrast might have been a helpful reminder to the Church of the Evangelist's day. It's a help to us today as well. We, who are about the work of the Church, often remain preoccupied and insensitive to what Jesus really hungers and thirsts for.

Perhaps the work of the Spirit in the Duquesne Weekend, and in the Charismatic Renewal which resulted from it, was to increase an awareness of the hunger and thirst of Jesus. It is, very simply put, the work of evangelisation, the work of sharing faith, of leading people to come and hear and experience the

Word of God more personally and more fully. It is the work of helping people learn what it means to worship the Father in spirit and truth and to drink more fully of that fountain of living water... the life which Jesus came to share with us.

I offer my own praise and thanks to God for the working of God's grace and the stirring of the Spirit in my life through the Duquesne prayer group. I close with this prayer from the letter to the Ephesians which I offer for all those who were part of my life at Duquesne, and for all those who will read this work:

> *For this reason, I kneel before the Father from whom every family in Heaven and on earth is named; that he may grant you in accord with the riches of his glory to be strengthened with power through his Spirit in the inner self, and that Christ may dwell in your hearts through faith. And that you, rooted and grounded in love, may have strength to comprehend with all the holy ones what is the breadth and length and height and depth, and to know the love of Christ that surpasses knowledge, so that you may be filled with all the fullness of God. Now to him who is able to accomplish far more than all we ask or imagine, by the power at work within us, to him be glory in the Church and in Christ Jesus to all generations, forever and ever. Amen (Eph. 3:14-21).*

THE THRESHOLD

A TESTIMONY BY JACK FLANAGAN

Jack Flanagan graduated from Duquesne University in 1969 with a B.A. in psychology. He participated in the first charismatic prayer meetings in Pittsburgh in 1967. Jack holds an M.B.A. from Eastern Michigan University and worked for AT&T in sales. He and his wife, Terri, have lived in Ypsilanti, Michigan, with their six children and have been members of the Word of God Community. Testimony and photo, 1992

I came to Duquesne University as a junior in the fall of 1967. I had just spent two years in the seminary, and although I stopped studying for the priesthood, I did not stop desiring God. I made a pact with the Lord that I would try to attend weekday liturgy on campus as frequently as I could. It was at those noon celebrations of the Eucharist that I met some people from *Chi Rho* who had a deep impact on my life.

Although I was never a member of *Chi Rho,* I was impressed by those members who were on the Duquesne Weekend. In December of 1967 the chaplain's office was sponsoring an Antioch Weekend, one of several that were scheduled for the school year. I felt it was significant that my particular Antioch Weekend took place the weekend we celebrated the First Sunday of Advent. In the Church year, Advent is a time when we celebrate the coming of the Lord Jesus. That Antioch Weekend for me was certainly an advent experience - a time when the Lord Jesus and the Holy Spirit came to me in a personal way.

The team giving the Antioch Weekend was comprised of people from the chaplain's staff as well as *Chi Rho* members who were already baptised in the Holy Spirit. I knew some of the young men and women who were baptised in the Spirit from campus.

Saturday night of the Antioch Weekend I was in the chapel praying when I began to shake all over. Then I started crying. I didn't know what was happening to me. I wondered if I was experiencing what the people on the Duquesne Weekend of February, 1967, had encountered.

As I listened to the talks that Weekend and conversed with the team members who were baptised in the Spirit, several things impressed me. First, it was very clear as I listened to people like Marybeth Mutmansky, David Mangan and Patti Gallagher, that God was not a conclusion or a deduction for them; He was a *person*. God was *real*. He wasn't *'something'* they figured out by the use of their reason alone. He was *'Someone'*, near at hand, who was revealing Himself to them. Even though I had been in the seminary for two years with other young men who were seriously pursuing the priesthood, I had not experienced that level of personal encounter with God before. I was meeting people that weekend who proclaimed a God who is alive and present. They spoke of him like they actually knew him.

Second, I could see that for them God was not only alive and present, He was *active*. The Duquesne Weekend folks actually *expected* God to act. They expected him to speak to them through Scripture. Now, I had always hoped it would be that way and I had some kind of expectation that God would speak, but it did not match the degree of expectant faith in this group.

It was striking to see the way Scripture came alive. God would give insight, wisdom, clarity and guidance through His word. We read that 'the word of God is living and active, sharper than any two-edged sword' *(Heb. 4:12)*. I began to experience how alive and powerful His word can be.

I remember that within a week of the Antioch Weekend, Patti Gallagher came up to me and asked, 'Jack, have you ever read

1 Corinthians 12?' As a matter of fact, I had just picked up my Bible that morning and it fell open to that very passage in 1 Corinthians 12 on the gifts of the Holy Spirit! 'Oh', she said, 'I thought the Lord was going to give that to you.'

Even though I'd studied the Scripture in the seminary, it had been more of an academic exercise. I found myself longing for God to reveal Himself to me in a personal way through His word. One day I prayed, 'Lord, speak to me like you do to Patti.' I parted the Bible at random and came upon this verse from Psalm 145:18, 'The Lord is near to all who call upon Him, to all who call upon Him in truth.' So, I began to respond to that word by calling upon the Lord saying, 'Thank you, Lord. I call upon your name. In truth do I call upon your name. I know that you are near to me, as it says in your word.' In prayer, I responded to the revelation I had received through God's word. And as I did, my relationship with him grew.

I remember that another time I asked the Lord a question in prayer. I said, 'Lord, why did you come?' Again I opened Scripture at random and read John 10:10. *'I have come that they may have life, and have it more abundantly.'* Here was God speaking to me, directly, personally - revealing himself as I reached out to him.

This expectation that God would speak his word to us was very evident at the charismatic prayer meetings I began attending after the Antioch Weekend. People brought their Bibles expecting to use them, and God spoke.

A third thing that impressed me about the Duquesne Weekend folks was that I could see evidence of the reality of God's call. They believed that God has a plan for our lives, that he reveals his plan as we seek him, and that we can begin to move ahead in response to God's will.

Some of these young men and women had been living in Mt. Vernon, New York, the previous summer. I heard testimonies about God's guidance and provision for them there. It was clear that the Lord was doing a powerful work by pouring out his Holy Spirit in the Church. I felt a deep desire to be part of that work as I heard their witness.

A fourth thing which impressed me about my Spirit-filled friends was their joy. Knowing God, responding to God's call, was a joyful experience. In the prayer meetings, in the songs, in the praise and worship, there was a sense of excitement. As college students, we could have been doing any variety of things with our time; there were obviously a variety of campus activities, including fraternity and sorority life. But being in the Lord's presence brought so much joy and life that this is what we chose.

The fifth thing God showed me through that group from the Duquesne Weekend was the place and importance of community. I could see in the early prayer meetings such a spirit of brotherly love. I didn't sense any ambition or rivalry. We were a group of Christians having a mutual experience of the Lord, each one contributing his or her gift for the common good. Later on, my apartment was used for prayer meetings. A real desire for community was born in me as a result of those experiences. Over the years that followed, I even relocated to be part of communities in Erie, Pennsylvania; Steubenville, Ohio; and finally Ann Arbor, Michigan, where my family and I now live as members of the Word of God Community.

Another thing which impressed me on that Antioch Weekend was the authenticity of the witness given. These folks were genuine and honest when they spoke about the Lord. They weren't pushing their experience on us. They were simply witnessing to the reality of God's love. I sensed that what was shared was said to glorify the Lord, not to glorify the speakers. They really seemed to want to lift Jesus up so that he might draw all to himself (cf. Jn. 12:32). They weren't out to win converts for themselves, either. I later heard from them that they were imprudent in some of their witnessing after the Duquesne Weekend. But by December, 1967 when I met them, they were more sensitive in sharing their experiences of the Lord.

And finally, I was struck by the reality of prayer. I had always been taught that prayer was a two-way communication. But in my experience until then, except in rare instances, prayer was more of a one-way communication. Here were people who actually encountered God in prayer. It was two-way communication. It had an almost contemplative quality to it. It was a deep encounter with God.

These were not just perceptions of what was happening to the people from the Duquesne Weekend. These things were becoming very real in my own life as well. For a hungry heart, these are realities that attract and draw. It's tremendous to know that God is real, personal and active; to know that he speaks through His word and reveals His plan; to know that in his presence there is fullness of joy; to know the companionship of brothers and sisters in Christ; to know the peace and power of personal prayer. I was attracted by these realities.

When I left to attend the December Antioch Weekend, I brought along a book I had acquired that preceding week, Teilhard de Chardin's *Letters from a Traveller.* I had hoped to find some time on the retreat Weekend to look up a letter I had used the previous year in seminary in some report, and to reflect on it. There was a statement in this letter to the effect that there is a threshold to be crossed, and when you cross this threshold you will know the freedom of being a son of God. I had hoped to identify that threshold on the Weekend and to cross it. However, the Antioch Weekend schedule was very full, and I never had time to even open the book, let alone look for this particular letter. I remember packing up the book Sunday night, and placing it at the bottom of my laundry bag, which served as my official collegiate suitcase. It was a hardback edition, so it went to the bottom, clothes followed and then papers, including a holy card from the retreat on top. When I returned to the dorm that night and dumped out the laundry bag contents, to my amazement, the holy card was in the de Chardin book. I wondered, 'Is this one of Patti's miracles?' I carefully opened the book where the card was now located, and sure enough, that was the page where the letter was located. The 'threshold' to the freedom of the sons of God for me was receiving the Baptism in the Holy Spirit. A whole new level of encounter with God and with His grace was opened to me.

After that Antioch Weekend I began attending the Friday night prayer meetings, where the Lord continued to manifest Himself in exciting ways. I recall that the morning of my second prayer meeting I had an interesting thought. I said to myself, 'Wouldn't it be funny if I spoke in tongues tonight?' Then I caught myself and said, 'Hey, the Lord hears those kind of thoughts.' And I had a two-fold reaction. One was fear… 'What's going to happen tonight?' The other was expectation and excitement…'What's going to happen tonight?'

It happened that there were three travelling ministers who came to our prayer meeting that night, because they had heard about the outpouring of the Holy Spirit among Catholics and had wanted to see it for themselves. When the meeting was over and I still had not spoken in tongues, I was somewhat disappointed and wondered if God really heard my prayer that morning. As I was thinking these things, one of the ministers approached me and asked if I was baptised in the Holy Spirit. I answered, 'I think so.' Then he asked if I had prayed in tongues. And I knew at that moment God was answering my prayer. When I told him no, he asked me if I wanted to. I knew God was giving me a choice. My answer was, 'Yes.'

We went into a back room where we prayed for the gift of

tongues. I could feel an anointing in my mouth and tongue, but I felt so embarrassed because all I had was two syllables. The syllables were 'Ah' and 'ba', 'Ah-ba', 'Ah-ba'. I began to speak them out and as I did the ministers became very excited and were thanking the Lord for this gift.

Later I realised that I was praying 'Abba, Abba,' which in Aramaic means 'Father, Father'. Then I remembered the passage in Galatians 4:6 where St. Paul says, 'And because you are sons, God has sent the spirit of His Son into our hearts, crying Abba! Father!' So through God you are no longer a slave but a son, and if a son then an heir.' And in Romans 8:14: 'For all who are led by the Spirit of God are sons of God. For you did not receive the spirit of slavery to fall back into fear, but you have received the spirit of sonship. When we cry, Abba! Father!' it is the Spirit himself bearing witness with our spirit that we are children of God...'

God brought me across that threshold to know the freedom of being his son when I met the folks from the Duquesne Weekend and received the Baptism in the Holy Spirit. When God gave me the gift of tongues, he made it plain that I was indeed his child as he led me to cry out, 'Abba! Father!' I praise and thank him for all his goodness in my life.

Baptism in the Holy Spirit and my growth in the Spirit since then haven't solved all my problems. I still battle temptation and repent for sin. But this experience has given me a close relationship with the Lord, and in this, a courage, a hope, and a foundation to enable me to approach the Lord daily to offer myself to him and to receive from him. 'Happy the people whose God is the Lord.' He continues to deeply satisfy and graciously meet my need for him. I also continue to experience great oneness with the Lord as I consider basic Gospel realities: he died and rose for me. He paid my debt. He took my sin upon himself to free me and bring me to life. He shed his blood to cleanse and free me as I confess my sins. His steadfast love and faithfulness is to every generation. These are truths and realities that form a foundation upon which to base our lives. I thank and praise him for all the goodness and mercy he has shown to me.

COME HOLY GHOST

Come, Holy Ghost, Creator blest,
And in our hearts take up Thy rest.
Come with Thy grace and heavenly aid
To fill the hearts which Thou hast made
To fill the hearts which Thou hast made.

O Comforter, to Thee we cry,
Thou heavenly gift of God most high
Thou fount of life and fire of love
And sweet anointing from above
And sweet anointing from above.

Praise be to Thee, Father and Son,
And Holy Spirit, with Them one
And may the Son on us bestow
The gifts that from the Spirit flow
The gifts that from the Spirit flow.

Al and Patti Mansfield on a return to the Ark and the Dove, 2007

PART FOUR
CURRENT OF GRACE

'You, the Charismatic Renewal,
have received a great gift from the Lord.
Your movement's birth was willed
by the Holy Spirit to be 'a current of grace
in the Church and for the Church'.
This is your identity: to be a current of grace.'

Pope Francis
37th Convocation of Renewal in the Spirit
Olympic Stadium, Rome, June 1, 2014

The Church's Greatest Need

You have just read the testimonies of people who say that they have experienced a personal Pentecost. The Holy Spirit has dramatically touched their lives, giving them a new love and power. Lest you conclude that this pentecostal grace, this outpouring of the Holy Spirit, is just reserved for a few privileged souls, I want to make it very clear: *The gift and the gifts of the Holy Spirit are meant for the whole Church!* The Church *needs* the Holy Spirit. The Church *needs* the gifts of the Holy Spirit as well. Read what Blessed Pope Paul VI described as the Church's greatest need at a General Audience on November 29, 1972 *(the italics are mine):*

> On several occasions we have been asked about the greatest needs of the Church… What do we feel is the first and last need of this blessed and beloved Church of ours?
>
> We must say it, almost trembling and praying, because as you know well, this is the Church's mystery and life: *the Spirit, the Holy Spirit.* He it is who animates and sanctifies the Church. He is her divine breath, the wind in her sails, the principle of her unity, the inner source of her light and strength. He is her support and consoler, her source of charisms and songs, her peace and her joy, her pledge and prelude to blessed and eternal life.
>
> *The Church needs her perennial Pentecost,* she needs fire in the heart, words on the lips, prophecy in the glance. She

> needs to be the temple of the Holy Spirit, that is, of complete purity and interior life...
> Living men, you young people, you consecrated souls, and you brothers in the priesthood — are you listening to us? *This is what the Church needs, she needs the Holy Spirit! The Holy Spirit in us, in each of us and in all of us together, in us who are the Church ... It is he, then, that the Church needs today, above all! And so may all of you always say to him: 'Come!'*[1]

Blessed Pope Paul VI, makes it clear that the Church's greatest need, its first need, is *'to live Pentecost'*.[2] All of us should place ourselves, in his words, *'windward of the breath of the Holy Spirit.'*[3] He reminded his listeners on one occasion of how frequently the Vatican Council made mention of the Holy Spirit - *two hundred fifty-eight times have been counted!*[4] With what insistence should we invoke the Holy Spirit, knowing that we will never do so in vain. Blessed Pope Paul VI, who may well be called *Pope of the Holy Spirit*, encouraged the Church to pray, *'Come, Holy Spirit; come Creator Spirit; come Consoling Spirit'*.[5]

Prophetic Women

Not only popes have spoken about a 'Perennial Pentecost' or a 'New Pentecost'. You remember the story of Blessed Elena Guerra, founder of the Oblates of the Holy Spirit in Lucca, Italy, and her many letters to Pope Leo XIII? God was using her at the turn of the last century to call for a New Pentecost. However, there are two other women, one from Mexico and another from

France, who were also inspired to speak of and to promote a New Pentecost. As a woman, I am very moved to know that the Lord was using prophetic women from around the world to announce his desire to renew the face of the earth as by a New Pentecost!

CONCHITA OF MEXICO

In 1971, I had the privilege to visit Mexico City for the first time to speak at some meetings organised by Msgr. (later Bishop) Carlos Talavera, one of the early leaders in the Catholic Charismatic Renewal in Mexico. While there, I met many priests who were part of a religious order I had never encountered, the 'Missionaries of the Holy Spirit'. They told me about their amazing foundress, Venerable Maria Concepción Cabrera de Armida, known simply as 'Conchita'. Conchita was born in San Luis Potosí, Mexico and lived from 1862 to 1937. She fulfilled all the vocations of a woman: fiancé, wife, mother of nine, grandmother, widow, and even, without being deprived of her family status, she died canonically as a religious in the arms of her children. Her prolific writings rival those of mystics like St. Catherine of Siena and St. Teresa of Avila. Conchita inspired five 'Works of the Cross' and experienced a profound mystical union with God in the midst of a seemingly ordinary family life.

Early in my marriage, my friend, Fr. George Kosicki, C.S.B., gave me a book entitled: *Conchita, A Mother's Spiritual Diary* by Fr. M.M. Philipon, O.P. I read with great interest about her experiences as a woman and a mother. I was especially captivated by what she wrote in her Diary between 1916 and 1928 about a New Pentecost. The life and mission of Conchita are not well-known, at least in the United States. Therefore, I am including excerpts from her Diary which detail what the Lord told her about a new coming of the Spirit. The Lord gave Conchita special messages for priests, as you will see. Here are some of her prophetic messages:

> On sending to the world a new Pentecost, I want it inflamed, purified, illumined, inflamed and purified by the light and fire of the Holy Spirit. The last stage of the world must be marked very specially by the effusion of the Holy Spirit. He must reign in hearts and in the entire world, not so much for the glory of his person as for making the Father loved and bearing testimony of me, although his glory is that of the whole Trinity (*Diary*, January 26, 1916).

> Tell the Pope that it is my will that in the whole Christian world the Holy Spirit be implored to bring peace and his reign into hearts. Only this Holy Spirit will be able to renew the face of the earth… May the whole world have recourse to this Holy Spirit since the day of his reign has arrived. This last stage of the world belongs very specially to him that he be honored and exalted… May the Church preach him, may souls love him, may the whole world be consecrated to him, and peace will come along with a moral and spiritual reaction, greater than the evil by which the world is tormented… May all at once this Holy Spirit

begin to be called on with prayers, penances and tears, with the ardent desire for his coming. He will come, I will send him again clearly manifest in his effects, which will astonish the world and impel the Church to holiness (*Diary*, Sept. 27, 1918).
Ask for this renewal, this new Pentecost for my Church has need of priests sanctified by the Holy Spirit. The world is foundering in the abyss since it lacks priests who will help it from falling in; priests who bear the light to shine on the paths of good; pure priests to pull out of the mud so many hearts; priests afire who will fill the entire universe with divine love... Ask, supplicate heaven that all my be restored in me by the Holy Spirit' (*Diary*, Nov. 1, 1927).

I want to return to the world in my priests. I want to renew the world of souls by making myself seen in my priests. I want to give a mighty impulse to my Church infusing in her, as it were, a new Pentecost, the Holy Spirit in my priests (*Diary*, Jan. 5, 1928).

To obtain what I ask, every priest must make a consecration to the Holy Spirit, asking him, through Mary's intercession to come to them as it were in a new Pentecost, to purify them, to fill them with love, possess them, unify them, sanctify them and transform them into me (*Diary*, Jan. 25, 1928).

One day not too far away, at the centre of my Church, at Saint

Peter's there will take place the consecration of the world to the Holy Spirit, and the graces of this Divine Spirit, will be showered on the blessed Pope who will make it... It is my desire that the universe be consecrated to the Divine Spirit that he may spread himself over the earth in a new Pentecost (*Diary*, March 11, 1928).

In 1992 when I wrote about Blessed Elena Guerra in the original edition of *As By A New Pentecost,* I had no idea that a young Brazilian priest named Fr. Eduardo Braga would one day read my book. He was moved by the story of Blessed Elena and later became Vice-Postulator of her cause for canonisation. Fr. Braga has made Blessed Elena Guerra well-known all over Brazil and it appears that the miracles needed for her canonisation will come from Brazil. As I quote from Venerable Maria Concepción Cabrera de Armida in this Golden Jubilee edition of *As By A New Pentecost,* I pray that many more people around the world will become familiar with Conchita and benefit from her teaching and her intercession. My friend, Fr. Raniero Cantalamessa, O.F.M., Cap., reminded me of Conchita's importance and her prophetic intuition concerning the new Pentecost. He remarked that Conchita was eager to see much more than simply a renewed devotion to the Holy Spirit, but a new Pentecost in all its fullness.

Marthe Robin and a Pentecost of Love

There is another woman who lived in the twentieth century named Venerable Marthe Robin, who also spoke of a New Pentecost, more specifically, a 'Pentecost of Love'. I think I first heard of Marthe Robin from Fr. René Laurentin when he visited one of our prayer meetings in New Orleans, Louisiana, in the early seventies. He told me about a French woman who had many extraordinary charisms and later, when I read her life, I discovered that indeed she was a uniquely gifted soul.

Marthe Robin was born in Chateauneuf-de-Galaure, France in 1902 and lived until 1981. Bed-ridden and blind for most of her life, she lived the virtues in a heroic fashion. She is reported to have suffered the Passion with Jesus every week for over 50 years. According to those responsible for her, she subsisted only on the Eucharist from 1930 until her death. Yet in the midst of this intense mystical life and suffering she founded, with the help of Fr. Finet, the Foyers of Charity in 1936. She received in her lifetime 100,000 visitors, including many priests who received from her a mother's love. Interestingly enough, several Catholic Charismatic Renewal communities in France, such as the Emmanuel Community and the Beatitudes Community, along with founders of many other ecclesial movements, shared a friendship with Marthe Robin.

As Martin Blake, one of Marthe Robin's biographers, has stated, '...one of the intriguing things said by Marthe to Fr. Finet, on February 10, 1936, was that God had foretold a 'new Pentecost of Love' that would be preceded by a renewal of the Church. And the laity were to have an important role to play.'[7] Remember, this was said long before the convening of the Second Vatican Council and long before the Charismatic Renewal! Blake continues,'... Pope John XXIII, twenty-three years after Marthe's prophetic statement, on May 10, 1959, asked for prayers' in order that 'a new Pentecost might gladden the Christian family', as a week later he announced that the celebration of the forthcoming Ecumenical Council would be the occasion of a New Pentecost.'[8]

On November 7, 2014, Pope Francis authorised the Congregation for the Causes of Saints to promulgate a decree recognising the heroic virtues of Marthe Robin. We await the Church's judgement on her life. From her writings we can see that she is another prophetic woman who announced the New Pentecost long before others were dreaming of it.

THE SURPRISES OF THE HOLY SPIRIT

The Lord was preparing his Church for a fresh outpouring of his Spirit through Vatican II which 'opened the windows'. Both the hierarchy and the laity were sensing a new time coming, full of opportunities and challenges. During the Second Vatican Council, Cardinal Suenens spoke forcefully in favor of the charisms, insisting that they were not just for the Church in its infancy, but for the Church of today. In 1967, just two years after the conclusion of Vatican II, the stage was set for what Cardinal Suenens called 'a surprise of the Spirit.'

This surprise of the Spirit came at the Duquesne Weekend when a group of young people were baptised in the Spirit with the manifestation of charismatic gifts, and what we now know as the Catholic Charismatic Renewal began to grow and spread around the world.

In fact, when Cardinal Suenens first heard about the Charismatic Renewal, he was writing a book called *The Holy Spirit Our Hope*. He stopped writing his book in order to investigate the reports of this possible action of the Holy Spirit, however surprising it might be. After his first personal encounter with the Renewal, he wrote the following:

> Suddenly, St. Paul and the Acts of the Apostles seem to come alive and become part of the present; what was authentically true in the past seems to be happening once again before our very eyes. It is a discovery of the true action of the Holy Spirit, who is always at work, as Jesus himself promised. He kept and keeps his 'word.' It is once more an explosion of the Spirit of Pentecost, a jubilation that had become foreign to the Church...[9]

Baptism in the Spirit Is Not Simply Personal Piety

Each testimony in this book, and the testimony of every person who has become involved in the Charismatic Renewal, refers to this grace of being baptised in the Spirit. Is it for everyone?

It is important to understand that Baptism in the Spirit is not a phrase invented by the Charismatic Renewal. All four gospels and the Acts of the Apostles (Acts 1:4-5) refer to being baptised in the Spirit. John the Baptist said, 'I baptise you with water; but he who is mightier than I is coming, the thong of whose sandals I am not worthy to untie; he will baptise you with the Holy Spirit and with fire' (Luke 3:16-17). For those who wish to refer to additional Scripture passages concerning the Baptism in the Spirit, please see Matthew 3:11, Mark 1:8, John 1:33, and Acts 11:16. Also read 1 Corinthians 12-14.

Some Catholics hold that Baptism in the Spirit is simply a matter of personal piety; an option, not a necessity. A landmark theological study by Fr. George Montague, S.M., and Fr. Kilian McDonnell, O.S.B., presents a different conclusion. Their extensive research in Scripture and Patristics has shown that the Baptism in the Spirit belongs, not in the realm of personal piety, but in the public liturgy of the Church. They have written two books: *Christian Initiation and Baptism in the Spirit: Evidence From the First Eight Centuries*, which is a scholarly work, along with a short companion booklet entitled, *Fanning the Flame: What Does Baptism in the Spirit Have to do with Christian Initiation?*[10] Consider the following excerpt from *Fanning the Flame*:

> Baptism in the Holy Spirit is captive to no camp, whether liberal or conservative. Nor is it identified with any one movement, nor with one style of prayer, worship or community. On the contrary, we believe that this gift of the Baptism in the Holy Spirit belongs to the Christian inheritance of all those sacramentally initiated into the Church.[11]

These books should be helpful in placing the Baptism in the Holy Spirit where it belongs - *at the very heart of the Church.* They illustrate that what millions are experiencing today in the

Charismatic Renewal was common in the early Church. Baptism in the Spirit is not the property of the Charismatic Renewal but is part of the heritage of every Christian.

A Big Grace!

There is a theology professor from Rome's Gregorian University who laughingly told his students he was going to give them a sophisticated theological description of the Baptism in the Holy Spirit. He said, 'Take out your pens and write this: It's a *big grace*!' A few years ago my husband and I prayed with another Jesuit from that same university to be baptised in the Spirit. One year later when we met him he told us, 'Everything in my life and priesthood is new!' And he looked like a new man! For him it was indeed 'a big grace!'

While there *are* real theological descriptions of this *big grace*, most of us who have been baptised in the Holy Spirit aren't equipped to give them. But what we *do* have is an experiential knowledge of a new love, a new peace, a new joy in the Lord... power from on high. Catholic Christian life is different than before. People like myself have looked for simple ways to describe the grace we have experienced.

We have some friends who shared a wonderful analogy to describe the Baptism in the Holy Spirit from a recent experience in their lives. For years they had noticed that the parts to their used car were unusually expensive. Then one day they learned that this vehicle had within it a police interceptor engine, more powerful than they had ever imagined. A few weeks later, the wife was on the road alone when a seedy looking character in a truck pulled up alongside her car. For miles he alternated between tailing her closely and taunting her by pulling next to her car. She felt uneasy and threatened until it dawned on her that she had within that car the very power she needed. *All she had to do was use it!* She then floored the gas pedal and that police interceptor engine propelled her to safety. Her taunter's truck was a tiny speck in the rearview mirror in no time. When she got home and told her husband, he remarked, 'It's the same thing we experienced with the Baptism in the Holy Spirit. The power was there all along. We just had to believe it and use it.' And he was right.

Our friend and coworker of 30 years, Fr. Harold Cohen, S.J., frequently used the following story to illustrate what happens in the Baptism in the Spirit. One night he was fixing a glass of chocolate milk for himself and a fellow Jesuit. Fr. Cohen poured some Hershey's chocolate syrup into the milk and it went straight to the bottom of the glass. He handed his friend a spoon and said, *'You've got to stir it up'*. Immediately he realised that he had before him a simple illustration of the Baptism in the Holy Spirit! The Holy Spirit is already present, poured out, so to speak, but we need to 'stir it up'. If the chocolate syrup is not stirred up, it remains at the bottom of the glass, and it seems to have made no difference in the flavor. But if it is stirred up, it permeates and transforms everything. It's the same thing with the power of the Holy Spirit in us. Fr. Cohen used to say, 'At the age of 40, I knelt down and asked some college kid to pray over me for the Baptism in the Holy Spirit. I felt foolish at the time, but my life has never been the same since. 'Life begins at 40' describes it for me.'

The Baptism in the Spirit is meant to be a life-changing experience of God's presence. There should be a 'before' and an 'after'. My dear friend, Fr. Jim Ferry, once told me about one of the shortest and most powerful testimonies he ever heard concerning the Baptism in the Holy Spirit. 'I had two lives; one before the Baptism in the Holy Spirit, and one after.' He attributed this statement to a Capuchin friar who visited Fr. Ferry at the House of Prayer in Convent Station, New Jersey, in 1977. Who was the friar? It was Fr. Raniero Cantalamessa, O.F.M., Cap. After being baptised in the Spirit, Fr. Cantalamessa felt led to leave his teaching position at the Catholic University of Milan and become an itinerant preacher of the Gospel. With his superior's permission, he resigned his post and made a retreat to prepare for his new mission. During that retreat he received word that Pope John Paul II had selected him to be 'Preacher to the Papal Household', a position he has held since 1980. Talk about a surprise of the Spirit!

A Definition of the Baptism in the Spirit

In 2012, the Doctrinal Commission for ICCRS, the International Catholic Charismatic Renewal Services, published an excellent pamphlet entitled *Baptism in the Spirit*. I highly recommend it! In the first pages this definition is given.

> Baptism in the Spirit is a life-transforming experience of the love of God the Father poured into one's heart by the Holy Spirit, received through a surrender to the lordship of Jesus Christ. It brings alive sacramental baptism and confirmation, deepens communion with God and with fellow Christians, enkindles evangelistic fervor and equips a person with charisms for service and mission.[12]

For me, there are at least three ways to understand what this Baptism in the Spirit is.

First, it can be understood as ***a release*** of the graces of Baptism and Confirmation which often lie dormant because of our lack of faith and expectation. This is the most common explanation.

Second, it can be understood as ***a new coming*** of the Spirit to help equip us for a new mission. Fr. Francis Sullivan, SJ, called attention to those passages in St. Thomas Aquinas wherein he refers to this 'new coming'. Pope Saint John Paul II also spoke of a new coming of the Holy Spirit upon Mary in the Cenacle to correspond to her new mission of universal motherhood given to her by her Son on the Cross.

Third, it can be understood as ***a special ecumenical grace*** being poured forth on Christians of all denominations to unite us, to help us preach the Gospel with power.

What Are the Effects of the Baptism in the Spirit?

Each testimony in this book details the effects of the Baptism in the Holy Spirit. They are manifold:

- a deepening awareness of the presence and love of God the Father
- a new understand of the Lordship of Jesus Christ
- a growth of intimacy with God in prayer
- a hunger for God's word and the sacraments
- a love for the Church
- a new power and desire to witness
- a growth in the fruit of the Spirit... peace, love, joy
- manifestations of charismatic gifts such as the gift of tongues
- an experience of the promptings and guidance of the Holy Spirit
- an awareness of the reality of spiritual warfare
- a call to purification and holiness
- a desire for Christian unity
- a call to serve the needs of others.

Countless Catholics have said that although they went through twelve years of Catholic education, they did not have a personal relationship with Jesus until they were baptised in the Spirit. They did not read the word of God nor witness to their faith. After being baptised in the Spirit, their faith came to life, they began to love God's word, to return to the sacraments, to look for ways to grow in holiness and service.

In a word, this is normal Christian life made possible by the power of the Holy Spirit! This is the kind of life Jesus calls all of us to as his disciples. In a talk Cardinal Suenens gave in Milwaukee, Wisconsin, in 1973, he made the following remarks which speak to this point:

> We don't trust him enough. We say, 'Yes, Holy Spirit, we are open to you, but not for everything. Don't give me this grace, or don't give me that one, I will choose for myself which graces you should give me… We ask to be opened and then we put our Baptism and all that it means... in a freezer... But if we are to live normal, full Christian lives, the power that we have received at Baptism has to come out of the freezer. We need a release of the Spirit within us. We need to say, 'Lord, if you are waiting to do your work in us, we accept that; have your way with us, Lord.'[13]

Many people have adapted the Cardinal's analogy in this way: Two men may have the same kind of steak, but if one steak is in the deep freeze and the other is on the fire, what a difference there is! The steak on the fire attracts attention by its aroma and nourishes the man who has it. The steak in the deep freeze is easily forgotten and remains but a promise of something good to come.

> *Out of the deep freeze and onto the fire… that's what the Baptism in the Holy Spirit has done to the faith experience of millions of Catholics all over the world in these many years since the Duquesne Weekend.*

Why then, if the effects of the Baptism in the Holy Spirit are so desirable, would any Catholic fail to seek it? Good question! Even after all these years of Charismatic Renewal in the Church, there are still vast numbers of Catholics who *don't even realise* that there is such an experience of the Holy Spirit available to them. My hope is that this book will open up the hearts and minds of many more Catholics to this marvelous grace of God in the Baptism in the Spirit.

Charismatic Gifts

Some people fail to seek a release of the Spirit because they are uncomfortable with what they perceive to be an unusual display of emotion at charismatic gatherings. In his book, *A New Pentecost?* Cardinal Suenens remarks that it may well be the deeply personal quality of the prayer that is really threatening someone who raises this objection. He writes that 'deeply personal prayer can present a challenge to our inhibitions'.[14] Charismatics smile, clap their hands, lift their arms in praise, pray aloud spontaneously and, in the opinion of some observers, do something exceedingly strange. They pray in tongues.

While it's true that such things are new to most Catholics, they are all found in Scripture. One has only to read the psalms to see evidence of laughter, tears, prayer with outstretched arms, loud vocal praise, and yes, even dancing. And in the gospels we see Jesus 'rejoicing in the Holy Spirit', weeping over Jerusalem, and prostrating himself as he prayed in Gethsemane. A display of emotion and bodily gestures in prayer is clearly appropriate and deeply human.

Having said all this, I must add that the Holy Spirit is a great respecter of persons. He will not manifest himself in such a way as to violate a person's normal manner of expression. I know charismatics of every possible temperament who have been baptised in the Spirit. The gentle, yet powerful, Holy Spirit can adapt Himself very easily to work through any one of us in our own particular way *if we give him permission*. You can be baptised in the Spirit and not clap your hands... but you will probably want to. You can be baptised in the Spirit and not lift your arms in prayer... but you will probably want to. You can be baptised in the Spirit and not pray in tongues... but you will probably want to - at least you will want to praise and worship God more than you have ever done before.

There is a particular beauty when a group worships together using the gift of tongues. Each person is praying or singing softly their words of praise at the same time. Yet, instead of a cacophony, there is a beautiful harmony. Fr. Ed O'Connor, C.S.C., commented on this in his book *The Pentecostal Movement in the Catholic Church*. The Holy Spirit unites that group of people singing together in tongues to create a symphony of praise. He remarks that accomplished musicians, upon hearing a group sing in tongues together, have commented that by all the laws of music, this is impossible. Yet it happens with people who have never sung together before.

Concerning the gift of tongues, Catholics generally do not hold to the belief commonly held in Pentecostal denominations which states that *unless* a person prays in tongues, he is not truly baptised in the Spirit. However, this particular charismatic gift is so commonly received by those baptised in the Spirit, it is almost 'a gateway' to the other charismatic gifts. It is a tremendous aid to entering into a deeper life in the Holy Spirit. As a priest friend of ours once said, 'Our question should not be whether we like the charismatic gifts, but whether *God* likes the charismatic gifts, and whether he's giving them in a new abundance today to evangelise a pagan and secularised world.'

A fear of the charismatic dimension, while understandable, can be overcome if one looks at the fruit of this life in the power of the Holy Spirit. The charismatic gifts are given to build up the Church. They are not adornments or 'spiritual merit badges'; they are tools for building God's Kingdom. They belong to him and he allows us to be his instruments as we yield to the action of the Holy Spirit. In 1974, Pope Paul VI said, *'How wonderful it would be if the Lord would again pour out the charisms in increased abundance, in order to make the Church fruitful.'*[15] The Lord has done just that. He has graced today's Church with a profusion of charismatic gifts that help us experience his great love and concern for his people.

One of the most stirring exhortations about the charismatic gifts came from our beloved Pope Saint John Paul II. He was meeting with Ecclesial Movements and New Communities in St. Peter's Square on May 30, 1998 and he said:

> Today, I would like to cry out to all of you gathered here

> in St. Peter's Square and to all Christians: Open yourselves with docility to the gifts of the Spirit! Accept gratefully and obediently the charisms which the Spirit never ceases to bestow on us! Do not forget that every charism is given for the common good, that is, for the benefit of the whole Church.[16]

To Revitalise All Ministries

The Catholic Charismatic Renewal has become well-known for its emphasis on prayer and evangelism. However, some people use this as an excuse for not seeking the Baptism in the Spirit. They conclude that if they feel a call to the social apostolate, the Renewal has nothing to offer them. On the contrary, the grace of the Baptism in the Spirit, so central to the Charismatic Renewal, can greatly enhance *all* ministries. There is almost no area of ministry in the Church which has not been revitalised by this move of the Holy Spirit. Those baptised in the Spirit have become active in pro-life work, service to the poor, nursing, education, prison ministry, and the permanent diaconate, to name just a few ministries.

Pope Saint John Paul II spoke about the power of the charisms that has been released in the Charismatic Renewal and in other movements.

> Some charisms given by the Spirit burst in like an impetuous wind, which seizes people and carries them to new ways of missionary commitment to the radical service

> of the Gospel, by ceaselessly proclaiming the truths of faith, accepting the living stream of tradition as a gift and instilling in each person an ardent desire for holiness.[17]

I have witnessed these charisms given by the Spirit in some magnificent communities and ministries that have grown out of the Renewal in less than five decades. I mention here only a few that I have visited personally on five different continents.

The Emmanuel Community in France numbers 8000 members in 57 countries with 233 priests, 100 seminarians, 4 bishops, and nearly 200 consecrated brothers and sisters. They evangelise 30,000 people through summer conferences in Paray-le-Monial, a pilgrimage site which has been entrusted to their care.

Our Lady's Youth Center in El Paso, Texas, where, according to reliable reports, food has been miraculously multiplied more than once to feed the poor after the director, Fr. Rick Thomas, SJ, was baptised in the Spirit (see *Miracles in El Paso?* Servant Books, 1982).

Kottongnae, South Korea, the largest social service agency in that country, which was founded by Fr. John Oh after he was baptised in the Spirit.

Canção Nova community in Cachoeira Paulista, Brazil. Fr. Jonas Abib was baptised in the Spirit 40 years ago and began with 12 young people. There is now a huge community that does 24/7 Catholic television evangelisation. They have built the largest covered stadium in Latin America and hold youth rallies that draw 40,000 teens, teaching them how to live chaste lives.

Emmaus Center in Kampala, Uganda. Fr. Ernest Sievers, M.Afr., was baptised in the Spirit and founded this evangelising community which has saved many priestly vocations. At their invitation, I spoke on the grounds of Namugongo, the Shrine of the Ugandan martyrs, to 10,000 persons who sat and slept outside in the '10,000 star hotel'!

Franciscan University of Steubenville, Ohio, a small college in decline until the former President, Fr. Michael Scanlan, T.O.R., was baptised in the Spirit and brought that grace to campus. They are now a thriving university that evangelises more than 52,000 people annually at summer conferences.

THE LORD IS NEAR

Thus far, I've been dealing with intellectual obstacles people raise when confronted with the Baptism in the Spirit. But if I were to venture a guess at what the greatest obstacle is for most Catholics, I would say that we are afraid to let God get too close. Cardinal Suenens describes this fear in his book, *A New Pentecost?*

> We have an instinctive fear of God intruding into our affairs, even if they are going badly. We stiffen in the face of any interference from outside; we regard it as an estrangement, and we fear a wisdom that does not obey

> our laws. The very idea of intervention on the part of God makes us uneasy. We usually steer clear of those passages in the Bible which do not conform to our categories. God's nearness disturbs us. We take exception whenever His action gets too close and upsets our daily routine. Our real fear, however, ought to be that we may not recognise God's coming in time, that we may not be there when He knocks at our door.[18]

The Cardinal's last sentence is crucial. It is entirely possible for many good people to miss the visitation of God because they are too afraid to welcome him *when he comes... as he really is... to let him be God (cf. Lk. 19:41-44).*

The Baptism in the Spirit is an experience of the love of God, and there is nothing to fear from his love. He has only good in mind for us. St. John expressed it so beautifully. 'There is no fear in love, but perfect love casts out fear. For fear has to do with punishment, and he who fears is not perfected in love. We love because He first loved us' *(1 Jn. 4:18-19).* The person who receives the Baptism in the Spirit experiences an immersion in God's love which is unconditional… full of mercy and kindness. Yes, it is true. It is 'a fearful thing to fall into the hands of the living God' *(Heb. 10:31).* But as long as we have repentant hearts, drawing near to God is fearful only in the sense that it is wonderful and awe-inspiring.

Living in the Spirit

All that I have experienced of the Lord since the Baptism in the Spirit bears this out. *God is love!* He is the source of all that is good, and for those who love him, he makes *everything* in their lives work together for the good - even times of trials and suffering *(cf. Rm. 8:28)*. In Hurricane Katrina, August 29, 2005, my family and I lost our home, our office and the retreat facility we used for our events. But God is so faithful and he demonstrated to us in countless ways that he really does make everything work together for good in the lives of those who are trying to love and serve him. His providence towards us was amazing. Just one year after the disaster, I made a long list of the blessings that came to us because of Hurricane Katrina.

Living in the power of the Holy Spirit is a magnificent adventure. No, all our problems are not automatically solved. There are times of dryness in prayer, difficulties with others, disappointments and broken dreams, even severe tragedies. But the difference is that now we are able to surrender more consciously to the Lordship of Jesus over our lives, and to trust in the power of his Spirit to carry us through whatever may come.

Growing in the Spirit means *finding our joy in doing God's will.* In a certain sense, it no longer matters so much whether we are being consoled or disciplined by the Lord at any particular moment. The mere fact that he is the one dealing with us and revealing himself to us is quite enough. As St. Paul writes, 'Nothing can happen to outweigh the supreme advantage of knowing Christ Jesus my Lord' *(Phil. 3:8)*. The Lord himself becomes our treasure...our 'portion and cup' as the psalmist expressed it *(cf. Ps. 16:5)*.

I share in greater detail my experiences of walking in the Spirit in my book, *Everyday Holiness: Bringing the Holy Spirit Home* (Vesuvius Press, 2014). Most of the lessons the Holy Spirit has taught me are drawn from my life as a wife and mother and grandmother, moving through the daily round of activities and concerns. One of the wonderful blessings of the Baptism in the Spirit is that any ordinary person, like you or me, can come to know God's presence in the midst of everyday life.

I always thought that a life of intimacy with God was reserved only for contemplatives. But my life has been far from quiet and contemplative while caring for a husband, raising four children, working within my home, and ministering through international travel as well. Yet the Lord is so humble that he willingly shares the joy of his presence with anyone who will receive him. As Jesus tells us in His word, 'Behold, I stand at the door and knock; if anyone hears my voice and opens the door, I will come in to him and eat with him and he with me' *(Rev. 3:20)*. Growing in intimacy with Jesus through the power of his Spirit can be a reality in the life of anyone who opens the door. If it has happened to me, it can happen to you.

There's More, There's So Much More

In June of 1991, while doing research for this book, I placed a phone call to Miss Flo Dodge in whose home the inter-denominational prayer meetings were held in Pittsburgh in 1967. I had only attended one of those meetings in March of

1967, therefore, I never anticipated that Flo would remember me. Not only did Flo remember me, but she asked me a startling question: 'What have you been up to lately, Patti? The Lord's been putting you on my heart, and I've been praying for you.' The Holy Spirit had awakened her to my need for prayer as I laboured over this book, even though we had not had any personal contact in twenty-five years! Now, to me, this is *amazing grace*! Just as Flo bore a burden in prayer for God's work among Catholics in 1967, he was once again calling her to intercede for what he wants to accomplish through the telling of the Duquesne Weekend story today. The Holy Spirit works in mysterious and marvellous ways!

In the course of our wonderful reunion by phone, Flo shared something that resonated deeply within me. After recalling the sovereign work of the Holy Spirit in 1967, Flo said, *'Patti, the prelude is nothing compared to what is coming, but we're not ready yet.'* The prelude is nothing compared to what is coming! It reminded me of a quote attributed to the late Kathryn Kuhlmann who was used so mightily in the charismatic gift of healing. After witnessing God's miracles for many years she said, *'There's more. There's so much more.'*

If indeed there is so much more of the Holy Spirit for us in the future, what can we do to dispose ourselves to receive him. How can we get ready? What does the Lord expect?

FIVE KEYS

As I've pondered these questions in my own life, I believe the Lord has shown me five keys to open the door to more of the Holy Spirit. They are: **Repentance. Humility. Prayer. Docility. Union with our Lady.**

Repentance:

We need to repent! Each one of us! God wants clean hands and a pure heart *(cf. Ps. 24)*. He wants us to be 'vessels for noble use, consecrated and useful to the master of the house, ready for any good work' *(cf. 2 Tim. 2:20-21)*. That means an honest and on-going examination of conscience. Thank God we Catholics have the sacrament of reconciliation to seek God's forgiveness of our sins. Have we lost our first love for Jesus? Then we must find it again by coming before the Lord and making a good confession. I've read that every confession can be like a new Pentecost. *'The eyes of the Lord roam over the whole earth, to encourage those who are devoted to him wholeheartedly' (2 Chron. 16:9).*

Humility

Humility attracts God's grace like nothing else! It seems to be the one thing he finds irresistible. 'The prayer of the humble pierces the clouds, and he will not be consoled until it reaches the Lord; he will not desist until the Most High visits him' (Sir. 35:17). 'Until the Most High visits him'... that's what we want, isn't it? A humble prayer, filled with faith, elicits a response from God. If we want to be ready for more of the Spirit, we must humble ourselves before the Lord.

Years ago I was fascinated as I read *Another Wave Rolls In,* the account of the Azusa Street revival of 1906. Frank Bartleman, a Pentecostal pioneer, wrote forcefully about the need for humility and prayer. Those who were instrumental in bringing to birth that outpouring of the Holy Spirit at the turn of the twentieth century, spent much time 'on their faces' before God, literally groaning under a burden of prayer for revival. God required of Bartleman and those who were with him, a deep spirit of repentance. He wrote, 'We must keep humble and little in our own eyes. Let us get built up by a sense of our own importance and we are gone... The depth of any revival will be determined exactly by the spirit of repentance that obtains.'[19]

Prayer with Desire

In her *Magnificat,* Mary proclaims, 'The hungry he has given every good thing, while the rich he has sent empty away' *(Lk 1:53).* God promises to fill those who are humble and hungry for him. The outpouring of the Holy Spirit has been preceded by a period of intense longing and prayerful hunger from the first Pentecost to the present day. Think back over the events related in the beginning of this book - the villagers in Czechoslovakia, Blessed Elena Guerra, the students at the Bethel Bible School, the prayer that surrounded the Second Vatican Council, the professors at Duquesne. In each case there was great hunger for God expressed through fervent prayer.

Our prayer does not change God's mind; it changes us. As we hunger after the things of God, as we beg for an increase of the Holy Spirit, our interior disposition becomes better prepared to receive *the very measure of blessing God himself longs to give us.* It is as if our hearts expand through prayer; we are stretched to contain His treasures. In St. Catherine's *Dialogue,* the Lord assures her that he is moved by constant, humble, holy prayer... that he is bound by the chain of holy desires, for he himself has given this chain.[20]

It is a mysterious thing. God calls us to labour in prayer to bring forth the very thing he is already longing to do. He draws us into his longing to bless mankind, by putting into our hearts a plea for mercy, for more of the Holy Spirit.

I have been captivated recently by these verses from Scripture: 'The eyes of all creatures look to you and you give them their food in due time. You open wide your hand, grant the desires of all who live' *(Ps. 145:15-16).*[21] You open *wide* your hand! God is not miserly in his dealings with us. His generosity is lavish, beyond our comprehension. In John 3:34 we read that 'it is not by measure that he gives the Spirit'. There is a limitless quality to his love which is difficult for us to grasp because we are so limited. But the saints have told us about it. All those who have drawn near to God experience it. 'They feast on the abundance of your house, and you give them drink from the river of your delights. For with you is the fountain of life; in your light do we see light' *(Ps. 36:8-9).* St. Teresa of Avila wrote in her *Autobiography,* 'He never tires of giving, nor can he exhaust his mercies. Let us not tire of receiving.'[22]

There is tremendous power in our prayer. Not only does God's grace change us when we pray, but Satan's plan is thwarted. Corrie ten Boom, survivor of a Nazi concentration camp and marvelous vagabond for the Lord, once wrote, 'The devil smiles when we make plans. He laughs when we get too busy. But he trembles when we pray - especially when we pray together.' [23]

Prayer makes us victorious over the power of evil. It unleashes grace. Prayer unlocks the key to the very heart of God. In prayer, God reveals to us his mind and his purpose; we catch a glimpse of the glory that is to come. A spirit of prayer and intercession is being awakened in God's people so that we may prepare for his fresh visitation.

Docility

And for what must we pray; for what must we hunger? *We must pray for the coming of the Holy Spirit, the greatest of all God's gifts!* To those not yet baptised in the Spirit, I make an appeal: Ask God to grant you this grace. Seek after it. Find others who will pray with you for a release of the Holy Spirit and the charismatic gifts in your life.

To those who are already baptised in the Spirit, I would say: The Lord is calling for a greater sensitivity, a greater docility to the promptings of his Holy Spirit. I believe that as we humble ourselves and hunger after him in prayer, we will experience the charismatic gifts flowing through us with a naturalness and a purity we have not known before. God wants to attune us to the sound of his voice, to accustom us to that gentle whisper, that subtle nudge. Do you remember the account in 1 Kings 19 when Elijah was waiting to hear the voice of the Lord? It did not come in the violent wind, rending the mountains and crushing the rocks. It did not come in the earthquake or in the fire. It was in the gentle breeze, the tiny whispering sound, that the Lord visited Elijah. And in awe, Elijah hid his face in his cloak. Sometimes as I sense the Holy Spirit coming, I am also moved to hide my face too, to literally bow down before his presence, to be very still and 'to know that he is God' *(cf. Ps. 46:11).*

The best analogy I can think of for what I am describing is that of a marriage. When a couple has been happily married for many years, they have come into a special kind of loving union. All it takes is a glance, a nod, a touch on the elbow and one person understands the other's intention. It is to that kind of docility that the Lord is leading us. We need to be very faithful and very obedient to every inspiration of the Holy Spirit... every impulse for doing good and bringing glory to God's name. This will mean obeying God's will and not our own, seeking his glory and not our own, building his Kingdom and not our own. In short, to let him rule and reign in us, that we may be his instruments.

Mary, Spouse of the Holy Spirit

It is natural for one's thoughts to turn to Mary when speaking of these things. She is the one who lived a life of total surrender to God. We Christians can rejoice for we have someone who is the exemplar of holiness, humility, ardent prayer, docility to the Spirit, and availability to the Spirit's gifts. *We have Mary.*

From the cross, Jesus entrusted St. John to Mary's care with the words, 'Woman, behold your son'.Then he entrusted his Mother, Mary, to St. John: 'Behold your Mother' (cf. Jn. 19:26-27). John, the beloved disciple welcomed Mary into his home. He received her as a parting gift from Jesus and he loved Mary with filial devotion.

We Catholics see in this scene a call to entrust ourselves to Mary's motherly care, to welcome her as one of the precious gifts Jesus has given us, and to ask for her powerful intercession. Just as at Cana Mary spoke to Jesus on behalf of those in need, we believe that she continues to intercede for the Church today.

Few Christians would deny the fact that Mary is a model for all those who seek the Lord. But she is much more than that. From the cross Jesus did not say, *'Behold your model'*. He said, *'Behold your Mother'*. Mary has a continuing role as Mother of all God's children, Mother of the Church. And her spiritual motherhood is intimately linked to the work of the Holy Spirit.

Pope John Paul II made clear this relationship. (Emphasis in original.) 'Mary embraces us all with special solicitude *in the Holy Spirit.* As we profess in our creed, he is 'the giver of life.' It is he who gives the fullness of life, open towards eternity. Mary's spiritual motherhood is therefore a *sharing in the power of the Holy Spirit,* of 'the giver of life.'[24]

In my own life in the Spirit these many years, Mary has been a tender mother to me, teaching me to yield to God... to say 'yes'.

To whatever measure I have been faithful to the Lord, it has been thanks to her example and to her prayer. I believe that an important element in preparing for a fresh outpouring of the Holy Spirit is our relationship with Mary as Mother. We need to heed the words of Jesus our Master: 'Behold your Mother'. As we entrust ourselves to the heart of Mary, she will lead us faithfully to the heart of Jesus her Son, the source of mercy.

Current of Grace

It was at the foot of the cross that the Lord Jesus first entrusted us to Mary as Mother. When we permit her to be a Mother to us, she will again lead us to this privileged place of grace… to the cross. There at the cross we can fix our gaze more clearly upon the Son of God who was slain for our sins and the sins of the world.

For me, the call to repentance, to humility, to prayer with desire, docility is, in fact, a call to come to the cross of Jesus in the company of Mary, my Mother. Strengthened by her prayer and her presence, I can begin to enter into the mystery of that cross… to unite myself to Jesus more fully... to learn the truth of St. Paul's words, 'I have been crucified with Christ; it is no longer I who live, but Christ who lives in me; and the life I now live in the flesh I live by faith in the Son of God, who loved me and gave himself for me' *(Gal. 2:20).*

I must witness to the fact that entrustment to Mary as my Mother has deepened my consecration to God… Father, Son and Holy Spirit. Entrusting myself to the heart of Mary has positioned me next to the pierced heart of Christ and has opened for me a door to greater intimacy with God. I long to bring others with me through that door.

I see now more clearly that it is at the pierced side of Christ from which blood and water flowed that we find mercy, that we can plead for mercy, and for more of the Holy Spirit. As Catholics, we see in the water and the blood a reference to the sacraments of Baptism and the Eucharist. The pierced heart of Jesus is the source of these sacramental gifts and of other immeasurable spiritual riches as well.

In the beautiful prayer, *Anima Christi (Soul of Christ),* we say to Jesus, 'In thy wounds I fain would hide, Ne'er to be parted from thy side.' This is more than poetry; it is spiritual reality. Hiding in the wounds of Christ, being bathed in his blood, brings peace and inspires confidence. It is by coming to the cross, meditating on Jesus' passion and death, pondering the love of his heart which was opened for our salvation, that we find life. The words of a marvellous old Protestant hymn express it yet another way:

> Rock of ages, cleft for me,
> Let me hide myself in thee;
> Let the water and the blood,
> From thy wounded side which flowed,
> Be of sin the double cure,
> Save from wrath and make me pure.[25]

When Jesus died on the cross, he yielded up his spirit. It is at the cross again today that Jesus imparts his Spirit. If we want more of the Holy Spirit, we must come to his pierced heart. What I am experiencing is this: as I draw near to the cleft in the rock from which living water flows, I feel myself caught up in its movement. It is the flow of the Holy Spirit.

At the cross of Jesus I experience what I would describe as a swiftly moving current of grace and mercy drawing me to God. Jesus said, 'And I, when I am lifted up from the earth, will draw all men to myself' (Jn. 12:32). This happens *not* because we are good, *but because he is good*; *not* because we are worthy, but *because he is worthy*. It is a pure gift. One cannot help but want everyone everywhere to draw near to this fountain of life, the pierced heart of Jesus the Lord, to be swept along in this current of grace and mercy.

If I were to say a word to others who have been baptised in the Holy Spirit it would be this: *We* are not the source of spiritual life and renewal; *God is*. He has in himself salvation and healing and mercy for the whole world.

The Holy Spirit is not our own property and possession. We should not attempt to be masters of this action of the Holy Spirit. Rather, we should yield to him and allow ourselves to be caught up in this swiftly moving current of grace and mercy destined to renew the face of the earth.

As I describe this current of grace and mercy, the outpouring of the Holy Spirit, I am reminded of the words of Cardinal Suenens in his book *Spiritual Journey*:

> To interpret the [Charismatic] Renewal as a 'movement' among other movements, is to misunderstand its nature: it is a movement of the Spirit offered to the entire Church, and destined to rejuvenate every facet of the Church's life. The soul of Renewal, 'Baptism in the Spirit', is a grace of pentecostal refreshment offered to all Christians… It is not a question of a 'Gulf Stream' which, here and there, reheats the coastlines, but of a powerful current destined to penetrate to the country's very heart...
>
> As for my friends in the Renewal all over the world I should like to say that the Renewal is destined for the entire Church, and that their constant preoccupation should be that the waters of the river flow into the sea in loyalty to their source. [26]

SEND FORTH YOUR SPIRIT!

Blessed Pope Paul VI said, 'If we really love the Church, the main thing we must do is to foster in it an outpouring of the Divine Paraclete, the Holy Spirit.' [27] In its own small way, I pray that what is written here may do just that… foster an outpouring of the Holy Spirit, the Lord, the Giver of Life!

I hope that the testimonies in this book have convinced you that the Baptism in the Holy Spirit is available for every person who desires it. The Lord Jesus wants to send the Holy Spirit to renew our personal lives, but he wants much more than that. *He wants to renew the whole Church! He wants to renew all men and women everywhere! He wants to renew the face of the earth!* God is preparing us for a new evangelisation. And there can be no new evangelisation without a new Pentecost!

Our Holy Father, Pope Francis, on more than one occasion, has spoken forcefully about the grace of the Baptism in the Spirit and what he expects of the Charismatic Renewal. I conclude this book with the words of our Holy Father himself. On June 1, 2014, in Olympic Stadium, Rome, Pope Francis said,

> **'I expect from you that you share with all, in the Church, the grace of Baptism in the Holy Spirit (expression that is read in the Acts of the Apostles).'**[28]

On June 13, 2015 in Rome at the Third Worldwide Priests Retreat organised by The Catholic Fraternity and the International Catholic Charismatic Renewal Services (ICCRS), Pope Francis exhorted 1000 priests in these words,

> **I ask each and all of you that as part of the current of grace of Charismatic Renewal you organise seminars of Life in the Spirit in your parishes, and seminaries, schools, in neighborhoods, to share Baptism in the Spirit; it is catechesis... so that it produces, by the work of the Holy Spirit, the personal encounter with Jesus who changes our life.**[29]

At the 38th Convocation of Renewal in the Spirit on July 3, 2015, Pope Francis continued his plea to share the grace of the Baptism in the Spirit in this directive.

> **'Organise seminars of Life in the Spirit for brothers and sisters living on the street, also for brothers and sisters marginalised by so much suffering in life'**[30]

Pope Francis has invited everyone in this 'current of grace' to celebrate the Golden Jubilee of the Catholic Charismatic Renewal in the Church by meeting with him in St. Peter's Square on the vigil of Pentecost, 2017. He said,

> **'We will gather to give thanks to the Holy Spirit for the gift of this current of grace, which is for the Church and for the world, and to celebrate the wonders that the Holy Spirit has worked in the course of these 50 years, changing the life of millions of Christians.'**[31]

As I bring this book to its conclusion, I am deeply moved in recalling these words of Pope Francis. Fifty years ago, who could have imagined that the Holy Father himself would be promoting the Baptism in the Spirit? Who could have dreamed that he would be encouraging us to give the Life in the Spirit Seminars far and wide? Who could have hoped that the Pope himself would invite us to celebrate our Golden Jubilee with him in St. Peter's Square?

As a twenty-year-old girl on the Duquesne Weekend in 1967, I wrote on a scrap of paper, 'I want a miracle!' And that miracle has been granted. **It is the miracle of the Divine Spirit renewing his signs and wonders in this our day as by a new Pentecost!**

NOTES

1. Pope Paul VI, Address at a General Audience, November 29, 1972. Quoted in Pope Paul and the Spirit: *Charisms and Church Renewal in the Teaching of Paul VI* by Edward D. O'Connor, C.S.C., (Notre Dame, Indiana: Ave Maria Press, 1978), p. 183.
2. Pope Paul VI, Address at a General Audience, Oct. 12, 1966. Quoted in O'Connor, op. cit., p. 142.
3. Pope Paul VI, Address at a General Audience, May 23, 1973. Quoted in O'Connor, op. cit., p. 190.
4. Ibid., p. 191.
5. Ibid., p. 191.
6. All quotes by Conchita taken from M.M. Philipon, O.P., *Conchita: A Mother's Spiritual Diary,* (New York, Alba House, 1978), p.211-212.
7. Martin Blake, *Marthe Robin and the Foyers of Charity,* (Nottingham, England, Theotokos Books, 2010), p. 68.
8. Ibid., p.95.
9. Léon-Joseph Cardinal Suenens, Memories and Hopes (Dublin, Ireland,Veritas Publications, 1992), p.267.
10. Kilian McDonnell and George T. Montague, *Christian Initiation and Baptism in the Holy Spirit: Evidence from the First Eight Centuries,* (Collegeville, Minnesota: The Liturgical Press, 1991). Kilian McDonnell and George T. Montague, Editors, *Fanning the Flame: What Does Baptism in the Holy Spirit Have to do With Christian Initiation?* (Collegeville, Minnesota: The Liturgical Press, 1991).
11. McDonnell and Montague, *Fanning the Flame,* p.10.
12. Doctrinal Commission of ICCRS, *Baptism in the Holy Spirit* (National Service Committee of the Catholic Charismatic Renewal in the U.S. Inc., 2012), p. 13.
13. Léon-Joseph Cardinal Suenens, Address in Milwaukee, Wisconsin, March 1973. Quoted in *New Covenant,* (October 1973), p.8.
14. Léon-Joseph Cardinal Suenens, *A New Pentecost?* (New York: The Seabury Press, 1974), p. 97.
15. Pope Paul VI, Address at a General Audience, October 16, 1974. Quoted in O'Connor, op. cit., pp. 210-212.

16. Pope John Paul II, Address to Ecclesial Movements and New Communities, May 30, 1998.
17. Ibid.
18. Suenens, op.cit., pp. 90-91.
19. Frank Bartleman, *Another Wave Rolls In*, (Northridge, CA: Voice Christian Publications, 1962), p. 24.
20. Catherine of Siena, *The Dialogue*, (Mahwah, NJ: Paulist Press, 1980), pp. 54, 57.
21. This translation is taken from the Liturgy of the Hours. It is an English translation prepared by the International Commission on English in the Liturgy (ICEL).
22. *The Collected Works of St. Teresa of Avila, Vol. I*, (Washington, DC: ICS Publications, 1976), p. 128.
23. Corrie ten Boom, *Don't Wrestle, Just Nestle*, (Old Tappan, NJ: Fleming H. Revell Company, 1978), p. 71.
24. Pope John Paul II, Homily at Fatima, May 13, 1982.
25. 'Rock of Ages,' Augustus M. Toplady from *Devotion and Praise*, Haldor Lillenas, ed., (Kansas City, MO: Nazarene Publishing House 1937), p. 167.
26. Léon-Joseph Cardinal Suenens,*Spiritual Journey*, (Ertvelde, Belgium: F.I.A.T. Publications, 1990), pp. 39, 41.
27. Pope Paul VI, Address at a General Audience, October 12, 1966. Quoted in O'Connor, op. cit., p. 143.
28. Pope Francis, Address to the 37th National Convocation of 'Renewal in the Spirit', Rome, 1 June 2014.
29. Pope Francis, Address to the Participants
30. Pope Francis, Message at the Third Worldwide Retreat of Priests, Basilica of St. John Lateran, Rome, 12 June 2015.
31. Pope Francis, Address to the 38th National Convocation of 'Renewal in the Spirit', Rome, 3 July 2015.
32. Ibid.

APPENDIX:

Papal Quotes to the Catholic Charismatic Renewal in its Various Expression

Address of Pope Paul VI on occasion of the First International Leaders' Conference, Grottaferrata, 10 October 1973.
'We rejoice with you, dear friends, at the renewal of the spiritual life manifested in the Church today, in different forms and in various environments. Certain common features appear in this renewal: the taste for deep prayer, personal and in groups, a return to contemplation and an emphasis on praise of God, the desire to devote oneself completely to Christ, an openness to the Holy Spirit, more assiduous reading of the Scriptures, generous brotherly devotion, a willingness to serve the Church. In all this, we can recognise the mysterious and hidden work of the Spirit, who is the soul of the Church.'[1]

Address of Pope Paul VI to the Catholic Charismatic Renewal on occasion of the Second International Leaders' Conference, Rome, 19 May 1975.
As we said. in the presence of some of you last October, the Church and. the world need more than ever that 'the miracle of Pentecost should be continued in history'.[2]

Nothing is more necessary for such a world, more and more secularised, than the testimony of this 'spiritual renewal', which we see the Holy Spirit bring about today in the most diverse regions and environments.[3]

How then could this 'spiritual renewal' be other than a blessing for the Church and for the world? And, in this case, how could we fail to take all means in order that it may remain so?[4]

Where the Spirit is concerned we are immediately alert, immediately happy to welcome the coming of the Holy Spirit. More than that, we invite him, we pray to him, we desire nothing more than that Christians, believing people, should experience an awareness, worship, a greater joy through the Spirit of God among us. Have we forgotten the Holy Spirit? Certainly not! We want him, we honour him and we love him, and we invoke him.[5]

We will say only this: today, either one lives one's faith with devotion, depth, energy and joy, or that faith will die out.[6]

Private Audience of Pope John Paul II with the ICCRO Council, Rome, 11 December 1979

I have always belonged to this renewal in the Holy Spirit. My own experience is very interesting. When I was in school, at the age of 12 or 13, sometimes I had difficulties in my studies, in particular with mathematics. My father gave me a book on prayer. He opened it to a page and said to me: 'Here you have a prayer to the Holy Spirit. You must say this prayer every day of your life'. I have remained obedient to this order that my father gave nearly 50 years ago, which I believe is no little while.

This was my first spiritual initiation, so I can understand all the different charisms. All of them are part of the riches of the Lord. I am convinced that this movement is a sign of his action. The world is much in need of this action of the Holy Spirit, and it needs many instruments for this action.[7]

Materialism is the negation of the spiritual, and this is why we need the action of the Holy Spirit. Now I see this movement, this activity everywhere. In my own country I have seen a special presence of the Holy Spirit. Through this action, the Holy Spirit comes to the human spirit, and from this moment we begin to live again, to find our very selves, to find our identity, our total humanity. Consequently, I am convinced that this movement is a very important component in the total renewal of the Church, in this spiritual renewal of the Church.[8]

Address of Pope John Paul II at the Fourth International Leaders' Conference, Rome, 7 May 1981

Pope Paul described the movement for renewal in the Spirit as 'a *chance* for the Church and for the world', and the six years since that Congress have borne out the hope that inspired his vision.[9]

Audience of Pope John Paul II with the National Service Committee of the Italian 'Renewal in the Spirit', Rome, 4 April 1998

The Catholic charismatic movement is one of the many fruits of the Second Vatican Council, which, like a new Pentecost, led to an extraordinary flourishing in the Church's life of groups and movements particularly sensitive to the action of the Spirit. How can we not give thanks for the precious spiritual fruits that the Renewal has produced in the life of the Church and in the lives of so many people? How many lay faithful - men, women, young people, adults and the elderly - have been able to experience in their own lives the amazing power of the Spirit and his gifts! How many people have rediscovered faith, the joy of prayer, the power and beauty of the Word of God, translating all this into generous service in the Church's mission! How many lives have been profoundly changed! For all this today, together with you, I wish to praise and thank the Holy Spirit.[10]

Message at the meeting between Pope John Paul II and the ecclesial movements and new communities in St. Peter's Square, Rome, 30 May 1998

Whenever the Spirit intervenes, he leaves people astonished. He brings about events of amazing newness, he radically changes people and history. This was the unforgetable experience of the Second Vatican Ecumenical Council, during which, under the guidance of the same spirit, the Church rediscovered the charismatic dimension as one of her constitute elements. 'It is not only through the sacraments and the ministries of the Church that the Holy Spirit makes holy the people, leads them and eniches them with his virtues. Allotting his gifts according as he wills', he also distributes special graces among the faithful of every rank. He makes them fit and ready to undertake various tasks and offices for the renewal and building up of the Church.

The institutional and charismatic aspects are co-essential as it were to the Church's constitution. They contribute, although differently, to the life, renewal and sanctification of God's people. It is from this providential rediscovery of the charismatic dimension that, before and after the Council, a remarkable pattern of growth has been established for ecclesial movements and new communities.[11]

Some charisms given by the Spirit burst in like an impetuous wind, which seizes people and carries them to new ways of missionary commitment to the radical service of the Gospel, by ceaslessly proclaiming the truths of the faith, accepting the living stream of tradition as a gift and instilling in each person an ardent desire for holiness.

Today I would like to cry out to all of you gathered here in St. Peter's Square and to all Christians: Open yourselves docilely to the gifts of the Spirit! Accept gratefully and obediently the charisms which the Spirit never ceases to bestow on us! Do not forget that every charism is given for the common good, that is, for the benefit of the whole Church.[12]

You have learned in the movements and new communities that faith is not abstract talk, nor vague religious sentiment, but new life in Christ instilled by the Holy Spirit.[13]

Address of Pope John Paul II to the participants at the Eighth meeting of the Catholic Fraternity of Charismatic Covenant Communities and Fellowships, Rome, 1 June 1998

From the very beginning of my ministry as the Successor of

Peter, I have considered the movements as a great spiritual resource for the Church and for humanity, a gift of the Holy Spirit for our time, a sign of hope for all people.[14]

Audience of Pope John Paul II with the participants at the Ninth International Leaders' Conference, Fiuggi, 30 October 1998

In greeting the International Conference for Catholic Charismatic Leaders 'I thank my God through Jesus Christ for all of you, because your faith is proclaimed throughout the world'. The Catholic Charismatic Renewal has helped many Christians to rediscover the presence and power of the Holy Spirit in their lives, in the life of the Church and in the world; and this re-discovery has awakened in them a faith in Christ filled with joy, a great love of the Church, and a generous dedication to her evangelising mision. In this year of the Holy Spirit, I join you in praise of God for the precious fruits which he has wished to bring to maturity in your communities and, through them, in the particular churches.[15]

Message of Pope John Paul II to members of the Executive and of the Council of the Catholic Fraternity of Charismatic Covenant Communities and Fellowships, Rome, 22 June, 2001

The Church and the world need saints! And all the baptised without exception are called to be saints! This is what the Second Vatican Council meant when it spoke of 'the universal call to holiness' (Lumen Gentium, 5)... For this is what the saints are: people who have fallen in love with Christ. And this is why the Charismatic Renewal has been such a gift to the Church: it has led a host of men and women, young and old, into this experience of the love which is stronger than death... I pray most fervently that your communities and the entire Charismatic Renewal will 'put out into the deep' of prayer in order to 'put out into the deep' of mission.[16]

Audience of Pope John Paul II with members of the National Service Committee and of the Council of the Italian Association 'Renewal in the Spirit', Rome, 14 March 2002

In our time that is so hungry for hope, make the Holy Spirit known and loved. Help bring to life that 'culture of Pentecost', that alone can make fruitful the civilization of love and friendly co-existence among peoples. With fervent insistence, never tire of praying 'Come Holy Spirit! Come! Come!'[17]

Homily delivered by John Paul II during vespers, in which he addressed a message to members of the Renewal in the Spirit, St. Peter's Square, 29 May 2004

The ecclesial movements and the new communities are a 'providential answer', 'inspired by the Holy Spirit' given the present need of new evangelisation, for which 'mature Christian personalities' and 'strong Christian communities' are needed. [18]

Angelus Address of Pope Benedict XVI, Vatican City, 13 January 2008, Libreria Editrice Vaticana

Christ's entire mission is summed up in this: to baptise us in the Holy Spirit...[19]

Regina Caeli Message of Pope Benedict XVI, Vatican City, 11 May 2008, Libreria Editrice Vaticana

'Today I would like to extend this invitation to everyone: Let us rediscover, dear brothers and sisters, the beauty of being baptised in the Holy Spirit…'[20]

Address of Pope Francis to the 37th National Convocation of 'Renewal in the Spirit', Rome, 1 June 2014, Libreria Editrice Vaticana

Dear Brothers and Sisters,

Thank you so much for your welcome. Someone must have told today's organisers that I really like the hymn: 'Jesus the Lord lives'. When I would celebrate Mass in the cathedral in Buenos Aires with the charismatic renewal, after the consecration and a few moments of adoration in tongues, we would sing this hymn with great joy and fervour, as you have today. Thank you! I felt at home!

I thank Renewal in the Spirit, ICCRS and the Catholic Fraternity for this opportunity to be with you, which is a source of great joy for me. I am grateful for the presence here of the first members of the renewal, who had an intense experience of the Holy Spirit's power. I believe that Patti is here… You, the charismatic renewal, have received a great gift from the Lord. Your movement's birth was willed by the Holy Spirit to be 'a current of grace in the Church and for the Church'. This is your identity: to be a current of grace.

What is the very first gift of the Holy Spirit? It is the gift of himself, the one who is love and who makes us fall in love with Jesus. And this love changes our lives. That is why we speak of 'being born again in the Spirit'. It is what Jesus told Nicodemus. You have received the great gift of diversity of charisms, the diversity which becomes harmony in the Holy Spirit, and in service to the Church.

When I think of charismatics, I think of the Church herself, but in a particular way: I think of a great orchestra, where all the instruments and voices are different from one another, yet all are needed to create the harmony of the music. Saint Paul speaks of this in the twelfth chapter of the First Letter to the Corinthians. As in an orchestra, no one in the renewal can think of himself or herself as being more important or greater than the others, please! Because when you think of yourselves as more important or greater, disaster is already on the horizon! No one can say: 'I am the head'. Like the Church, you have only one head, one Lord: the Lord Jesus. Repeat with me: Who is the head of the renewal? The Lord Jesus! Who is the head of the renewal? *[the crowd:]* The Lord Jesus! And we can say this with the power given us by the Holy Spirit, since no one can say 'Jesus is Lord' without the Holy Spirit.

As you may know – because news gets around – in the first years of the charismatic renewal in Buenos Aires, I didn't care very much for charismatics. I used to think: 'They strike me as some kind of samba school!' I didn't share their style of prayer or the many new things which were happening in the Church. Later, I got to know them and I finally realised all the good that the charismatic renewal was doing for the Church. And this story which began with the 'samba school' had an unexpected ending: a few months before entering the conclave, I was named the spiritual assistant for the charismatic renewal in Argentina by the Conference of Bishops.

The charismatic renewal is a great force meant to serve the preaching of the Gospel in the joy of the Holy Spirit. You received the Holy Spirit and he has made you appreciate God's love for all his children; he has also made you love God's word. In the early days, they used to say that you charismatics always carried around a Bible, the New Testament... Do you still carry one today? *[the crowd:]* Yes! – I'm not so sure! If not, return to this first love, and always carry the word of God in your pocket or bag! And read a bit of it. Keep the word of God with you always.

You, the people of God, the people of the charismatic renewal, must be careful not to lose the freedom which the Holy Spirit has given you! The danger for the renewal, as our dear Father Raniero Cantalamessa often says, is that of getting too organised: the danger of excessive planning.

Yes, you need organisation, but never lose the grace of letting God be God! *'Yet there is no greater freedom than that of allowing oneself to be guided by the Holy Spirit, renouncing the attempt to plan and control everything to the last detail, and instead letting him enlighten, guide, and direct us, leading us wherever he wills. The Holy Spirit knows well what is needed in every time and place. This is what it means to be mysteriously fruitful!'* (Evangelii Gaudium, 280).

Another danger is that of becoming *arbiters* of God's grace. Many times, leaders (I prefer the name 'servants') of a group or community become, perhaps without intending to, 'managers' of grace, deciding who can receive the prayer of outpouring or baptism in the Spirit and who cannot. If any of you are doing this, I ask you to stop; no more! You are *dispensers* of God's grace, not its *arbiters*! Don't act like a tollhouse for the Holy Spirit!

In the Malines Documents, you have a guide, a reliable path to keep you from going astray. The first document is *Theological and Pastoral Orientations*. The second is *Ecumenism and Charismatic Renewal*, written by Cardinal Suenens himself, an outstanding figure of the Second Vatican Council. The third is *Charismatic Renewal and Social Action*, written by Cardinal Suenens and Bishop Helder Camara.

This is your path: *evangelisation, spiritual ecumenism, caring for the poor and needy, and welcoming the marginalised.* And all of it is based on *worship!* The foundation of the renewal is *worshiping God!*

They asked me to tell you what the Pope expects of you.
The first thing is conversion to the love of Jesus which changes our lives and makes each Christian a witness to God's love. The Church expects this witness of Christian life from us, and the Holy Spirit helps us to *live the Gospel fully and consistently for our own growth in holiness.*

I expect you to share with everyone in the Church the grace of baptism in the Holy Spirit (a phrase we find in the Acts of the Apostles).

I expect you to evangelise with the word of God, which proclaims that Jesus lives and that he loves all men and women. To give a witness of spiritual ecumenism to all our brothers and sisters of other Churches and Christian communities who believe in Jesus as Lord and Saviour.

To remain united in the love that the Lord Jesus asks us to have for all people, and in prayer to the Holy Spirit for the attainment of this unity which is necessary for evangelisation in the name of Jesus. Remember that *'the charismatic renewal is de facto ecumenical in nature… The Catholic renewal rejoices in what the Holy Spirit is accomplishing in the other Churches'* (1 Malines 5,3).

Be close to the poor and to those in need, so as to touch in their flesh the wounded flesh of Jesus. Please, draw near to them!

Seek unity in the renewal, because unity comes from the Holy Spirit and is born of the unity of the Trinity. Who is the source of division? The devil! Division comes from the devil. Flee from all infighting, please! Let there be none of this among you!

I wish to thank ICCRS and Catholic Fraternity, the two groups of pontifical right of the Pontifical Council for the Laity which are at the service of the worldwide renewal and are entrusted with preparing the world meeting of priests and Bishops in June of next year. I know that they have decided to work together and to share office space as a sign of unity and to make better use of their resources. This makes me very happy. I would also like to thank them because they are already working on preparations for the great jubilee of 2017.

Brothers and sisters, remember: Worship the Lord your God. This is fundamental! Worship God. Seek holiness in the new life of the Holy Spirit. Be dispensers of the grace of God. Avoid the danger of excessive organisation.

Go out into the streets and evangelise. Proclaim the Gospel. Remember that the Church was born 'on the move', that Pentecost morning. Draw close to the poor and touch in their flesh the wounded flesh of Jesus. Let yourselves be guided by the Holy Spirit, in freedom; and please, don't put the Holy Spirit in a cage! Be free!

Seek unity in the renewal, the unity which comes from the Trinity!

And I am waiting for all of you, charismatics the world over, to celebrate with the Pope your great jubilee on the feast of Pentecost 2017 in Saint Peter's Square! Thank you![21]

Address of Pope Francis to members of the Catholic Fraternity of Charismatic Covenant Communities and Fellowships, Paul VI Audience Hall, 31 October 2014

The Charismatic Renewal has reminded the Church of the necessity and importance of the prayer of praise. When we speak of the prayer of praise in the Church, Charismatics come to mind. When I spoke of the prayer of praise during a homily at Mass in Santa Martha, I said it is not only the prayer of Charismatics but of the entire Church! It is the recognition of the Lordship of God over us and over all creation expressed through dance, music and song.[22]

Meditation of Pope Francis at Third World Retreat of Priests, Basilica of St. John Lateran, Rome, 12 June

Grace is not purchased; it is free, it is grace and, speaking of dispensers of grace I ask each and all of you that as part of the current of grace of Charismatic Renewal you organise seminars of life in the Spirit in your parishes and Seminaries, schools, in neighborhoods, to share Baptism in the Spirit; it is catechesis *(applause)*... it is catechesis so that it produces, by the work of the Holy Spirit, the personal encounter with Jesus who changes our life. I speak to you from experience: when I began to know the Charismatic Movement, this current of grace, I was a young priest, it made me very angry; it seemed to me that they all had something in their head and once, in a sermon speaking of the Holy Spirit, I said that today, some Christians convert the Holy Spirit into a 'school of samba'; the years went by and I realised how mistaken I was -- it was a grace, a grace. [23]

Address of Pope Francis to the 'Renewal in the Spirit', St. Peter's Square, 3 July 2015

Unity in working together for the poor and the needy, who are also in need of the Baptism of the Holy Spirit. It would be so beautiful to organise seminars of life in the Spirit, together with other Christian Charismatic realities, for brothers and sisters who live on the street: they, too, have the Spirit within who impels them, so that someone will open wide the door from the outside... I remind you: Charismatic Renewal is a Pentecostal grace for the whole Church... And then, if the Lord gives us life, I expect you all together at the meeting of the ICCRS and of the Catholic Fraternity, which are already organising it, all of you and all those who wish to come at Pentecost in 2017... here in St Peter's Square to celebrate the Golden Jubilee of this current of grace - an opportunity for the Church, as Blessed Paul VI said in St Peter's Basilica in 1975. We will gather to give thanks to the Holy Spirit for the gift of this current of grace, which is for the Church and for the world, and to celebrate the wonders that the Holy Spirit has worked in the course of these 50 years, changing the life of millions of Christians.[24]

NOTES

1. Address of Pope Paul VI on occasion of the First International Leaders' Conference, Grottaferrata, 10 October 1973, included in *Then Peter Stood Up...: Collection of the Popes' Addresses to the Catholic Charismatic Renewal from its origin to the year 2000; compiled by Oreste Pesare, (Rome: International Catholic Charismatic Renewal Services, 2000)*, p. 15.
2. Address of Pope Paul VI to the Catholic Charismatic Renewal on occasion of the Second International Leaders' Conference, Rome, 19 May 1975, Ibid., p. 17.
3. Ibid., p. 17.
4. Ibid., p. 19.
5. Ibid., p. 25.
6. Ibid., p. 25.
7. Private audience of Pope John Paul II with the ICCRO Council, Rome, 11 December 1979, Ibid., p. 76.
8. Ibid., p. 77.
9. Address of Pope John Paul II at the Fourth International Leaders' Conference, Rome, 7 May 1981, Ibid., p. 35.
10. Audience of Pope John Paul II with the National Service Committee of the Italian 'Renewal in the Spirit', Rome, 4 April 1998, Ibid., p. 65.
11. Message at the meeting between Pope John Paul II and the ecclesial movements and new communities in St. Peter's Square, Rome, 30 May 1998, Ibid., pp. 91-92.
12. Ibid., p. 93.
13. Ibid., p. 95.
14. Address of Pope John Paul II to the participants at the Eighth Meeting of the Catholic Fraternity of Charismatic Covenant Communities and Fellowships, Rome, 1 June 1998, Ibid., p. 69.
15. Audience of Pope John Paul II with the participants of the Ninth International Leaders Conference, Fiuggi, 30 October 1998, Ibid.,p.71.

16. Address of Pope John Paul II to the Catholic Fraternity of Charismatic Covenant Communities and Fellowships, 22 June, 2001, included in *Then Peter Stood Up…: A Collection of Popes' Messages to the Catholic Charismatic Renewal from its origin to the year 2012;* compiled by Oreste Pesare, (Rome: International Catholic Charismatic Renewal Services, 2012), p. 86.
17. Audience of Pope John Paul II with members of the National Service Committee and of the Council of the Italian Association *Rinnovamento nello Spirito Santo*, Rome, 14 March 2002, Ibid., p.90.
18. Homily delivered by John Paul II during vespers, in which he addressed a message to members of the Renewal in the Spirit, St. Peter's Square, 29 May 2004, Ibid., p. 98.
19. Angelus Address of Pope Benedict XVI, Vatican City, 13 January 2008, Libreria Editrice Vaticana.
20. Regina Caeli Message of Pope Benedict XVI, Vatican City, 11 May 2008, Libreria Editrice Vaticana.
21. Address of Pope Francis to the 37th National Convocation of 'Renewal in the Spirit', Rome, 1 June 2014, Libreria Editrice Vaticana.
22. Address of Pope Francis to members of the Catholic Fraternity of Charismatic Covenant Communities and Fellowships, Paul VI Audience Hall, 31 October 2014, Libreria Editrice Vaticana.
23. Meditation of Pope Francis at Third World Retreat of Priests, Basilica of St. John Lateran, Rome, 12 June 2015, Innovative Media.
24. Address of Pope Francis to 'Renewal in the Spirit', St. Peter's Square, 3 July 2015, Libreria Editrice Vaticana.

A Final Word

And my Spirit continues in your midst;
do not fear!
For thus says the Lord of hosts:
One moment yet, a little while,
and I will shake the heavens and the earth,
the sea and the dry land.
I will shake all the nations,
and the treasures of all the nations will come in.
And I will fill this house with glory,
says the Lord of hosts.
Mine is the silver and mine the gold,
says the Lord of hosts.
Greater will be the future glory of this house
than the former, says the Lord of hosts;
And in this place I will give peace,
says the Lord of hosts!

Hag. 2:5-9

Further copies of this book can be obtained from

Goodnews Books
Upper level
St. John's Church Complex
296 Sundon Park Road
Luton, Beds. LU3 3AL

www.goodnewsbooks.co.uk
orders@goodnewsbooks.co.uk

01582 571011